ANXIETY:
THE COGNITIVE PERSPECTIVE

Anxiety:
The Cognitive
Perspective

MICHAEL W. EYSENCK

Royal Holloway and Bedford New
College, University of London

LEA LAWRENCE ERLBAUM ASSOCIATES, PUBLISHERS LEA
Hove (UK)   Hillsdale (USA)

Lawrence Erlbaum Associates Ltd., Publishers
27 Palmeira Mansions
Church Road
Hove
East Sussex, BN3 2FA
U.K.

British Library Cataloguing in Publication Data

Eysenck, Michael W.
Anxiety: The Cognitive Perspective. – (Essays in Cognitive
Psychology Series, ISSN 0959-4779
I. Title II. Series
152.4

ISBN 0-86377-071-1 (Hbk)

Printed and bound by BPCC Wheatons, Exeter.

TO MY DAUGHTER, FLEUR,
AND TO AMY

A professor should know at least everything.
(Juliet Eysenck, aged four years)

Contents

Preface

The notion that it is fruitful to consider emotions from the cognitive perspective has become increasingly popular in recent years. Richard Lazarus, Irwin Sarason, Nico Frijda, Aaron Beck, and Gordon Bower are just a few of the well-known theorists who have espoused that notion. As a cognitive psychologist myself, I have always been sympathetic to the cognitive approach to the emotions. It seems to be the case that this approach has considerably enhanced our understanding of many human emotions, perhaps especially anxiety and depression.

The particular focus of this book is on the emotion of anxiety, and on the ways in which the cognitive perspective can shed light on individual differences in anxiety among normal and clinical populations. Collaboration is increasingly common in scientific research, and the programme of research reported in this book is no exception. The list of those who have been actively involved in the research programme includes the following: Anna Eliatamby, Christos Halkiopoulos, Jan Graydon, Jos van Berkum, Andrew Mathews, Colin MacLeod, Karin Mogg, Jon May, Anne Richards, John Kentish, James Walsh, Frank Tallis, Manuel Calvo, and Angela Byrne. While I owe much to all of them, the greatest debt of gratitude is undoubtedly to Andrew Mathews. He was instrumental in developing the research programme on generalized anxiety disorder which forms a major part of this book, and he was responsible for many of the key theoretical ideas. It was originally our intention that we should co-author this book, but his numerous other commitments forced him to withdraw.

I am also especially grateful to Manuel Calvo. He has made numerous important theoretical and empirical contributions in the area of anxiety and performance, and collaboration with him has had a substantial impact on my thinking. It has also been very agreeable to visit him and his family in the sunny climes of Tenerife in the Canary Islands!

My family provided constant support and encouragement to me during the writing of this book. This book is dedicated to my elder daughter Fleur and her good friend Amy Harland. They wanted the book dedicated to them because, being young, they believe that with fame comes fortune.

Michael W. Eysenck
January 1992

CHAPTER ONE

The Cognitive Approach

INTRODUCTION

This book is concerned with individual differences in anxiety from the cognitive perspective. Two major lines of research are relevant. The first involves comparing clinically anxious patients with normal controls, and the second involves comparing normal individuals high and low in proneness to anxiety. Historically, these two lines of research have developed in relatively splendid isolation from each other. The reasons for this are not altogether clear. However, one major reason is probably that the goals of researchers in the two areas have been somewhat different. Those engaged in clinical research have focused primarily on cognitive factors involved in the aetiology and maintenance of clinical anxiety, whereas those investigating cognition in normal groups have concentrated on the ways in which anxiety affects performance (e.g., Sarason, 1988).

One of the few points of agreement among most researchers in the field of anxiety is that anxiety is a complex phenomenon, and one which can fruitfully be studied from a number of different perspectives. For example, Lang (1971, 1985) argued that there are three separate response systems involved in anxiety. These three systems are the behavioural, the physiological, and the verbal or cognitive. Situations that would be expected to produce anxiety typically have effects on all of these response systems. However, there is plentiful evidence that the three systems often exhibit failures of concordance or agreement, and so cannot be regarded as equivalent.

An example of such lack of concordance is provided by the work of Craske and Craig (1984) in a study of competent pianists under the stressful condition of performing in public. In essence, they discovered that measures belonging to the same response system mostly correlated with each other, whereas measures from different response systems did not. An implication of this, and similar findings is that it is generally desirable to obtain measures from all three response systems. If this is not done, then erroneous conclusions may be reached.

There are various reasons for a lack of concordance among the three response systems. In most cases, the reactions assessed vary from one response system to another. As Thorpe (1989) pointed out, "It should not surprise us when different measures of anxiety do not agree with each other when we confound 'question asked' with 'response mode'" [p. 192]. However, a lack of concordance can happen for other reasons. In many situations, behaviour is the response system most influenced by social constraints and the physiological response system is the one least influenced. For example, the 'natural' behavioural response of passive avoidance is generally socially unacceptable, and is thus not produced. It could be argued that blushing and other physiological manifestations of anxiety (e.g., trembling) are also socially unacceptable, but most people find it much harder to control physiological reactions than behavioural ones.

There may also be more theoretically interesting reasons why the various response systems show a lack of concordance. For example, Schwartz (1983) argued that repressors are stressed individuals who fail to attend to indications of distress. As a consequence, they should appear low in anxiety when verbal measures are used, but rather high in anxiety with other measures (e.g., physiological or behavioural). Repressors can be identified by administering a test of trait anxiety (= susceptibility to anxiety as a personality dimension) and the Marlowe–Crowne Social Desirability Scale (Crowne & Marlowe, 1964), which is a measure of defensiveness, protection of self-esteem, and affect inhibition. Those who score low on trait anxiety but high on the Marlowe–Crowne Social Desirability Scale are regarded as having a repressive coping style. Weinberger, Schwartz, and Davidson (1979) discovered that subjects with a repressive coping style appeared to be more stressed than low-anxious subjects (i.e., those low on both trait anxiety and the Marlowe–Crowne) on six different measures (three physiological and three behavioural). In fact, the repressors were even more stressed than high-anxious subjects (i.e., those high on trait anxiety but low on the Marlowe–Crowne) on most of the measures, in spite of the fact that they all had low scores on trait anxiety.

Similar findings to those of Weinberger et al. (1979) were reported by Fox, O'Boyle, Barry, and McCreary (1989). Anxiety in stressful dental surgery was assessed by two oral surgeons. Repressors appeared to be considerably more anxious than low-anxious patients and were approximately as stressed as high-anxious patients.

In sum, anxiety is a complex phenomenon encompassing three different response systems. A complete theory of anxiety would need to account for the dynamic interrelationships among these systems, and in so doing would explain the typical failures of concordance of response measures across systems. For the present, however, all theories of anxiety (including the one proposed in this book) fall well short of such completeness.

WHY A COGNITIVE PERSPECTIVE?

If one accepts the view that anxiety is a complex phenomenon involving several different response systems, then it is clearly necessary to justify adopting an almost purely cognitive approach in this book. There are, in fact, various reasons why a cognitive perspective is especially important. These reasons are explored in this section of the chapter.

Affect and Cognition

Anxiety, and other emotional reactions, often occur in response to environmental stimuli or situations. An important theoretical issue is whether it is essential for stimuli or situations to be processed cognitively before the emotional reaction can occur. If it is the case that affective responses to all stimuli depend on prior cognitive processing, then it would seem to follow that theories of anxiety and other emotions should have a distinctly cognitive flavour. However, some theorists have claimed that the affective evaluation of stimuli involves basic processes which can function without the intervention of the cognitive system. For example, Zajonc (1984) argued as follows:

> Affect and cognition are separate and partially independent systems and ... although they ordinarily function conjointly, affect could be generated without a prior cognitive process [p. 117].

Zajonc (1980) discussed various studies which he claimed supported his theoretical position. In most of these studies, stimuli were presented either subliminally or while the subjects were involved in a different task. Performance on a subsequent test of recognition memory was at chance level, but the subjects nevertheless preferred the previously presented stimuli to new ones. According to Zajonc (1980), these studies demonstrate a positive affective reaction to the old stimuli (as assessed by the preference judgements) without the involvement of cognitive processing (assessed by recognition-memory performance).

Lazarus (1982) disagreed with Zajonc's (1980) conclusion. As he pointed out, the studies cited by Zajonc (1980) appear to have rather little to do with ordinary emotional states. More importantly, concluding that a failure of recognition memory means that the stimuli were not processed cognitively makes little sense. This conclusion might be acceptable if cognition were to be equated with consciousness, but very few cognitive psychologists would be prepared to make that equation. It is entirely possible that there was extensive pre-conscious processing involving automatic (= fast and inaccessible to consciousness) and other processes in all of the studies discussed by Zajonc (1980).

It has not proved possible so far to obtain definitive evidence on the issue of whether cognitive processes necessarily precede affective responses to environmental stimuli. However, it seems extremely likely that there is always at least some cognitive processing of the meaning of a stimulus before an emotional reaction is triggered. As Lazarus (1982) argued, "Cognitive appraisal (of meaning or significance) underlies and is an integral feature of all emotional states" [p. 1021]. An implication of this position is that an adequate theory of anxiety would need to consider the cognitive processes involved in the evaluation of stimuli as threatening or non-threatening; only the former stimuli generate anxiety.

The Nature of Anxiety

In considering the potential value of a cognitive approach to anxiety, it is important to consider anxiety from the evolutionary perspective. Anxiety is an unpleasant and aversive state, and it is perhaps not immediately obvious what (if any) biological significance it might have. However, it is clear that rapid detection of the early warning signs of danger possesses considerable survival value. It can be fatal, for example, if one ignores the smell of burning in a house or the initial malfunctioning of a car. The key purpose or function of anxiety is probably to facilitate the detection of danger or threat in potentially threatening environments. While it is important to detect danger, some anxious individuals (e.g., clinical patients) may have such highly developed danger-detection processes that they become hypervigilant and grossly exaggerate the number and severity of threatening or dangerous events in the environment. Of course, anxiety becomes dysfunctional in such clinical cases.

If the anxious system is specially adapted for the purpose of threat detection, then one must address the issue of the processes producing facilitated threat detection. Almost certainly, pre-attentive and/or attentional processes are centrally involved. Thus, the cognitive system is of crucial significance with respect to the primary purpose of anxiety.

One of the major functions of the cognitive system is its involvement in thinking about, and planning for, the future. The fact that most people know approximately what they will be doing next week, next month, and even next year reflects the functioning of the cognitive system. This capacity of the cognitive system to anticipate the future is highly relevant to anxiety. According to *Collins English Dictionary*, anxiety is "a state of uneasiness or tension caused by apprehension of possible future misfortune, danger, etc.; worry." The notion that thoughts about possible future aversive events are of great significance in anxious states has been endorsed by several theorists. For example, Beck and Emery (1985) argued as follows:

> The anxious patient anticipates possible damage to his relations with others, to his goal and objectives, to his ability to cope with problems and perform adequately, and to his health or survival [p. 104].

There is some empirical evidence to support this general viewpoint. Anxious patients report that situations threatening future misfortunes often precede the onset of clinical anxiety (Finlay-Jones & Brown, 1981). Normal subjects asked to think of major episodes of anxiety they have experienced in the past typically report that these episodes were triggered off by events which at that time lay in the future (Eysenck & Adams, in preparation).

The clearest way in which the future time orientation of anxiety involves the cognitive system is via the phenomenon of worry. Worry manifestly involves the cognitive system, and worry content relates primarily to possible future aversive states of affairs ('if ..., then ...'). As is discussed in Chapter 6, worry is of central importance in anxiety. Individuals high in trait anxiety report worrying considerably more than those low in trait anxiety, and worry is the crucial defining feature of generalized anxiety disorder according to the Third Revised Edition of the American Psychiatric Association's *Diagnostic and Statistical Manual of Mental Disorders* DSM-IIIR, 1987). Thus, it would not seem possible to provide a detailed theoretical account of the role played by worry in anxiety without adopting a cognitive orientation.

Cognitive Therapy

One of the most important changes in the treatment of anxiety disorders in recent years has been the marked growth of cognitive therapy (see Eysenck, 1990 b). There are several varieties of cognitive therapy which have been applied to the treatment of clinical anxiety, including those advocated by Beck (1976), Ellis (1962), and Meichenbaum (1977). In spite of the differences among them, all of these cognitive therapists agree that patients suffering from anxiety disorders have unrealistic negative and self-defeating thoughts about themselves and about their circumstances, and that therapy designed to normalize patients' thought patterns can lead to recovery. Thus, for example, Ellis (1962) argued along the following lines:

> If he [i.e., the individual] wants to be minimally disturbable and maximally sane, he'd better substitute for all his absolutistic 'It's terrible', two other words which he does not parrot or give lip-service to but which he incisively thinks through and accepts — namely, 'Too bad!' or 'Tough shit'!

It is notoriously difficult to evaluate the efficacy of most forms of therapy, and cognitive therapy is no exception. However, the available evidence suggests that cognitive therapy is comparable to, or more effective than, other therapies in the treatment of anxiety disorders (Brewin, 1988). The therapeutic success of cognitive therapy indicates strongly (although it does not demonstrate conclusively) that cognitive factors are of major significance in the anxiety disorders. It is not clear as yet that cognitive therapy has contributed much to our theoretical understanding of the part played by cognition in clinical anxiety. Most forms of cognitive therapy involve a number of different ingredients, and it is usually difficult to identify which ingredient or ingredients are most effective in facilitating recovery.

A limiting characteristic of cognitive therapy is that it is very largely confined to thoughts and beliefs of which the patient is consciously aware. As a consequence, it is uninformative about the role of cognitive processes operating below the level of conscious awareness. Some cognitive therapists are unconcerned about this state of affairs. For example, Sacco and Beck (1985) argued as follows: "The concept of unconscious processes is largely irrelevant to cognitive therapy" [p. 5]. This seems an unduly restricted view. Many (or possibly all) conscious processes have pre-conscious processes as antecedents, and so to understand even conscious processing in anxiety disorders it will be necessary to focus on pre-conscious processes as well.

In sum, a consideration of cognitive therapy suggests that anxious patients differ from normal controls in their cognitive functioning, and that reducing or eliminating these differences can help to produce recovery. However, cognitive therapy is not based securely on empirical research, and cognitive therapists have made only modest progress in the task of identifying the cognitive factors involved in the aetiology and maintenance of clinical anxiety. There is thus a pressing need for additional empirical and theoretical work by cognitive psychologists to provide a more solid foundation for the practice of cognitive therapy. This is especially the case as far as pre-conscious processes are concerned.

COGNITIVE PSYCHOLOGY:
EXPERIMENTAL vs. SOCIAL

There are, in principle, a number of different cognitively-based theoretical and empirical approaches to anxiety which could be adopted. For example, Brewin (1988) proposed a valuable distinction between experimental cognitive psychology and cognitive social psychology. Experimental cognitive psychologists are concerned primarily with basic aspects of human information processing such as attention, perception, learning, thinking, and memory. A range of relatively standard laboratory tasks is used to investigate the information processing system. In contrast, cognitive social psychologists focus on conscious attitudes, expectancies, and beliefs, all of which are assessed by means of self-report questionnaires. This basic distinction between experimental cognitive psychology and cognitive social psychology is discussed in more detail by Eysenck (1991 b).

One of the major assumptions made in this book is that the approach of experimental cognitive psychology is greatly to be preferred to that of cognitive social psychology. Many of the reasons for preferring the approach of experimental cognitive psychology to that of cognitive social psychology relate to the severe limitations of most self-report questionnaires as a means of assessing cognitive processes. As Nisbett and Wilson (1977) pointed out, numerous experimental studies have shown that introspective evidence is often very inaccurate and distorted, especially when people are asked to identify the causal factors influencing their own behaviour. Self-report measures are also susceptible to distortion because of social desirability and other biases. Finally, and perhaps most importantly, while self-report questionnaires can provide evidence about the consciously available products of pre-conscious cognitive processes, they are uninformative about those pre-conscious processes.

In contrast, properly designed cognitive tasks are largely immune from these criticisms of self-report questionnaires. They permit the accumulation of detailed knowledge of pre-conscious and conscious processes under conditions in which deliberate bias in performance is either unlikely or can be assessed separately. It is assumed here that automatic processes, pre-attentive processes, attentional processes, and conscious thoughts all occur within the cognitive system, and that all should be regarded by any theorist who is interested in anxiety from the cognitive perspective. It is unnecessarily limited to do as cognitive social psychologists often do, namely, to treat conscious processes in isolation from processes occurring below the level of conscious awareness. The reason is that the two kinds of processes have dynamic effects on each other.

The assumption that psychologically important processes within the cognitive system can occur in the absence of conscious awarenesss, and can affect ongoing emotion and action, has attracted much controversy and is by no means universally accepted. Therefore, it must be considered in some detail. Within this general area, there has been special interest in the more specific issue of whether the meanings of stimuli can be accessed outside of awareness. In an influential review, Holender (1986, p.1) discussed studies of dichotic listening, parafoveal vision (= outside the central foveal area of the retina), and visual pattern masking. His conclusions concerning the existence of preconscious semantic processing were essentially negative:

1. Dichotic listening cannot provide the conditions needed to demonstrate the phenomenon. These conditions are better fulfilled in parafoveal vision and are realized ideally in pattern masking.
2. Evidence for the phenomenon is very scanty for parafoveal vision, but several tentative demonstrations have been reported for pattern masking. It can be shown, however, that none of these studies has included the requisite controls.
3. On the basis of current evidence it is most likely that these stimuli were indeed consciously identified.

If Holender (1986) is correct, then it would be difficult to argue for the theoretical importance of pre-attentive processes in anxiety. However, there are at least three reasons for rejecting his conclusions. First, Holender (1986) defined lack of awareness in visual pattern masking studies as the inability to make a voluntary discriminative response to the masked stimulus (e.g., to decide accurately whether it was a word). This is sometimes known as the objective threshold, whereas the subjective threshold of awareness is defined in terms of whether or not there is conscious awareness. The objective threshold probably provides an insufficiently stringent criterion for awareness. This is shown by the fact that subjects often demonstrate 'awareness' of a stimulus as assessed by the objective threshold, even when they totally deny seeing it (Cheesman & Merikle, 1985).

Secondly, Holender (1986) adopted a 'head-counting' approach in which he argued in effect that access to word meaning outside of conscious awareness does not occur because most studies have failed to provide acceptable evidence of its existence. As Marcel (1986) wittily remarked, "This is equivalent to seeking evidence of black swans in ten samples of swans, finding them in two of the samples, and then concluding that the bulk of the evidence goes against their existence!" [p. 40].

Thirdly, Holender (1986) ignored some important areas of research. One example is the phenomenon of 'blindsight', which has been observed in patients with lesions in the primary visual projection area of the cortex. These patients generally insist that they cannot see anything, but are nevertheless able to discriminate between two stimuli in a forced-choice task (see Weiskrantz, 1990).

It has been claimed that blindsight and other phenomena such as perceptual defence are paradoxical, in that they seem to imply that people can 'perceive without perceiving'. However, these phenomena are paradoxical only if one assumes that perception is an either/or event. If, as seems probable, perception is a multi-stage process taking place over time (cf., Erdelyi, 1974), then there is no interpretive problem. The early stages of perceptual processing occur below the level of conscious awareness, and it is only the later stages of processing of which the perceiver may become aware. Thus, it is entirely possible for extensive perceptual processing to occur in the absence of conscious awareness.

The argument that preconscious processes should be considered within a cognitive approach to anxiety would be strengthened if there were convincing evidence that such processes can produce anxiety. Tyrer, Lewis, and Lee (1978) claimed to have obtained such evidence. In one experiment, they presented anxiety-related words either supraliminally or subliminally. State or experienced anxiety was assessed before and after the stimuli were presented. Both forms of presentation were associated with increased state anxiety. In a second experiment, subjects were shown a speeded-up film of a drive through a busy city taken from a car (allegedly anxiety-provoking) and a neutral film of a swan floating on a lake. One group of subjects viewed the first film subliminally and the second film supraliminally, and a second group viewed the first film supraliminally and the second film subliminally. There were indications that anxiety increased following subliminal presentation of the emotional film and decreased after subliminal presentation of the neutral film.

While the results of Tyrer et al. (1978) seem impressive, they cannot be accepted at face value. The first experiment suffers from the very severe deficiency of having no control group, so the reasons for the increased state anxiety after presentation of the anxiety-related words cannot be determined. The second experiment did not involve genuinely subliminal presentation, because some of the subjects reported seeing 'flickering'. The sight of flickering may have caused uncertainty and anxiety, but not as a result of pre-conscious processes.

Kemp-Wheeler and Hill (1987) reported a study which was methodologically superior to that of Tyrer et al. (1978). Emotionally unpleasant or neutral words were presented subliminally 10% below each subject's own detection threshold. Subliminal presentation of the emotionally unpleasant words produced increased state anxiety on a self-report measure, whereas subliminal presentation of the neutral words produced a decrease.

EXPERIMENTAL COGNITIVE PSYCHOLOGY: EVOLUTIONARY PERSPECTIVE

Even if one accepts that individual differences in anxiety should be studied from the perspective of experimental cognitive psychology, there are still important decisions to be made about the central focus of theory and research. There are numerous differences in cognitive processes and performance between those high and low in anxiety, and theorists vary in terms of which differences they regard as of major significance. For example, J.T. Spence and K.W. Spence (1966) emphasized the view that anxiety affects the retrieval of information from long-term memory by changing the effects of intra-task response competition. In contrast, Humphreys and Revelle (1984) claimed that anxiety has major effects on on-task effort, arousal, short-term memory, and sustained information transfer. According to Beck and Emery (1985), some of the cognitive symptoms most frequently reported by patients with anxiety disorders are difficulties of concentration (found in 86% of cases), fear of losing control (76%), fear of being rejected (72%), inability to control thinking (72%), and confusion (69%).

How can one distinguish among these very different cognitive approaches to anxiety? One obvious possibility is to rely on the available empirical evidence. However, while the evidence clearly pinpoints deficiencies in some theoretical positions (e.g., that of J.T. Spence and K.W. Spence, 1966; see Eysenck, 1982), it does not resolve all of the issues. In essence, the problem is that it is not possible from the research evidence alone to decide which of these effects are of fundamental importance and which are less consequential.

The approach taken in this book is that full account should be taken of the biological and evolutionary significance of anxiety. The primary function of anxiety is to facilitate the detection of danger or threat in potentially threatening environments, and theory and research should reflect that fact. In other words, the pre-attentive, attentional, and other processes involved in threat detection are of central significance within a cognitive approach to anxiety, as are the processes (e.g., worry) triggered by threat. In contrast, most (but not all) effects of anxiety on cognitive processing which are not specific to threat are of lesser theoretical importance. These include effects on intra-task response competition, short-term memory, sustained information transfer, difficulties of concentration, and inability to control thinking. Most of these effects are simply by-products of pre-attentive and attentional processes in anxious individuals (see Chapter 7).

Oatley and Johnson-Laird (1987) have espoused a similar theoretical position. They argued that threats to the self-preservation goal produce a state of anxiety. In this anxious state, the individual stops, attends vigilantly to the environment, or escapes. They also made the interesting suggestion that anxiety and other emotions are cognitively based states which serve to co-ordinate processes in the nervous system, especially when the probability of the success of a plan changes considerably.

Four cognitive theories of anxiety are discussed in Chapter 2. One of the bases on which they were selected is that they all address theoretical issues relating to the detection and processing of threat-related stimuli by anxious individuals. To a greater or lesser extent, the evolutionary perspective argued for here is incorporated into all of those theories, although generally in a less wholehearted fashion than would be desirable.

SUMMARY AND CONCLUSIONS

Anxiety is a complex phenomenon which can be studied in a number of different ways. Individual differences can be investigated in either clinical or normal populations. In terms of measures of anxiety, it is possible to identify at least three different response systems: behavioural; physiological; and verbal. Measures taken from the various response systems typically exhibit a lack of concordance which is difficult to account for theoretically.

Since anxiety can be approached in a variety of different ways, it is necessary to justify adopting the cognitive perspective. There are reasons for claiming that at least some cognitive processing always precedes the experience of anxiety, which means that the cognitive system is importantly involved in anxiety. If it is accepted that a prime function of anxiety is to facilitate the rapid detection of threatening stimuli, then pre-attentive and attentional processes within the cognitive system are involved. Worry, which is a major component of anxiety, is essentially cognitive in nature. Cognitive therapy has proved successful in the treatment of anxiety disorders, presumably because the functioning of the cognitive system differs in clinically anxious patients.

Experimental cognitive psychology and cognitive social psychology are the two major cognitive approaches which could be used to investigate anxiety. Experimental cognitive psychology has a number of advantages over cognitive social psychology. In particular, it permits the assessment of pre-conscious processes, and it is less susceptible to some of the biasing factors which can invalidate the self-report data associated with cognitive social psychology.

There are numerous findings within experimental cognitive psychology which point to differences between individuals high and low in anxiety. Those of greatest theoretical interest relate to the evolutionary significance of anxiety, and especially its role in ensuring the rapid detection of potential threat.

CHAPTER TWO

Theories of Anxiety and Cognition

INTRODUCTION

Theorists attempting to provide a cognitive theory of individual differences in anxiety might focus either on normals of varying levels of anxiety or on clinical groups suffering from anxiety disorders. Those interested in normal individuals have mostly considered the personality dimension of trait anxiety. This dimension was defined by Spielberger, Gorsuch, and Lushene (1970) as "relatively stable individual differences in anxiety proneness" [p. 3].

As the 1987 Third Revised *Diagnostic and Statistical Manual* of the American Psychiatric Association (DSM-IIIR) made clear, there are a number of different anxiety disorders. These disorders include various phobias, panic disorder, obsessive-compulsive disorder, post-traumatic stress disorder, and generalized anxiety disorder. Cognitive theorists have mostly assumed that there is some commonality in the cognitive functioning of these different clinically anxious groups. However, there has so far been insufficient research to be confident about the extent of the commonality (but see Chapter 8).

What are some of the major issues which should be addressed by a comprehensive approach to individual differences in anxiety from the cognitive perspective? First, it is important to consider the salient differences in cognitive functioning between clinically anxious patients and normal individuals. Second, these differences in cognitive functioning need to be investigated fully, including both non-conscious and conscious aspects of cognition. This requires the use of tasks developed by cognitive psychologists. Third, the causal relationships between clinical anxiety and non-normal cognitive functioning require consideration. Some aspects of the non-normal functioning of anxious patients may pre-date the onset of psychopathology and play a part in its development; these aspects would form a cognitive vulnerability factor. Other aspects of non-normal cognitive functioning may simply be secondary consequences of clinically anxious mood state. This issue needs to be addressed in the light of relevant experimental evidence.

Fourth, a comprehensive theory would identify those personality or other individual differences associated with vulnerability to clinical anxiety. Trait anxiety has been proposed most frequently as the personality dimension of greatest relevance to vulnerability. Fifth, it is important to place the functioning of the cognitive system in a broader context. Anxious individuals differ from non-anxious individuals in their physiological functioning and behaviour as well as in their cognitive functioning. The dynamic interrelationships at the cognitive, physiological, and behavioural levels need to be identified.

The rest of this chapter is devoted to four theories which address at least some of the major issues delineated above. Gray (1982) proposed a theory of trait anxiety with potential applicability to clinical anxiety, and his viewpoint is considered first. Then the important theoretical work of the cognitive therapist Aaron Beck (e.g., Beck & Emery, 1985) is analysed. His primary focus is on clinical anxiety and cognition. Penultimately, Bower's (1981) theoretical position is presented and evaluated. He has proposed the most influential theory of mood and cognition. Finally, the important theory of cognition and emotional disorders proposed by Williams, Watts, MacLeod, and Mathews (1988) is discussed.

This analysis of cognitive theories of anxiety serves a number of functions. Nearly all new theories in psychology relate to a greater or lesser extent to previously formulated theoretical positions, and the theory to be presented in this book is no exception. Thus, a consideration of relevant theories will provide a theoretical context for what is to come. It also introduces a number of themes which are developed in the rest of the book.

GRAY'S NEUROPSYCHOLOGICAL THEORY

Gray (1982, 1985) proposed an ambitious neuropsychological theory which was designed (among other things) to explain individual differences in trait anxiety and to account for some of the main categories of clinical anxiety. The research strategy which he adopted consisted of two interrelated stages. The first stage involved measuring the behavioural consequences of anti-anxiety drugs on a number of species. The second stage involved a search for those interventions in the brain which produced effects resembling those resulting from the administration of anti-anxiety drugs.

Gray's (1982) theory and the relevant evidence are discussed at length by Eysenck (1992), and so only a succinct summary will be presented here. Various anti-anxiety drugs have been investigated (mainly the benzodiazepines, barbiturates, and alcohol), and interest has centred on those behavioural effects which are common to all three types of drugs. Shared effects are assumed to reflect impaired functioning of the system mediating anxiety, which Gray (1982) termed the 'behavioural inhibition system'. Research has indicated that there are four types of stimuli which can activate the behavioural inhibition system: signals of punishment; signals of non-reward; novel stimuli; and innate fear stimuli. The activated behavioural inhibition system fulfils a number of functions which were listed by Gray (1975):

(a) to inhibit all ongoing behaviour; ... and (b) to perform the maximum possible analysis of current environmental stimuli, especially activity in this system. The other major outputs are an initial inhibition of all previously operative behaviour patterns, coupled with an increment in arousal level, i.e., an increment in the intensity of whatever behaviour finally does occur [p. 354].

Research with rats has indicated that lesions to the septo-hippocampal system produce effects which are very similar to those produced by anti-anxiety drugs. There are 19 different performance measures for which lesion and drug data are both available, and on 18 of them septo-hippocampal lesions and anti-anxiety drugs have similar effects (Gray, 1985). The implication is that anti-anxiety drugs affect behaviour by impairing the functioning of the septo-hippocampal system. There is some research support for the more specific hypothesis that anti-anxiety drugs reduce the noradrenergic input to the septo-hippocampal system.

Gray (1982) also considered cognitive functioning. He claimed that the hippocampus is part of a system which functions as a comparator. The comparator receives information about the current state of the world as well as a prediction as to what that state should be. If the comparator decides that there is a match between the predicted and actual events, then it checks the next actual event. If a mismatch is detected (i.e., there is a discrepancy between actual and expected events or there is a stimulus warning of an event which could disrupt planned behaviour), then the outputs of the behavioural inhibition system are activated.

Individual differences in trait anxiety are accounted for very straightforwardly within this theory. According to Gray (1982), individuals who are high in trait anxiety have a much more active behavioural inhibition system than those who are low in trait anxiety, being more sensitive to signals of punishment, signals of non-reward, and novelty. It is assumed that individual differences in trait anxiety are affected by genetic factors, an assumption which is supported by twin-study evidence (Eysenck, 1992).

In terms of self-reports of physiological activity, it is certainly true that individuals high in trait anxiety indicate much greater activity than those low in trait anxiety. However, the picture is very different when it comes to psychophysiological studies. Fahrenberg (1987) reviewed the psychophysiological evidence relating to trait anxiety and to the highly related personality dimension of neuroticism. He came to the following pessimistic conclusion:

> Psychophysiological research on physiological correlates of the established emotionality (neuroticism) trait dimension has come to a standstill. Findings of questionnaire studies generally support the postulated psychophysiological relationship, but research that employs objectively measured physiological parameters in large-scale, methodologically well-controlled and replicated investigations has not substantiated these hypotheses [p. 117].

The implication would appear to be that there is very little support for Gray's (1982) general theoretical position from psychophysiological studies on normals. However, the psychophysiological measures which have been used provide no more than a rather indirect reflection of septo-hippocampal system activity. As a consequence, it could be argued that the research discussed by Fahrenberg (1987) is of little relevance to Gray's (1982) theory.

Finally, Gray's (1982) theory provides an account of clinical anxiety. Obsessive-compulsive neurosis can occur if the comparator's checking system is over-active. Phobic states may involve the comparator detecting too many mismatches in the presence of relevant innate fear stimuli (e.g., snakes, spiders). Generalized anxiety states are thought to arise from high sensitivity of the behavioural inhibition system to all classes of triggering stimuli. It is individuals who are high in trait anxiety who are most likely to develop anxious symptoms.

One of the distinctive features of Gray's (1982) theory is the emphasis which is placed on the similarities between anxiety in man and anxiety in other species. This may be correct so far as the brain structures mediating anxiety are concerned, but it seems much less likely that the cognitive processes associated with anxiety are the same. As Hallam (1985) pointed out:

> Even if the layman or clinician were to accept that perceiving events as, say, signals of punishment or non-reward brought forth biological responses that we have in common with other species one might still argue that the cause of complaints of anxiety was in perceiving events in this way, and not in possessing the biological mechanism of these responses [p. 218].

From the cognitive perspective, the comparator is of particular interest. However, it is doubtful whether it functions in exactly the fashion assumed by Gray (1982). For example, while the notion that an novel stimulus will produce a mismatch is entirely reasonable, the assumption that this will always produce activity in the behavioural inhibition system and thus anxiety is implausible. There is surely a fundamental distinction between mismatches where the predicted event is preferable to the actual event and mismatches where the opposite is true. Mismatches of the former type may, indeed, produce anxiety, but mismatches of the latter type obviously produce more positive emotional states. Support for the view that a distinction should be drawn between the two kinds of mismatches was obtained by Rachman and Lopatka (1986 a, b). They compared the amount of fear predicted and experienced by snake phobics who were repeatedly exposed to a snake. In general, under-predictions of fear led to increased fear, in line with Gray's (1982) theory. However, mismatches involving over-prediction of fear led to reduced fear, which does not seem to be in accord with expectations from Gray's (1982) theory.

According to Gray (1982), cognitive analysis of stimuli by the comparator is limited to an assessment of whether they are anticipated or not anticipated and whether they are aversive or non-aversive. This seems to be an over-simplified account if it is compared to the theoretical position of Lazarus (e.g., Lazarus & Averill, 1972). Lazarus has identified three kinds of cognitive processes which together help to determine emotional states:

1. Primary appraisal processes, which compare stimuli against information in long-term memory to assess danger and/or distress;

2. Secondary appraisal processes, which consider stimuli and events in relation to the individual's available resources (e.g., coping skills); and

3. Reappraisal processes, which are activated when actions have been initiated and are beginning to affect the threatening situation.

In approximate terms, Gray (1982) has included primary appraisal as the major function of the comparator, but has largely ignored secondary appraisal and reappraisal. Part of the reason for this may stem from the fact that Gray (1982) has studied rats. It may well be that most species engage in primary appraisal, but that secondary appraisal and reappraisal are far more prevalent in the human species than in any other.

Since our major concern is with individual differences in anxiety, it is important to evaluate Gray's (1982) theoretical views on this issue. With respect to trait anxiety, Gray (1982) emphasized the sensitivity of the behavioural inhibition system. This may well be one of the factors which differentiates those high and low in trait anxiety, but there are other factors which are relatively neglected by Gray (1982). As is discussed in Chapters 4 and 5, the cognitive system functions rather differently among those high and low in trait anxiety. As a consequence, high- and low-anxiety individuals differ both in which stimuli they process and how they process them. In addition, the contents of long-term memory probably vary as a function of trait anxiety. This presumably affects the functioning of the comparator, since predictions about events are determined on the basis of information in long-term memory. Therefore, our theoretical approach to trait anxiety differs from that of Gray (1982) in that we stress individual differences in cognitive functioning whereas he does not. This issue is considered further in Chapter 3.

The final aspect of Gray's (1982) theory to be evaluated is the one dealing with clinical anxiety. The main advantage of his theoretical treatment is that the main forms of clinical anxiety can all be identified with different functions of the comparator and/or the behavioural inhibition system. However, his account is descriptive rather than explanatory. The causes of clinical anxiety are not made clear, nor is it explained why individuals vary in the specific form of clinical anxiety which they exhibit.

BECK'S SCHEMA THEORY

Easily the most influential theoretical account of anxiety disorders from a cognitive perspective is that of Aaron Beck (e.g., Beck & Clark, 1988;

Beck & Emery, 1985). His approach was initially based almost entirely on clinical observations, and owed little to experimental research. It is assumed that the major features of anxiety disorders are cognitive in nature, but that the cognitive system is not causally involved in the aetiology of clinical anxiety. In the words of Beck and Emery (1985):

> We consider that the primary pathology or dysfunction during a depression or an anxiety disorder is in the cognitive apparatus. However, that is quite different from the notion that the cognition *causes* these syndromes — a notion that is just as illogical as an assertion that hallucinations cause schizophrenia [p. 85].

In spite of the above apparently unequivocal statement, Beck and Emery (1985) include certain kinds of cognitions (e.g., unrealistic goals; unreasonable attitudes) among those factors predisposing to anxiety disorders. Other predisposing factors allegedly include hereditary predisposition, certain physical diseases, developmental traumata, and inadequate personal experiences.

This issue was clarified by Beck and Clark (1988). They argued that certain schemas (= "functional structures of relatively enduring representations of prior knowledge and experience"; Beck & Clark, 1988, p. 24) play an important role. More specifically, "by possessing latent maladaptive schemas, some individuals evidence a cognitive vulnerability for developing anxiety or depression" [p. 24]. Psychopathology was said to result from an interaction between cognitive vulnerability and relevant life stressors.

The central construct used by Beck and Emery (1985) and by Beck and Clark (1988) in their cognitive theory of clinical anxiety is that of the *schema*. The first systematic schema theory was developed by Bartlett (1932), who regarded a schema as an integrated body of knowledge stored in long-term memory. Bartlett (1932) assumed that schemata (or 'schemas' in American English) influence memory processes, and other theorists have argued that schemata also affect perceptual, attentional, and comprehension processes (see Eysenck & Keane, 1990, for a review). The essence of the schema theory approach to the anxiety disorders was expressed succinctly by Beck and Clark (1988):

> Cognitive structures [i.e., schemas] guide the screening, encoding, organizing, storing and retrieving of information. Stimuli consistent with existing schemas are elaborated and encoded, while inconsistent or irrelevant information is ignored or forgotten ... the maladaptive

schemas in the anxious patient involve perceived physical or psychological threat to one's personal domain as well as an exaggerated sense of vulnerability [pp. 24-26].

In addition to schemas or schemata, there is a superordinate organizing principle termed a 'mode'. Each mode consists of various groups of rules and concepts which are organized in terms of general themes. In the case of anxiety disorders, it is the vulnerability or danger mode which is dominant.

How do schemas or schemata influence cognitive functioning? In essence, they serve to direct processing resources to those aspects of the external or internal environment which are congruent with them. In other words, anxious patients will attend to stimuli which present a physical or psychological threat, ambiguous stimuli will be interpreted in a threatening fashion, and threatening information will be readily retrieved from memory.

Those individuals who possess maladaptive schemata concerned with physical or psychological threat will not necessarily exhibit the pattern of schema-congruent processing described above. In general, maladaptive schemata remain latent until they are triggered by relevant life stressors.

Beck (1967, 1987) has proposed a rather similar schema theory of clinical depression. Depressed patients are assumed to have maladaptive schemata which incorporate negative information about the self, the world, and the future, in addition to other schemata based on personal loss. As is the case with the maladaptive schemas or schemata of anxious patients, those of depressed patients systematically affect information processsing by favouring schema-congruent information.

According to Beck, there are major similarities in information processing between anxious and depressed patients. In both groups, maladaptive schemata systematically distort the processes involved in the perception, storage, and retrieval of information. In terms of differences between the two groups, Beck and Clark (1988) proposed the content-specificity hypothesis. According to this hypothesis: "it is primarily the content of the faulty information processing system that distinguishes anxiety and depression" [p. 31]. There is some support for the content-specificity hypothesis. For example, Beck et al. (1987) compared the performance of anxious and depressed patients on the Cognitions Checklist. The anxious group reported more anxiety-relevant thoughts and images than the depressed group, whereas the depressed group reported significantly more negative cognitions.

So far we have considered Beck's schema theory of anxiety at a rather general level. Beck and Emery (1985) made a number of more specific predictions about cognitive functioning in anxious patients, some of which have been submitted successfully to experimental test. One such prediction is that "an anxious patient will be hypersensitive to any aspects of a situation that are potentially harmful but will not respond to its benign or positive aspects" [p. 33]. There is plentiful evidence that anxious individuals selectively allocate processing resources to threatening rather than to non-threatening stimuli (e.g., D.E. Broadbent & M. Broadbent, 1988; Eysenck, MacLeod, & Mathews, 1987; MacLeod, Mathews, & Tata, 1986).

Another prediction which is consistent with much of the evidence is that "the range of stimuli that can evoke anxiety in generalized anxiety disorder may increase until almost any stimulus is perceived as a danger" (Beck & Emery, 1985, p. 32). One of the implications of this prediction is that anxious patients are more likely than normal controls to interpret ambiguous stimuli in a threatening fashion. There is accumulating evidence that this is, indeed, the case (e.g., Eysenck et al., 1987, 1991; Mathews, Richards, & Eysenck, 1989).

A further prediction made by Beck and Emery (1985) is as follows:

> Because the patient 'uses up' a large part of his cognitive capacity by scanning for threatening stimuli, the amount available for attending to other demands is severely restricted [p. 31].

It is well established that anxious individuals have reduced processing capacity (e.g., Darke, 1988 a; Eysenck, 1979 a, 1982, 1983, 1985; Eysenck & Calvo, in press). However, it is not clear that this reduced capacity occurs because of environmental scanning. Indeed, many theorists (e.g., Eysenck, 1979 a; Wine, 1971) have argued that processing of worries and other self-concerns by anxious individuals is responsible for the reduced processing capacity they demonstrate on most complex cognitive tasks.

Evaluation

Beck's theoretical approach has the great merit that it was the first systematic attempt to provide a comprehensive cognitive theory of clinical anxiety. In particular, the notion that maladaptive schemas or schemata influence the processing of threat-related information in a top-down or conceptually driven manner is a valuable one. Anxious individuals do frequently exhibit the schema-congruent processing predicted by this schema theory. It is of particular interest and importance that cognitive functioning in anxious patients appears to be very similar whether observed in clinical settings by Beck and his colleagues or in controlled laboratory conditions by cognitive psychologists.

While the pioneering value of Beck's schema theory is indisputable, the validity of his theoretical edifice is open to question on several grounds. First, schema-congruent processing in both anxious and depressed groups is less extensive in scope that is anticipated on schema theory (see MacLeod & Mathews, 1991 a, for a review). More specifically, anxious patients usually fail to show any evidence of schema-congruent retrieval biases (e.g., Mogg, 1988; Mogg, Mathews, & Weinman, 1987), and depressed individuals do not exhibit schema-congruent attentional or perceptual biases (e.g., Gotlib, McLachlan, & Katz, 1988; MacLeod et al., 1986). These anomalies will be considered in more detail in Chapter 5. For present purposes, the main point is that they can be resolved only by considering information processing in more detail than is done by Beck and Emery (1985) and by Beck and Clark (1988).

Second, according to the content-specificity hypothesis, the cognitive functioning of anxious and depressed patients differs in terms of content rather than process. In fact, as we have just seen, the actual differences in cognitive functioning between anxious and depressed patients are much greater than can be accommodated by the content-specificity hypothesis. There are some theoretical speculations on the significance of these differences in Chapter 5.

Third, the central theoretical construct of 'schema' is amorphous, and often seems to mean little more than 'belief'. This imprecision is of some importance when it comes to evaluating the theory. For example, Beck and Clark (1988) argue that maladaptive threat or danger schemas cause anxious patients to attend selectively to threat-related stimuli. The notion that stimuli which are consistent with the expectations of a currently active schema are preferentially processed may sound plausible, but it appears to be inconsistent with much of the available evidence. Berlyne (e.g., 1960) discovered that attention was directed mainly to stimuli that conflicted with expectations. Friedman (1979) found that visual stimuli which were inconsistent with the prevailing frame or schema were looked at for twice as long as consistent stimuli.

Fourth, while Beck argues that there may be individuals who possess latent maladaptive danger schemas, and who therefore have a cognitive vulnerability for developing clinical anxiety, he has not attempted to identify these individuals. It would obviously strengthen the theory considerably if it were possible to demonstrate in a prospective study that individuals characterized by latent maladaptive danger schemas had a greater probability than other individuals of subsequently becoming clinically anxious.

Fifth, while the major theoretical emphasis of Beck and Emery (1985) and Beck and Clark (1988) is on stable, long-term individual differences in underlying schemas, the contrast between active and 'latent' schemas allows for change over time. The existence of latent schemas is inferred when there is no behavioural evidence of schema-based processing biases in individuals who are assumed to possess maladaptive schemas (e.g., individuals who have recovered from clinical anxiety). An alternative possibility, of course, is that the measures taken (e.g., verbal reports) are simply insufficiently sensitive, and that measures of preconscious processes would indicate that the underlying schemas are not really latent. This alternative possibility deserves to be explored.

Sixth, there is the issue of causality. According to Beck and Emery (1985), cognitive factors do not directly cause anxiety disorders; instead, non-normal cognitive functioning is often the first indication of the onset of an anxiety disorder, and it can lead to malfunctioning of the affective and behavioural systems. These views are rather limited. It is probably over-simplified to assume that all aspects of non-normal cognitive functioning relate to anxiety disorders in the same way. Some aspects (e.g., reported anxious and irrational thoughts) may form part of the anxiety disorder itself, whereas others (e.g., automatic processes to threatening stimuli) may be predisposing factors to clinical anxiety. Beck and Emery (1985) do not consider such a possibility, nor do they address the complex issue of how to obtain evidence to elucidate these issues.

Seventh, Beck and Emery (1985) and Beck and Clark (1988) make extensive use of introspective evidence. Introspective evidence can obviously be distorted by demand or expectancy effects, and it is uninformative about pre-conscious processes. An additional limitation of the research approach of Beck and his associates is that they have generally not obtained data from non-anxious control groups, and so the significance of their introspective reports from anxious patients is difficult to assess.

BOWER'S ASSOCIATIVE NETWORK THEORY

Bower (1981) proposed a theory concerned with the relationship between mood and memory. This theory was subsequently extended by Bower and Cohen (1982), Gilligan and Bower (1984), and Bower (1987). The starting point for this theoretical approach is the notion that long-term memory can be regarded as a semantic associative network in which concepts are represented as nodes. This notion has informed several well-known theories of semantic memory (e.g., Collins & Loftus, 1975). What is more original about Bower's (1981) theory is the way in which emotions are treated. They are also represented as nodes within the semantic network.

When any node (whether or not it is an emotion node) is activated by external or internal stimuli, activation from that node spreads in a selective fashion to other related nodes. Accessing information in any node requires a critical level of activation in that node. There is substantial evidence from the priming literature (e.g., Neely, 1977) that activation does, indeed, spread from an initially activated node to associatively related nodes.

When an individual is in an emotional state (e.g., anxious), the node for that emotion is activated and activation speads to associated nodes. These associated nodes will typically contain information which is congruent in mood with the experienced emotion. Thus, in the case of anxiety, concepts such as 'failure', 'danger', 'stupid', would become activated when a person was feeling anxious. The basic prediction is that all tasks involving access to stored information should demonstrate mood-congruent effects because of this increased activation of mood-congruent information. Thus, for example, there should be mood congruity in learning, with emotionally toned information being learned best when its affective value corresponds to that of the learner's current mood state. There should also be thought congruity, in which an individual's free associations, thoughts, and interpretations tend to be thematically congruent with his or her mood state. There should also be mood-state-dependent recall, in which recall is best when the mood at recall is the same as that at the time of learning.

The basic network theory was extended by Bower and Cohen (1982). They pointed out that, within the original theory, activation of any emotion node would automatically lead to the experience of that emotion. In reality, of course, it is perfectly possible to think about anxiety without actually becoming anxious. To handle this, Bower and Cohen (1982) introduced the idea of a 'blackboard', which corresponds closely to the notion of 'working memory' (Baddeley & Hitch, 1974). In essence, to re-experience the emotion associated with a given event, it is necessary to recreate the state of the blackboard or working memory as well as activating the appropriate emotion node.

A more consequential change to the original theory was proposed by Bower (1987). He pointed out that mood-state-dependent recall had proved difficult to obtain; indeed, he admitted that, "the effect seems a will-of-the-wisp that appears or not in different experiments in capricious ways that I do not understand" [p. 451]. These disappointing findings led him to propose the causal belonging hypothesis. According to this hypothesis, mood-state-dependent recall is found only when the learner causally attributes his or her emotional state at the time of learning to the to-be-learned stimulus. The reason is that causal attribution leads to an effective association between the emotional state and the stimulus, a state of affairs which is lacking when the emotional state is induced prior to the introduction of the learning task.

Bower has been mainly concerned to provide a theoretical account of the effects of current mood state on information processing. His research reflects this concern, since he has typically carried out mood-manipulation studies on normal groups. However, the theory does have potential application to mood-disordered clinical patients for at least two reasons. First, induced mood in normals may have the same effects on cognition as current mood state in anxious and depressed patients. Second, individuals differ in the richness of the associative connections surrounding each emotion node, with anxious patients presumably tending to have more nodes strongly associated with the anxiety node than normals. Such differences in the semantic network could underlie relatively long-term differences in cognitive functioning (see Ingram, 1984, for an attempt to develop such a theory).

Evaluation

Bower's network theory has provided an excellent focus for research on mood and cognition. Indeed, his is the leading theory in that area, and it has generated a considerable volume of research (see the review by Blaney, 1986). In general terms, mood-induction studies have provided some support for the notion of mood-congruent effects in perception, learning, and memory (e.g., Bower, Gilligan, & Monteiro, 1981; Clark & Teasdale, 1982; Schare, Lisman, & Spear, 1984). However, it is becoming increasingly clear that mood-congruent effects are considerably less widespread than is predicted by the theory. For example, as we have already seen, it has proved difficult to obtain good evidence for mood-state-dependent recall. In addition, it follows from Bower's (1981) theory that the same pattern of mood-congruency effects should be found in anxious and depressed mood states, but this is by no means the case. Mood-congruency effects involving memory have been difficult to demonstrate with anxiety, and mood-congruency effects involving attention are not usually found with depression (see MacLeod, 1990, for details).

There have also been other failures to replicate findings. The evidence suggests that the predictions of network theory are more often confirmed when subjects are in positive moods than when they are in negative moods. There are several cases in which negative moods have reduced the learning and recall of affectively positive information but have failed to enhance the learning and recall of negative information.

While it is not known exactly why negative moods do not always lead to enhanced learning and memory for affectively negative information, it is possible to suggest a plausible reason. It is probably reasonable to assume that anyone who is in a negative mood is motivated to improve that mood. Even if the negative mood activates negative associations as Bower (1981) proposed, it may well be that efforts are then made to counteract the negative consequences by focusing on non-congruent or positive associations (Fiske & Taylor, 1984).

Doubts about the interpretation of some of the findings have been raised. For example, W.J. Perrig and P. Perrig (1988) obtained fairly typical 'mood-congruent effects' in subjects who were instructed to behave as if they were depressed or happy, despite the fact that the experimenters made no attempt to induce any mood state. This suggests that to some extent subjects may be simply behaving in the way they believe the experimenter wants them to behave.

In spite of the fact that network theory has many successful predictions to its credit, it is clearly over-simplified in a number of ways. Emotions or moods and cognitive concepts are both represented as nodes within a semantic network, and are thus treated in a rather similar way theoretically. In reality, however, moods and cognitions are very different from each other. Moods are diffuse and difficult to classify with accuracy, whereas cognitive concepts are usually readily differentiated. Moods tend to increase or decrease gradually in intensity, whereas cognitions tend to be all-or-none and there is often rapid change from one cognition to another. In view of these pervasive differences between emotions and cognition, it seems highly probable that emotions are more than just nodes in a semantic network.

Bower's (1981) theory is also over-simplified in the account which it provides of mood-congruency effects. In essence, associative priming is the mechanism allegedly responsible for such effects. This mechanism is relatively passive and 'bottom-up' or data-driven, and does not allow adequately for the involvement of 'top-down' or conceptually driven processes. In other words, priming may be involved in mood-congruency effects, but it is improbable that it is the only mechanism which needs to be considered.

Finally, there are some criticisms which can be levelled at semantic network theories simply as models of long-term memory. It is inherently improbable that the passive spread of activation from node to node in a semantic network can account for more than a small fraction of language processing. For example, concepts can be associated or related to each other in numerous different ways, and most network theories fail to reflect this complexity (see Power & Champion, 1986). Furthermore, the nodes in Bower's (1981) semantic network theory represent words. As we saw with Beck's schema theory, there are many purposes for which larger meaningful units (e.g., schemata) need to be postulated.

WILLIAMS ET AL. (1988)

Williams, Watts, MacLeod, and Mathews (1988) put forward an ambitious theory encompassing both anxiety and depression. However, since our primary focus is on anxiety and cognition, we will refer only in passing to their theoretical account of cognitive factors in depression.

A central theoretical distinction for Williams et al. (1988) is that between integration or priming and elaboration. This distinction was originally proposed by Graf and Mandler (1984). According to them, priming is an automatic process in which a stimulus word produces activation of the various components comprising its internal representation. This automatic activation strengthens the organization of the internal representation, and means that the word will subsequently be accessed more readily when only a fraction of its features are presented. In contrast, elaboration is a strategic process in which the activation of the internal representation of a presented word leads to the activation of other, associated internal representations. This speed of activation either strengthens existing inter-connections among words or forms new inter-connections. Elaboration has the effect of making the presented word easier to retrieve subsequently. The distinction between priming and elaboration is relevant during retrieval as well as during encoding. Words may be retrieved in a relatively automatic and effortless fashion, or they may be retrieved only as a result of an active search of long-term memory.

The distinction between integration or priming and elaboration provided Williams et al. (1988) with a potentially important advantage at the theoretical level over some other theories. Bower's (1981) semantic network theory and Beck and Emery's (1985) schema theory both predict that biases involving affect-congruent effects should be pervasive throughout the cognitive processing system. In contrast, it is entirely possible within the theoretical framework of Williams et al. (1988) for an affect-congruent bias to be relatively circumscribed. A bias may be apparent in tasks involving priming but not in those involving integration, or vice versa. Indeed, Williams et al. (1988) argued that precisely this kind of dissociation characterizes anxiety and depression, although the nature of the dissociation differs with the two emotional disorders:

anxiety preferentially affects the passive, automatic aspect of encoding and retrieval, whereas depression preferentially affects the more active, effortful aspects of encoding and retrieval [pp. 173-174].

The detailed model proposed by Williams et al. (1988) indicates more clearly the circumstances in which anxiety is associated with a bias in the processing of threatening information. At the pre-attentive stage, stimulus input is processed by an affective decision mechanism. This mechanism assesses the threat value of the stimulus or stimuli presented, and this information is then passed to the resource allocation mechanism. This mechanism directs attention towards or away from threatening sources. State anxiety affects the output of the affective decision mechanism by increasing the subjective threat value of presented stimuli. Trait anxiety "may represent a permanent tendency to react to input from the ADM [affective decision mechanism] by directing attention towards or away from the location of threat" [p. 175].

These theoretical assumptions provide a way of understanding why trait and state anxiety interact with each other in some situations. In essence, high trait anxiety provides a constant tendency to direct attention towards threat and low trait anxiety is associated with a tendency to direct attention away from threat. These directional biases become greater in magnitude as the level of state anxiety increases. Precisely this interactional pattern has been obtained in a number of studies concerned with selective allocation of attention (e.g., D.E. Broadbent & M. Broadbent, 1988; MacLeod & Mathews, 1988; MacLeod, 1990).

As far as the development of anxiety disorders is concerned, the theory predicts that those high in trait anxiety are more vulnerable than those low in trait anxiety because of their cognitive processing of threatening stimuli. However, this vulnerability will typically lead to psychopathology only when the level of state anxiety is high, which increases the attentional bias towards threat. This is an example of the diathesis-stress model, according to which psychopathology is interactively determined by individual vulnerability or diathesis and by environmentally determined stress. A high level of trait anxiety constitutes the diathesis and the stress is provided by life events or other factors producing high levels of anxiety. Only a few details of how cognitive biases might precipitate anxiety disorders are supplied by Williams et al. (1988). However, it is clear that a strong attentional bias towards sources of threat would make the environment seem subjectively to be very threatening. This could ultimately raise an individual's anxiety to clinical levels.

As Williams et al. (1988) pointed out, the verbal reports of anxious patients are consistent with the notion that they focus selectively on threatening stimuli. This is especially the case so far as phobic patients are concerned. They generally attribute the source of their anxiety to specific kinds of threatening stimuli (e.g., other people, enclosed spaces).

According to Williams et al. (1988), the cognitive functioning of anxious and non-anxious individuals differs primarily when threatening or potentially threatening stimuli are being processed. However, there are numerous studies in which anxious and non-anxious groups have been found to differ in their performance of cognitive tasks in which only non-threatening stimuli were presented (see Chapter 7). The most commonly found difference is that the performance of anxious individuals is inferior to that of non-anxious individuals on a variety of cognitive tasks. These impairments may occur in anxious individuals because of "the pre-attentive switching of attention away from a task in hand to other mood-relevant concerns. Such switching is likely to occur even when neutral or ambiguous stimuli occur in the environment of the individual if such material is easily disambiguated as negative" [p. 179].

Evaluation

There are several attractive features of the theoretical model proposed by Williams et al. (1988). Probably its greatest success is in explaining the differences in cognitive functioning which characterize anxiety and depression. Theorists such as Bower (1981) and Beck and Emery (1985) have emphasized the similarities of the effects of anxiety and depression. As a consequence, they find it difficult to account for differences. In fact, anxiety affects pre-attentive and attentional processes more frequently than memory, whereas the opposite pattern is found with depression. These contrasting patterns can be accounted for in approximate fashion by invoking the distinction between priming or integration and elaboration. As far as anxiety is concerned, it certainly appears to be the case that pre-attentive and attentional processes involving priming or integration are of crucial significance.

The theoretical assumptions concerning some of the factors involved in the development of anxiety disorders are plausible although somewhat speculative. It is reasonable to regard high trait anxiety and the associated attentional bias towards threat as vulnerability factors for anxiety disorders. It is also reasonable to assume that stressful circumstances create high levels of state anxiety which magnify or exacerbate pre-existing processing biases. However, the processes mediating between an attentional bias and an anxiety disorder are not clearly specified. For example, worry is the central defining feature of generalized anxiety disorder according to DSM-IIIR (1987). Thus, in order to understand the development of generalized anxiety disorder it is presumably necessary to consider the factors causing worry. However, worry is scarcely discussed by Williams et al. (1988).

Williams et al. (1988) set themselves the ambitious task of producing a more comprehensive cognitive theory of anxiety and depression than any previous theory in the area. They were entirely successful in achieving this goal. In addition, they established a sound theoretical framework within which more specific theories could be developed. Indeed, in many ways the theory proposed in this book owes its origins to the pioneering efforts of Williams et al. (1988). Of course, it is the fate of most pioneers to take some false steps, and there are various criticisms that can be made of the theory of Williams et al. (1988).

First, their account of anxiety and attention is too limited. They stress the notion that anxious individuals have an attentional bias towards threat, but de-emphasize other attentional phenomena associated with anxiety. As is discussed in Chapter 4, there are theoretical and empirical reasons for arguing that anxiety affects the breadth of attention, attentional scanning, and distractibility, and that all of these attentional processes are influenced by anxiety even in the absence of threat-related stimuli. In other words, anxiety affects more aspects of attentional functioning than is suggested by Williams et al. (1988).

Second, the theory is more explicit at the *descriptive* level of identifying cognitive differences between anxious patients and normal controls than at the *explanatory* level of pinpointing those differences which form part of a cognitive vulnerability factor. This deficiency, although readily explicable because of the lack of relevant empirical evidence available to Williams et al. (1988), is crucial. Differences between anxious patients and normals which relate to cognitive vulnerability are of greater theoretical significance than those which are merely secondary consequences of being in a clinically anxious state.

Third, while the distinction between priming or integration and elaboration has proved theoretically fruitful, it has limited applicability. Many tasks involve both priming and elaboration, and it is often extremely difficult to disentangle the relative contributions of these two processes to performance. Furthermore, it is improbable that more than a small fraction of the processes involved in cognitive functioning can meaningfully be categorized as involving either priming or elaboration.

Fourth, while Williams et al. (1988) acknowledge that the nature of any cognitive bias may differ from one anxiety disorder to another, most of their theorizing involves the implicit assumption that there are important similarities in cognitive functioning across the anxiety disorders. There is insufficient evidence available at present to evaluate this assumption properly (but see Chapter 8). However, there are indications that the anxiety disorders differ considerably from each other in various ways. As Torgersen (1990) has pointed out, there is strong evidence for genetic influences in the aetiology of panic disorder, but generalized anxiety disorder does not seem to show any genetic transmission. The notion that panic disorder and generalized anxiety disorder have very different aetiology is supported by the findings of Noyes, Clarkson, and Crowe (1987), who carried out a family study of anxiety disorders. They discovered that panic disorder was the only diagnosis which was more common in relatives of probands with panic disorder than in relatives of controls, and generalized anxiety disorder was the only diagnosis with enhanced frequency among the relatives of probands with generalized anxiety disorder. It remains possible that the same cognitive vulnerability factors are involved in the aetiology of all anxiety disorders, but the major differences among the anxiety disorders should not be obscured.

Fifth, as Williams et al. (1988) admitted, "The model is based largely on studies with word stimuli" [p. 178]. As a consequence, the extent to which the theory can appropriately be extrapolated to cover other kinds of stimuli is currently unknown. In particular, threatening situations often require thinking of appropriate action strategies, whereas visually presented words do not. There must also be a suspicion that theoretical constructs such as 'priming' and 'elaboration' can be applied with greater precision to simple, discrete stimuli such as words than to complex and/or continuous stimuli (e.g., films).

Sixth, the theory is concerned mainly with the early stages of threat appraisal. This can be seen if we consider the appraisal processes postulated by Lazarus (e.g., Lazarus & Averill, 1972). He distinguished between primary and secondary appraisal processes. The former processes are concerned with comparing stimuli against relevant stored information, whereas the latter relate to coping skills and other resources available to handle the situation. Most of the theoretical views and research discussed by Williams et al. (1988) are of much more relevance to primary than to secondary appraisal processes. In other words, only a partial account is given of the cognitive processes triggered off by threatening stimuli and situations.

SUMMARY AND CONCLUSIONS

The four theoretical positions discussed in this chapter can be considered with respect to the five major issues relevant to individual differences in anxiety and cognition which were discussed in the introduction to this chapter. These issues are as follows:

1. cognitive differences between clinically anxious and normal groups;
2. experimental investigation of conscious and non-conscious processes relevant to (1);
3. aetiology of anxiety disorders, especially cognitive vulnerability factors, with relevant evidence;
4. personality dimensions relevant to vulnerability; and
5. interrelationships among the cognitive system, the physiological system, and behaviour.

Gray, in his neuropsychological theory, dealt with individual differences in personality (i.e., trait anxiety) which may be relevant to anxiety disorders. He also addressed the issue of non-normal cognitive functioning in clinically anxious patients. Finally, Gray considered the relationship between cognitive and physiological functioning. However, cognitive tasks designed to investigate conscious and non-conscious processing in anxious and non-anxious individuals are not explored, and there is little analysis of possible cognitive vulnerability factors.

Beck has focused on differences between anxiety disordered patients and normals in cognitive functioning. He has also shown increased interest in the use of experimental tasks to identify these differences. Furthermore, he has addressed the issue of cognitive vulnerability, albeit in the absence of direct empirical evidence. Personality dimensions in normals which might predispose to clinical anxiety are not considered in detail by Beck, and little of his theorizing is devoted to the relationships among the cognitive, physiological, and behavioural systems.

Bower has concentrated on mood and cognition, and has devised a number of tasks to explore affect-congruent effects in cognition. He has made numerous contributions in this area, but has not considered in detail how individual differences in personality or in patient status might influence cognition. The interrelationships among cognition, physiology, and behaviour are also not analysed.

The theory of Williams et al. (1988) clearly comes closest of the four theories to addressing the major issues. The only one of the five issues which is not examined at length is the one concerned with the interrelationships among the systems involved in cognition, physiology, and behaviour. It is, therefore, the most comprehensive theory discussed in this chapter. This is one of the reasons why the theory put forward in this book resembles the theory proposed by Williams et al. (1988) more than any of the other theories.

If one looks across the four theories, then there are two issues which have received less attention than they deserve. The first such issue is that of cognitive vulnerability factors for anxiety disorders. This issue is considered in several later chapters, and is of major importance within the theoretical framework adopted in this book. The second relatively neglected issue is that of the role of the cognitive system *vis-à-vis* other systems (e.g., the physiological and the behavioural). This issue is also neglected in this book. The reason is that the optimal strategy is probably to form an understanding of the cognitive system in anxious individuals before attempting to elucidate how the cognitive system relates to other systems.

CHAPTER THREE

Vulnerability to Anxiety

INTRODUCTION

As we saw in Chapter 2, those interested in individual differences in anxiety can focus either on high- and low-anxious normal groups, or they can concentrate on patients suffering from anxiety disorders. While trait anxiety is the personality dimension which has been of greatest interest to those investigating normal groups, it should be noted that other personality dimensions such as neuroticism and repression-sensitization are fairly closely related to trait anxiety. According to a review by Watson and Clark (1984), trait anxiety correlates approximately +0.70 with neuroticism, and it correlates approximately +0.80 to +0.85 with repression-sensitization as measured by the Repression-Sensitization Scale.

As far as the anxiety disorders are concerned, the main theoretical focus in this book is on generalized anxiety disorder. Generalized anxiety disorder is one of the categories of anxiety disorder identified by the Third Revised *Diagnostic and Statistical Manual of Mental Disorders* (DSM-IIIR), which was issued by the American Psychiatric Association in 1987. The presence in at least two areas of life of unrealistic worries lasting for a minimum of six months is the central defining feature of generalized anxiety disorder (see Chapter 6). Other diagnostic features are signs of motor tension, autonomic hyperactivity, and vigilance.

The theoretical approach to generalized anxiety disorder which is proposed in this book conforms to the diathesis-stress model. In other words, it is assumed that generalized anxiety disorder occurs mainly (although not exclusively) in those individuals who are semi-permanently vulnerable and who are exposed to stressful life events. Vulnerability may depend in part on genetic factors (e.g., H.J. Eysenck, 1967), although the evidence provides little support for that view (Torgersen, 1983). It is assumed that there is a cognitive vulnerability factor, and that this vulnerability involves systematic biases in the cognitive system which influence the emotional impact of environmental events.

It is, therefore, an important issue to identify those individuals who are vulnerable to generalized anxiety disorder. In essence, it is assumed that high levels of trait anxiety predispose to generalized anxiety disorder. The best method of testing this assumption would be by means of a large-scale prospective study in which trait anxiety was measured in a normal sample. Those who subsequently suffered from generalized anxiety disorder could then be compared with those who did not in terms of their initial levels of trait anxiety. Unfortunately, such a study has never been carried out, so that one must of necessity rely on indirect evidence.

A study of some relevance was reported by McKeon, Roa, and Mann (1984). They compared obsessive-compulsive patients rated as having a highly anxious premorbid personality with patients having low premorbid anxiety. The former group had experienced only half as many life events on average as the latter group during the year preceding the onset of the disorder. The implication of this finding is that individuals having an anxious personality are more vulnerable to stress than those low in trait anxiety, and therefore few life events are needed to precipitate an anxiety disorder. If the environment is exceptionally threatening (e.g., on the battlefield or in a concentration camp), then even individuals having very non-anxious personalities can develop anxiety disorders (Eitinger, 1980; Von Baeyer, 1969).

An alternative way of attempting to ascertain premorbid levels of trait anxiety is to study individuals who have recovered from clinical anxiety. Of course, this approach is useful only to the extent that trait anxiety levels following recovery from clinical anxiety are the same as premorbid levels. They would not be the same if, for example, the experience of suffering from clinical anxiety produces lasting adverse effects so that the recovered levels of trait anxiety are more or less permanently elevated above the corresponding premorbid levels. Alternatively, there may be a 'contrast' effect with recovered anxious patients underestimating their trait anxiety because they feel relatively less anxious than they did in the clinical state. Yet another possibility is that those who have recovered from clinical anxiety may underestimate their trait anxiety level because they want to convince themselves that they are now functioning normally.

One of the earliest relevant studies was reported by Ingham (1966). The Maudsley Personality Inventory was administered to a sample of anxious patients, and then re-administered three years later. The Maudsley Personality Inventory includes a measure of neuroticism. Recovered patients who were 'very much better' had neuroticism scores resembling those of a normal random sample.

We (e.g., Eysenck et al., 1991) have obtained basically the same findings as Ingham (1966) in a number of studies. That is to say, the mean level of trait anxiety in recovered generalized anxiety disorder patients is typically rather close to population norms. While these findings are disappointing, we have already indicated various reasons why the trait anxiety scores of recovered patients may not provide an accurate assessment of premorbid scores.

Even if it were demonstrated conclusively that high trait anxiety predisposes to generalized anxiety disorder, it would still be necessary to identify the precise reasons why this was the case. A major orienting assumption throughout this book is that high levels of trait anxiety predispose to generalized anxiety disorder at least in part because of a cognitive vulnerability factor. As a consequence, it is important to investigate differences in cognitive functioning between normal groups high and low in trait anxiety. The characteristics of cognitive functioning in normals high in trait anxiety may well provide insights into the nature of the cognitive vulnerability factor in clinical anxiety. This point is developed more fully later in the chapter.

In spite of the fact that this book is concerned primarily with generalized anxiety disorder, it is assumed that the general theoretical approach adumbrated here is also of relevance to the other anxiety disorders. There is at present insufficient evidence available to permit definitive conclusions about the similarities and differences among the anxiety disorders from the cognitive perspective. However, panic disorder and post-traumatic stress disorder are considered in Chapter 8, and some speculations are offered about possible cognitive differences between patients belonging to those diagnostic categories and those suffering from generalized anxiety disorder.

In sum, our approach assumes that it is valuable to move towards a theoretical model which is applicable to trait anxiety in normals as well as to generalized anxiety disorder and to the other anxiety disorders. It is assumed that a cognitive vulnerability factor plays a significant role in the aetiology of clinical anxiety. Finally, it is assumed that the

methods of experimental cognitive psychology are the most appropriate
way of investigating cognitive functioning in anxious groups, and that
introspective evidence must be used with great caution.

TRAIT ANXIETY

Most theorists have drawn a distinction between trait anxiety and state
anxiety. Trait anxiety is a personality dimension, whereas state anxiety
is "characterized by subjective, consciously perceived feelings of tension
and apprehension, and heightened autonomic nervous system activity"
(Spielberger et al., 1970, p. 3). However, some theorists have claimed
that the distinction is of minor significance. For example, Allen and
Potkay (1981) argued as follows:

> The distinction between state and trait is arbitrary rather than explicit
> and discrete as has been taken for granted by lay and professional
> persons ... No ... criteria for determining whether a person's behaviours
> fit state or trait are currently available [p. 917].

In essence, they claimed that the state-trait distinction relates
mainly to temporal duration: States typically last for relatively short
periods of time, whereas traits remain essentially unchanged for
considerably longer. According to Allen and Potkay (1981), the fact that
states and traits both vary considerably in stability over time means
that the state-trait distinction is unclear.

The major problem with the position adopted by Allen and Potkay
(1981) is that they disregarded other criteria in terms of which traits
and states can be distinguished. Traits are assumed to stem from distant
causal factors such as heredity or the experiences of early childhood,
whereas states depend upon the current situation. The trait-state
distinction resembles that between disposition and occurrence (Ryle,
1949). A disposition is a property of an organism or object which is
inferred from predictable responses in the appropriate circumstances,
whereas an occurrence is a single observable event. As Fridhandler
(1986) pointed out, the addition of this criterion serves to clarify the
conceptual distinction between traits and states.

Physiologically based Theories

Historically, individual differences in trait anxiety or neuroticism have
usually been considered from the physiological perspective (H.J.
Eysenck, 1967; Gray, 1982; see Chapter 2). Since the approach to trait

anxiety and neuroticism adopted in this book is very different in its emphasis on the cognitive system, it is worth considering the limitations of these earlier theories. However, even if there are significant problems with existing physiologically based theories, that does not mean that the physiological system should not be considered. As Eysenck (1988 a) argued, "a complete theory of trait anxiety would indicate how the physiological, cognitive, and behavioural systems combine to determine how each individual deals with threatening and stressful situations" [p. 471].

According to the theories of H.J. Eysenck (1967) and Gray (1982), individual differences in trait anxiety or neuroticism are due mainly to heredity, and so an individual's level of trait anxiety or neuroticism will remain fairly constant over time. Heredity serves to determine individual differences in the responsiveness of certain physiological systems. According to H.J. Eysenck (1967), individual differences in neuroticism depend upon the functioning of the so-called 'visceral brain', which consists of the hippocampus, amygdala, cingulum, septum, and hypothalamus. According to Gray (1982), individual differences in trait anxiety depend upon the septo-hippocampal system, its neocortical projection in the frontal lobe, and its monoaminergic afferents from the brain-stem. It is also assumed that individuals with highly responsive physiological systems will be anxious across virtually all stressful situations, whereas low trait-anxious individuals will experience rather little anxiety in any situation; this we may term the 'unidimensional view' of trait anxiety. Of course, there are likely to be some idiosyncratic anxiety responses due to particular unpleasant experiences, but the essence of the unidimensional view is that there is a single anxiety factor rather than several.

There is evidence that all of these assumptions are incorrect. The first assumption is that heredity plays a major role in determining trait anxiety or neuroticism. According to H.J. Eysenck (1967), "the evidence suggests fairly strongly that something like 50 per cent of individual differences in neuroticism and extraversion ... is accountable for in terms of hereditary influences" [p. 210]. According to Gray (1982), "Studies ... of the personality traits of neuroticism and extraversion ... estimate the contribution of heredity to these conditions at about 50 per cent of the variance" [p. 438]. The research of Shields (1962) provides some support for these views. He discovered on a test of neuroticism that the correlation between monozygotic (MZ) twins brought up apart was +0.53, compared to +0.38 for MZ twins brought up together, and +0.11 for dizygotic (DZ) twins brought up together. The high correlation between MZ twins brought up apart seems to point to a strong genetic determination of neuroticism.

More recent findings have suggested that the role of genetic factors in determining neuroticism may be rather limited. Langinvainio, Kaprio, Koskenvuo, and Lonnqvist (1984) reported correlations of +0.25 for MZ twins brought up apart, +0.32 for MZ twins brought up together, and +0.10 for DZ twins brought up together. Pedersen et al. (1984) obtained correlations of +0.18 for MZ twins brought up apart, +0.37 for MZ twins brought up together, and +0.18 for DZ twins brought up together. The findings of Langinvainio et al. (1984) and of Pedersen et al. (1984) differ substantially from those of Shields (1962), and suggest a markedly smaller genetic involvement. As Torgersen (1990) concluded in his review of the evidence, "The development of the relatively normally distributed neuroticism or anxiousness may be modestly influenced by genetic factors ... However, by far the most important source of variance seems to be individual environmental factors" [p. 285].

The crucial assumption that there are consistent individual differences in the responsiveness of the 'visceral brain' or septo-hippocampal system has been considered in numerous studies (see H.J. Eysenck & M.W. Eysenck, 1985, and Fahrenberg, 1987, 1992 for reviews). As we saw in Chapter 2, there is very little good evidence for psychophysiological differences between individuals, high and low in trait anxiety or neuroticism (see H.J. Eysenck & M.W. Eysenck, 1985; Fahrenberg, 1987). This negative conclusion holds regardless of whether psychophysiological measures were taken under stressed or non-stressed conditions. However, the measures which have been taken provide only indirect evidence of activity within the visceral brain or septo-hippocampal system.

The fact that it is extremely difficult to identify any consistent psychophysiological differences between those high and low in trait anxiety is difficult to reconcile with the finding that high trait-anxious individuals indicate the existence of considerably more physiological symptoms than low trait-anxious subjects on self-report questionnaires (e.g., Spielberger's State-Trait Anxiety Inventory). It is true that correlations between reported symptoms and actual physiological measures are generally modest, averaging approximately +0.30 (Pennebaker, 1982). Nevertheless, the substantial discrepancy between actual and reported physiological symptoms as a function of trait anxiety is an apparent paradox.

The resolution of the paradox is not known at present. However, there is a plausible hypothesis which merits further consideration. As is discussed in Chapters 4 and 5, high trait-anxious individuals tend to attend selectively to threatening external stimuli, and they tend to interpret ambiguous stimuli in a threatening fashion. These processing characteristics, if applied to internal physiological stimuli, would lead high trait-anxious individuals to report more physiological symptoms than low trait-anxious individuals even if there were no actual differences in physiological functioning.

Evidence that attentional processes can affect reported physiological symptoms was discussed by Pennebaker (1982). He used the cold pressor test, in which subjects place their hand in a jar of very cold water. Some of the subjects were told to pay close attention to their hand while it was in the water, whereas other subjects were instructed to think about the Rotunda of the University of Virginia. Subjects in the former condition reported the onset of pain in much less time than did those in the latter condition.

High trait-anxious individuals may have greater expectations than low trait-anxious individuals of experiencing various physiological symptoms, and these expectations may affect attentional processes. Pennebaker and Skelton (1981) carried out a study in which subjects were told that ultrasonic noise might increase or might decrease skin temperature. They were then led to believe that they were being exposed to ultrasonic noise, although none was actually presented. Those subjects told that ultrasonic noise might increase their skin temperature reported attending more to sensations of increasing skin temperature and less to sensations of decreasing skin temperature than did subjects instructed that their skin temperature might decrease. The former subjects reported their finger temperatures as becoming warmer as a result of the alleged exposure to ultrasonic noise, whereas the latter subjects reported a modest change in the direction of decreased warmth.

The assumption that trait anxiety or neuroticism is constant or static over time has been considered in detail by Conley (1984). Test-retest reliability over long periods of time is often relatively low. However, this is due in part to the intrinsic unreliability of the questionnaires used. When the influence of this intrinsic unreliability is eliminated statistically, it turns out that the consistency from one year to the next is 0.98. This may sound high, but still implies that fairly large changes in trait anxiety or neuroticism often occur over a period of a few years. The level of year-by-year consistency is lower than that of intelligence, which is 0.99.

The uni-dimensional view of trait anxiety has been challenged by several theorists. For example, Endler (1983) has proposed replacing the uni-dimensional view of trait anxiety with a multi-dimensional conceptualization in which there are five different dimensions of trait anxiety. According to this multi-dimensional approach, the increase in state anxiety produced by a threatening environment will be greater among those high in trait anxiety than among those low in trait anxiety only when there is *congruence* between the nature of the threat and the dimension or facet of trait anxiety possessed by the individual. This prediction has been confirmed several times, but primarily when the dimensions of social evaluation and physical danger have been investigated (Donat, 1983; Kendall, 1978). Indeed, these are the only dimensions for which there is convincing empirical support.

In sum, physiologically based theories of trait anxiety or neuroticism have proved relatively unsuccessful. Such theories are typically based on assumptions about the importance of heredity, the longitudinal stability of trait anxiety or neuroticism, individual differences in psychophysiological responsiveness, and the uni-dimensional nature of trait anxiety. Since it is probable that all of these assumptions are partially or totally erroneous, it is clear that alternative accounts of trait anxiety and neuroticism are required.

The Cognitive Approach

The various inadequacies of the physiological approach to trait anxiety and neuroticism arise to a large extent because environmental influences and the role of learning are de-emphasized. As soon as one considers learning, then the importance of the cognitive system becomes obvious. Information is added to long-term memory over time. This additional information may increase or decrease the level of trait anxiety depending on whether it is predominantly anxiety-related or positive in affect. These changes within the cognitive system allow for dynamic changes in trait anxiety over time.

The cognitive approach can also potentially account for the multi-dimensional nature of trait anxiety. An individual's previous experience in stressful situations of a particular type will influence the information which is stored in long-term memory. This will in turn have an impact on that individual's susceptibility to anxiety in that type of situation.

The cognitive approach has the further advantage that it is not embarrassed by the failure to discover consistent psychophysiological differences between individuals high and low in trait anxiety or neuroticism. In essence, it is assumed by the cognitive approach that those high and low in trait anxiety differ in terms of the functioning of the cognitive system. It is entirely possible that there are also physiological differences, but such differences are not required by the cognitive approach.

The specific cognitive theory of trait anxiety proposed in this book has developed out of earlier theoretical formulations (e.g., Eysenck, 1979 a, 1986, 1987; Eysenck & Mathews, 1987). It has as its starting point the assumption that the major function of anxiety is to facilitate the early detection of signs of threat or impending danger in potentially threatening environments (see Chapter 1). This suggests that individuals high and low in trait anxiety are more likely to differ in their pre-attentive and/or attentional functioning than in other aspects of cognitive functioning (e.g., memory). More specifically, if threat is to be detected as rapidly as possible, then the attentional system needs to possess certain characteristics. Attention needs to be selective, favouring threat-related stimuli over neutral stimuli; there needs to be at least some processing of all of the stimuli in the environment to assess their threatening potential; and there needs to be constant attentional scanning of the environment. In addition, threat-related stimuli might be detected more readily if the attentional beam were broad initially, but became narrower after potential threat was detected.

The issue arises as to whether high trait-anxious individuals exhibit these characteristics of attentional functioning most of the time, or whether they are most likely to exhibit them when they are stressed or in a potentially threatening environment. There would be clear disadvantages in having an attentional system that was constantly scanning the environment and engaging in only limited processing of non-threatening stimuli. Accordingly, it is assumed that the attentional system in high-trait anxious normals is geared to detect threatening stimuli primarily when such individuals are in potentially threatening situations and/or high in state anxiety.

Eysenck (1991 c) has proposed what he called hypervigilance theory, according to which a crucial characteristic of anxious individuals is hypervigilance. Theoretically, hypervigilance can manifest itself in various sense modalities; however, it is generally most straightforward to investigate hypervigilance in the visual modality. In the case of normal individuals high in trait anxiety, this hypervigilance may manifest itself in a variety of different ways:

- general hypervigilance, which is demonstrated by a propensity to attend to any task-irrelevant stimuli which are presented; this is generally known as distractibility;
- a high rate of environmental scanning, which involves numerous rapid eye movements throughout the visual field;
- specific hypervigilance, which is demonstrated by a propensity to attend selectively to threat-related rather than neutral stimuli;
- a broadening of attention prior to the detection of a salient (e.g., threatening, task-relevant stimulus); and
- a narrowing of attention when a salient stimulus is being processed.

There are some additional assumptions which are incorporated within hypervigilance theory. First, it is assumed that the above aspects of attentional functioning will be more apparent when high trait-anxious normals are high in state anxiety than when they are low in state anxiety. Secondly, and more speculatively, it is assumed that hypervigilance forms an important part of a cognitive vulnerability factor for clinical anxiety. Individuals who have a hypervigilant attentional style perceive the environment as much more threatening than those who do not, and this increases the probability that they will develop clinical anxiety. Finally, it is assumed that most (or all) of the components of hypervigilance are latent in the sense that they will be manifest in vulnerable individuals especially in conditions of high stress and/or high state anxiety.

GENERALIZED ANXIETY DISORDER

Relatively little headway has been made in identifying the causes of generalized anxiety disorder. According to Rosenhan and Seligman (1989), "While the symptoms of generalized anxiety disorder are quite clear, its causes remain a mystery" [p. 232]. The limited evidence available suggests that genetic factors do not play a role in the aetiology of generalized anxiety disorder. Torgersen (1983) discovered that the frequency of anxiety disorders among the co-twins of sufferers from generalized anxiety disorder was 17% for MZ twins and 20% for DZ twins. However, the incidence of generalized anxiety disorder among first-degree relatives of patients with generalized anxiety disorder is 20%, compared to 4% among controls (Noyes et al., 1987). These findings, when combined with those of Torgersen (1983), suggest that there is purely environmental familial transmission of generalized anxiety disorder. Further support for this viewpoint comes from Torgersen (1986). He discovered that patients with generalized anxiety disorder had been subjected to far more traumata as children in the family environment than had patients with panic disorder.

One way of approaching the study of generalized anxiety disorder is to consider its various symptoms. Many of the symptoms are either cognitive or physiological in nature, as Gleitman (1987) pointed out:

> The [generalized anxiety disorder] patient is constantly tense and worried, feels inadequate, is oversensitive, can't concentrate or make decisions, and suffers from insomnia. This state of affairs is generally accompanied by any number of physiological concomitants — rapid heart rate, irregular breathing, excessive sweating, frequent urination, and chronic diarrhoea [p. 516].

Koksal, Power, and Sharp (1991) analysed the symptoms of generalized anxiety disorder patients in more detail. They made use of the Four Systems Anxiety Questionnaire, which provides measures of four relatively independent components of anxiety: affect, cognitive, behavioural, and somatic. This questionnaire was administered to generalized anxiety disorder, agoraphobic, simple phobic, panic disorder, and obsessive-compulsive patients. The patients with generalized anxiety disorder were the second highest scorers (out of the six groups) on affect and on the somatic component, and they were the third highest scorers on the cognitive and behaviour components. In other words, patients with generalized anxiety disorder have rather elevated scores on all four anxiety components.

It would be possible to attempt to develop a theory of generalized anxiety disorder which took all four components of anxiety into account. However, the theory proposed in this book focuses mainly on the cognitive component, and has relatively little to say about the other components. Why is this so? Some of the arguments for the central role of the cognitive system in anxiety were put forward in Chapter 1. It was argued there that the cognitive system is of crucial significance in achieving the primary function of anxiety, which is the rapid detection of threat. It was also argued that emotional reactions to stimuli are always preceded by some cognitive processing of those stimuli. A further reason is that it is assumed theoretically that cognitive processes often have important consequences for the other components of anxiety (i.e., affect, behaviour, and somatic symptoms). At present, however, there is very little evidence to support or disconfirm that particular assumption.

According to the cognitive perspective adopted in this book, generalized anxiety disorder can appropriately be considered within the framework of the hypervigilance theory proposed above. According to that theory, it is assumed that the attentional functioning of patients with generalized anxiety disorder resembles that of normal individuals with high trait anxiety. It is also assumed that hypervigilance forms part of a cognitive vulnerability factor for generalized anxiety disorder. Other cognitive processes and structures (e.g., those involved in learning and memory) may also contribute to a cognitive vulnerability factor, but they are of subsidiary importance to those involved in hypervigilance.

It should be emphasized that much of the theoretical account of generalized anxiety disorder developed in this book has been expressed previously by other theorists. For example, Beck and Emery (1985) argued as follows on the basis of their clinical experience:

The [anxious] patient is hypervigilant, constantly scanning the environment for signs of impending disaster or personal harm ... The anxious patient selectively attends to stimuli that indicate possible danger and becomes oblivious to stimuli that indicate that there is no danger" [p. 31].

While Williams et al. (1988) consider the anxiety disorders in general rather than focusing on generalized anxiety disorder, their general theoretical approach has much in common with the one developed here for generalized anxiety disorder. In spite of the similarities between hypervigilance and other theories of anxiety and cognition, there are also some important differences. First, it is assumed within hypervigilance theory that there are at least five different effects of anxiety on the functioning of the pre-attentive and attentional systems. In contrast, a smaller range of effects is considered by Beck and Emery (1985) and especially by Williams et al. (1988). Secondly, and related to the first point, one of the assumptions of hypervigilance theory is that a number of the effects of anxiety on attentional processes can occur in the absence of any threatening stimuli in the environment. These effects include a high rate of environmental scanning, general distractibility, broadening of attention prior to the detection of a threatening stimulus, and narrowing of attention after a salient stimulus has been detected. On the other hand, Beck and Emery (1985) and Williams et al. (1988) emphasize the effects of anxiety on attention to, and processing of, threat-related stimuli.

ASSESSING COGNITIVE VULNERABILITY

In essence, the research programme has consisted of two stages. The first stage was basically *descriptive*, and consisted of an attempt to delineate the main differences in cognitive functioning between anxious patients and normal controls. The second stage is more *explanatory*. It involves attempting to discover why the differences identified in the first stage have occurred. The emphasis here is on the causality issue; that is to say, on whether the cognitive differences reflect anxious mood state or whether they are due to stable characteristics associated with vulnerability to clinical anxiety. It is important to distinguish between two rather different forms of cognitive vulnerability, which we may term manifest vulnerability and latent vulnerability. Manifest vulnerability is involved if the non-normal cognitive functioning of anxious patients is present much of the time both before and after the time during which they are clinically anxious. In contrast, latent vulnerability is involved if non-normal cognitive functioning is observed before and after the period of clinical anxiety only under conditions of stress or high state anxiety. Some of the relevant theoretical and empirical issues are discussed by Eysenck (1989 c; 1991 e).

Prospective Studies

There is no doubt that the optimal way of distinguishing between a mood state and a vulnerability interpretation of non-normal cognitive functioning in anxious patients would be a prospective study. In essence, premorbid normals who subsequently developed generalized anxiety disorder would be compared on cognitive performance with currently anxious patients and with normal controls. There are three major possible outcomes. If non-stressed premorbid normals resembled current patients in their cognitive performance, but differed from normals who did not thereafter develop generalized anxiety disorder, then it could be concluded that cognitive functioning was part of a manifest vulnerability factor. If premorbid normals needed to be tested in stressful conditions in order to perform comparably to current anxious patients, this would indicate the existence of a latent vulnerability factor. Finally, if premorbid normals were similar to normal controls in their cognitive performance, but differed from currently anxious patients, then the implication would be that the non-normal cognitive functioning of currently anxious patients was due to their clinical anxious mood state.

There are considerable practical difficulties associated with the use of prospective studies. These difficulties are discussed in detail by Eysenck (1990 a), and so only some of the major ones will be considered here. For example, a very large sample of normals needs to be tested in order to ensure that it includes a sufficient number of premorbid individuals. Such a study would obviously need to be longitudinal, and would necessitate following up on a very large sample over a period of years. In view of these requirements, a prospective study would be extremely expensive.

Recovered Patient Studies

Since the practical problems meant that it was not feasible to carry out a prospective study, an alternative research strategy was adopted for much of the research discussed in this book. This research strategy involved administering various cognitive tasks to three different groups of subjects: currently anxious patients suffering from generalized anxiety disorder; recovered anxious patients who had recovered from generalized anxiety disorder for at least six months prior to experimental testing; and normal controls. The tasks selected were those on which currently anxious patients differ significantly from normal controls. It was assumed that those aspects of cognitive performance which reflect a manifest vulnerability factor would distinguish the normal controls from both of the other groups. In contrast, those aspects of cognitive performance reflecting current clinically anxious mood state or a latent vulnerability factor would distinguish the currently anxious patient group from the other two groups. Realistically, of course, it is also possible that some aspects of non-normal cognitive performance in currently anxious patients reflect an amalgam of the vulnerability factor and current mood state. In that case, the performance of the recovered patient group would be intermediate between that of the currently anxious patients and the normal controls.

There are various problems of implementation and interpretation with this particular research strategy. It is extremely difficult to be sure that putatively 'recovered' patients have genuinely recovered fully and do not have any residual symptoms. It is also difficult to provide an unequivocal interpretation of the performance data from recovered patients. Recovered patients may resemble currently anxious patients in some aspects of cognitive functioning because there are permanent effects of anxiety disorder on the cognitive system, rather than because of the existence of a cognitive vulnerability factor. Another reason why recovered patients might resemble currently anxious patients is simply that non-normal cognitive functioning reverts to normal more slowly than the other, non-cognitive aspects of generalized anxiety disorder. However, we attempted to guard against this possibility by stipulating that all of the recovered anxious patients had to have been recovered for a period of at least six months prior to testing.

There are different interpretative problems if recovered anxious patients are similar to normal controls in their cognitive performance but differ from currently anxious patients. While the non-normal cognitive performance of currently anxious patients may reflect their current anxious mood state, there are at least three other possibilities. First, there may be a cognitive vulnerability factor in generalized anxiety disorder, but this vulnerability factor may be latent and require stressful conditions and/or high state anxiety to reveal itself. Secondly, there may be a manifest cognitive vulnerability factor, but therapy has been successful in eliminating it. Thirdly, it is likely that many recovered anxious patients are highly motivated to demonstrate that they have, indeed, recovered. This could have the effect of making their performance misleadingly appear to be normal on at least some cognitive tasks. This interpretative difficulty can be obviated to some extent by selecting cognitive tasks which are unlikely to be affected by such bias.

The research strategy as described so far is rather limited. For example, consider the case in which recovered anxious patients perform comparably to normal controls on a variety of cognitive tasks. Such findings would certainly tend to disconfirm the notion that there is a manifest cognitive vulnerability factor. However, as we have already pointed out, they would not distinguish between two other possible explanations for non-normal cognitive functioning in currently anxious patients: A latent cognitive vulnerability factor or a secondary consequence of clinically anxious mood state. These two possibilities could be distinguished by testing recovered anxious patients under stressful conditions, if that were ethically acceptable. If the recovered patients showed non-normal cognitive functioning under those conditions, that would favour the explanation in terms of a latent vulnerability factor; if they did not, it would favour the view that a clinically anxious mood state is required for non-normal cognitive functioning to be observed.

Studies on Normals

If one is willing to make the assumption that high trait anxiety predisposes to generalized anxiety disorder, it then becomes possible to investigate cognitive vulnerability by comparing the cognitive functioning of normals high and low in trait anxiety. This approach is particularly valuable if the effects of trait and state anxiety are both considered. However, since trait and state anxiety often correlate rather highly with each other, it can be difficult to separate out their effects. As a consequence, it is generally advisable to compare high and low trait-anxious individuals under stressed and non-stressed conditions in order to clarify the situation.

The potential relevance of this approach can be seen if the three main alternative interpretations of non-normal cognitive functioning in anxious patients are considered in turn: a secondary consequence of clinically anxious mood state; a manifest vulnerability factor; and a latent vulnerability factor. If some aspect of cognitive functioning in anxious patients occurs only in response to a clinically anxious mood state, it should not be found in high trait-anxious normals under either stressed or non-stressed conditions. If a manifest vulnerability factor is involved, then high trait-anxious individuals should exhibit comparable non-normal cognitive functioning to anxious patients under both stressed and non-stressed conditions. If a latent vulnerability factor is involved, then high trait-anxious individuals should be more likely to perform equivalently to anxious patients under stressed than under non-stressed conditions. Performance under non-stressed conditions would depend on the level of state anxiety exhibited by high trait-anxious individuals, since they are sometimes high in state anxiety even in apparently relaxing circumstances (cf., Watson & Clark, 1984).

SUMMARY AND CONCLUSIONS

It is assumed that the aetiology of generalized anxiety disorder can be understood within the framework of the diathesis-stress model. It is further assumed that normal individuals high in trait anxiety are predisposed to develop generalized anxiety disorder. While this vulnerability of high trait-anxious normals might reside within the physiological system, it has proved extremely difficult to identify any consistent differences between high and low trait-anxious individuals in physiological functioning. However, there are several differences between the two groups in cognitive functioning, and it is assumed that there is a cognitive vulnerability factor for generalized anxiety disorder. More specifically, the assumption is made that an important difference between normals high and low in trait anxiety is in hypervigilance, and that hypervigilance constitutes the central ingredient of a cognitive vulnerability factor. Finally, it is assumed that most or all of the aspects of hypervigilance form a latent vulnerability factor, meaning that they primarily become manifest under conditions of stress and/or high state anxiety. In terms of testing for the existence of a cognitive vulnerability factor, it is useful to consider data from high and low trait-anxious normals under stressed and non-stressed conditions. It is also useful to collect data from patients who have recovered from generalized anxiety disorder. In essence, the notion that hypervigilance is a latent vulnerability factor for generalized anxiety disorder would be supported if hypervigilance were found in patients currently suffering from generalized anxiety disorder and in high trait-anxious normals under stressed conditions, but not in non-stressed high trait-anxious normals or non-stressed recovered anxious patients. If hypervigilance were a manifest vulnerability factor, then it would be found in high trait-anxious normals and in recovered anxious patients under both stressed and non-stressed conditions. Finally, if hypervigilance were simply a secondary consequence of being in a clinically anxious mood state, then hypervigilance would not be found in high trait-anxious normals under any circumstances or in recovered anxious patients whether stressed or non-stressed.

CHAPTER FOUR

Attentional Processes

INTRODUCTION

The issue of the biological significance of anxiety was considered in Chapter 1. In essence, it was argued there that anxiety possesses considerable survival value. It serves to facilitate the rapid detection of signs of threat or impending danger, and is especially valuable in potentially threatening environments. While anxiety does thus fulfil a useful function, it is clear that the processes involved in threat detection are used excessively by generalized anxiety disorder patients. They are so hypervigilant to threat that even ambiguous and non-threatening situations are often interpreted as threatening. In other words, many of the cognitive symptoms which characterize patients with generalized anxiety disorder represent the over-development of processes having genuine survival value.

It is presumably a combination of pre-attentive and attentional processes which make anxious individuals more sensitive to threat-related stimuli than are non-anxious individuals. Indeed, it is one of the central contentions of this book that many of the most important differences in cognitive functioning between anxious and non-anxious individuals lie within the pre-attentive and attentional systems. If the cognitive system of anxious individuals is geared to the rapid detection of threat, then this has several implications for attentional functioning; some of these implications are discussed below.

Hypervigilance theory was discussed in Chapter 3. It was proposed within that theory that anxiety might lead initially to the extraction of information from a broad area of the visual environment, followed by narrowly focused processing of any apparently salient (e.g., task-relevant; threatening) stimuli. It might also lead to constant scanning of the environment for the detection of threat-related stimuli. Anxiety might additionally produce heightened distractibility, in the sense that performance of a task would be disrupted by the concurrent presentation of task-irrelevant stimuli. Such disruption would probably be greater if the distracting stimuli were threat-related rather than neutral. Finally, anxiety might lead to a selective bias, in which threatening stimuli were preferentially processed in situations in which threatening and neutral stimuli were presented concurrently. The remainder of this chapter is devoted to an examination of the evidence relating to these various predictions.

BREADTH OF ATTENTION

Easterbrook (1959) proposed a very influential hypothesis, according to which states of high emotionality, arousal, and anxiety all reduce the breadth of attention and increase attentional selectivity. More specifically, he argued that the range of cues used (basically the breadth of attention) reduces as anxiety or arousal increases, which "will reduce the proportion of irrelevant cues employed, and so improve performance. When all irrelevant cues have been excluded, however ... further reduction in the number of cues employed can only affect relevant cues, and proficiency will fall" [p. 193].

The most common way in which Easterbrook's (1959) hypothesis has been tested is by assessing subjects' performance on concurrent primary and secondary tasks. The basic prediction is that high levels of anxiety should have a more adverse effect on performance of the secondary than of the primary task. However, findings consistent with Easterbrook's (1959) provide less convincing support for it than is usually thought to be the case. As Eysenck (1982) pointed out, "There are nine possible combinations of main-task and subsidiary-task performance, only three of which are clearly incompatible with Easterbrook's hypothesis; in those cases, arousal either has a less detrimental effect or a greater enhancing effect on the subsidiary task than on the main task" [pp. 50–51].

Ten experimental tests of Easterbrook's (1959) hypothesis with respect to anxiety were discussed by Eysenck (1982). In most cases, anxiety was manipulated by selecting high and low scorers on a questionnaire measure of trait anxiety, but in two of the studies

(Weltman & Egstrom, 1966; Weltman, Smith, & Egstrom, 1971) anxiety was created by using what appeared to be dangerous environments. The modal findings were that there was no effect of anxiety on performance of the primary task, but that high anxiety significantly impaired performance on the secondary task.

A problem with several of the above studies designed to test Easterbrook's (1959) hypothesis is that the subsidiary task involved incidental learning which was assessed several seconds or minutes later. While reduced incidental learning is consistent with a narrowing of attention, a range of non-attentional mechanisms involved in storage, consolidation, and retrieval of information may also be implicated.

More convincing evidence of a narrowing of attention was reported by Weltman et al. (1971). There was a central visual acuity task and a secondary task which involved pressing a button when a light flashed in the periphery of vision. Some of the subjects carried out the experiment in a pressure chamber, and thought that they were performing a 60 foot dive. As a consequence, they were more anxious than the control subjects. The two groups performed comparably on the central task, but the anxious group detected only half as many peripheral lights as the control group.

Additional evidence of attentional narrowing was obtained by Levinson (1989). He presented anxiety disordered patients and controls with a visual display of seven elephants under various conditions, and asked the subjects to indicate how many elephants could be seen clearly. The anxious patients had a much smaller perceptual span than the controls in all three conditions. This appears contrary to the prediction of hypervigilance theory, since anxious individuals should show a broadening of attention when salient stimuli are presented in the periphery. However, hypervigilance theory refers to detection rather than to clear perception. Furthermore, it is possible that the results were affected by response bias, with the anxious patients adopting a more stringent criterion (Mogg, pers. comm.).

According to Easterbrook (1959), the attentional narrowing under high anxiety revealed in the various findings described above is due to a relatively passive and automatic process. However, a rather different theoretical account may well be preferable. For example, since anxiety reduces the available capacity of working memory (see Chapter 7), it would be an appropriate strategy for anxious individuals to restrict their limited processing resources to those stimuli forming part of the primary task. Other theoretical accounts will be discussed a little later.

It is still generally believed that Easterbrook's hypothesis provides a reasonably accurate account of the effects of arousal and anxiety on the breadth of attention. However, there is an apparent conflict between this hypothesis and the central theoretical orientation proposed in this book. We have assumed throughout that the cognitive system in anxious individuals functions in such a way as to maximize the probability of detecting threatening environmental stimuli. This is presumably best achieved by extracting information from a wide area rather than reducing the range of cues used. As Shapiro and Lim (1989) pertinently pointed out,

> if an organism is experiencing a state of anxiety (e.g., fear), it might be to that organism's advantage to employ its peripheral detection mechanisms (either peripheral vision or audition) to locate and be prepared to respond to a source of stimulation. The superior detection and/or localization properties of the peripheral visual or auditory system, given its larger receptive field, make them better candidates for choice under these circumstances [p. 350].

How is the notion that extracting information from a broad area is optimal for threat detection in anxious individuals to be reconciled with the evidence indicating that anxious individuals actually show narrowing of attention? As is proposed within hypervigilance theory (see Chapter 3), at least part of the answer appears to be that anxiety reduces the breadth of attention only when peripheral information is of little or no relevance to the subject's primary task. When peripheral information is of as much relevance as central information, then anxiety seems to be associated with a broad sampling of information. Of course, this is precisely the state of affairs in everyday life when anxious individuals find themselves in an uncertain environment.

One of the first studies in which peripheral information was relevant was reported by Cornsweet (1969). She measured choice response times to central lights on the left and the right of the fixation point. On some trials, a peripheral light was presented 300 msec before the central light on the same side of the fixation point. Those subjects who were threatened with electric shocks responded faster to the central lights when preceded by a peripheral light, whereas control subjects did not. The implication is that aroused and/or anxious subjects made more use of peripheral information than did those at lower levels of arousal and/or anxiety.

The most convincing evidence that anxiety can be associated with broadened attention was reported by Shapiro and Lim (1989). They created anxious and non-anxious mood states by playing Stravinsky's *The rite of spring* and Fauré's *Ballad for piano and orchestra* respectively. The subjects were instructed to fixate on a central fixation point. On most trials, a central or a peripheral visual signal was presented, and the subjects had to respond as rapidly as possible by pressing the relevant response key. On 20% of the trials, the central and peripheral stimuli were presented at the same time, and the subjects had to respond by pressing the key corresponding to the stimulus they detected first. The main finding was that the anxious subjects were far more likely than the non-anxious subjects to respond to the peripheral stimulus: The respective percentages were 49.9% and 11.1%. This finding suggests that the induction of an anxious mood produces greater sensitivity to peripheral stimuli and a broadening of attention.

Rather similar results were reported by Shapiro and Johnson (1987) using the same paradigm that was subsequently employed by Shapiro and Lim (1989). They created anxiety and/or arousal in some of their subjects by giving them a number of electric shocks. When central and peripheral stimuli were presented together, the aroused (or anxious) subjects were much more likely than the control subjects to detect the peripheral stimulus first.

If, as we have assumed, anxious individuals endeavour to use their attentional system so as to ensure that threatening stimuli are detected as rapidly as possible, then a further prediction is possible. As Shapiro, Egerman, and Klein (1984) pointed out, "If one considers the relative advantage of the auditory system's 360-deg detection capability over the visual system's more localized detection properties, it is to an animal's advantage in most aversive situations to attend to audition over vision" [p. 552]. They investigated this hypothesis in a task in which visual and auditory stimuli were presented at the same time. Subjects were instructed to respond to whichever stimulus was detected first under shocked or non-shocked conditions. Non-shocked subjects showed visual dominance, but this was significantly attenuated among shocked subjects. Thus, arousal and/or anxiety can cause a shift of attention away from the visual modality and towards the auditory modality.

In order to make sense of the findings on anxiety and attentional selectivity, we need to take account of some of the characteristics of visual attention (see Eysenck, 1984 a; Eysenck & Keane, 1990, for details). The first point is that the visual spotlight has a variable beam, in the sense that the area it covers can be enlarged or decreased (LaBerge, 1983). The second point is that the location of a stimulus can be detected in peripheral vision, but only stimuli within the attentional spotlight receive full semantic processing. The third point is that we need to distinguish between focused attention and attentional search (D.E. Broadbent, M. Broadbent, & Jones, 1986). Focused attention is used when the location of a target is known in advance, whereas attentional search is used when the location is unknown.

The above considerations suggest that anxiety may have two rather different effects on attentional breadth. When it is not known which part of the visual environment may contain a threatening stimulus or significant (e.g., task-relevant) information (and so attentional search is required), the anxious individual's optimal strategy is to extract information from as broad an area as possible in order to facilitate rapid detection. However, when a salient stimulus is detected (and so focused attention can be used), it then becomes optimal to focus attention on that stimulus in order to ascertain the amount of threat which it poses. In other words, anxious individuals may shift from an initial stage involving broad sampling of environmental information to a subsequent stage of highly focused visual attention.

There has been a fair amount of theoretical speculation in this section, and other theoretical possibilities are worth considering. For example, if a narrow attentional beam were combined with very rapid scanning of the environment in anxious individuals, then rapid detection of threat would still be possible. A broad attentional beam combined with rapid scanning would obviously permit very rapid visual perception of the visual environment, but this might be achieved at a considerable cost in terms of ability to extract usable information.

SCANNING

What pattern of eye fixations might one anticipate if high- and low-anxious subjects were given the naturalistic task of inspecting a visual display in the absence of explicit instructions as to which part of the display should be fixated? If the attentional functioning of anxious individuals is such as to maximize the probability of detecting threatening environmental stimuli as quickly as possible, then it is reasonable to assume that they would tend to scan the environment more rapidly and more thoroughly than non-anxious individuals. In terms of the analogy between visual attention and a spotlight, it is clear that a threatening stimulus would on average be detected most rapidly if the spotlight scanned rapidly and thoroughly over the visual environment. In addition, following detection of a threatening stimulus, anxious individuals are likely to devote more eye fixations to it than non-anxious individuals.

Various theorists have proposed that scanning is greater in anxious individuals. Wachtel (1967) argued as follows:

> If we postulate that a primary effect of anxiety is to narrow ... the width of the attentional beam, then we might expect that at extremely high levels of anxiety, the attentional field may become so narrow that no stable orientation toward the environment can be maintained [p. 421].

As a consequence, the very anxious individual's attention is "like a narrow beam which roams all over the field" [p. 421]. In similar fashion, Beck and Emery (1985) argued that the anxious patient is "hypervigilant, constantly scanning the environment for signs of impending disaster or personal harm" [p. 31].

There is surprisingly little evidence on the effects of anxiety on attentional scanning. One of the few relevant studies was reported by Haley (1974). He considered the eye movements of subjects of varying levels of repression-sensitization while watching a moderately stressful film about wood-working shop accidents. The sensitizers (= high in trait anxiety) and the repressors (= low in trait anxiety) both showed greater scanning during the film than did those with intermediate scores on the Repression-Sensitization Scale. Additional evidence suggested that the sensitizers were scanning in order to attend to the stressful content of the film, whereas the repressors were scanning in order to avoid that content.

Rather different results were obtained by Luborsky, Blinder, and Schimek (1965). Their subjects were presented with a mixture of neutral, sexual, and aggressive pictures one at a time. Repression as assessed by the Rorschach inkblot test was negatively correlated with scanning, and this relationship was stronger for the two sexual pictures. The differences in results between the two studies may be due to the fact that Luborksy et al. (1965) used static stimuli, whereas Haley (1974) used dynamic, moving stimuli. As Haley (1974) pointed out, "with static displays an avoidant defence can be expressed in lower looking about, but with a dynamic stimulus situation, higher scanning is necessary as a defence" [p. 93].

The extent to which threat-related stimuli are fixated by repressors and sensitizers has been examined by Olson and Zanna (1979) and by Halperin (1986). Olson and Zanna (1979) discovered that repressors tended to avoid fixating paintings which they had decided not to keep for themselves, perhaps because these paintings caused a certain amount of cognitive dissonance. In contrast, sensitizers fixated such paintings as frequently as paintings they had decided to keep. Halperin (1986) presented a series of injury, sexual, and neutral slides for one minute each. The injury and sexual slides contained key areas which were largely responsible for their emotional impact. The sensitizers spent much longer than the repressors fixating these key areas (approximately 40% of the time versus 25%). The sexual slides were rated as pleasant, so that it cannot be assumed that sensitizers differ from repressors only in their eye fixations on threat-related stimuli.

In sum, there is currently insufficient evidence to provide a proper evaluation of the hypothesis that anxious individuals typically scan the environment more rapidly and more thoroughly than non-anxious individuals. However, there is slight support for that view in the work of Luborksy et al. (1965). There is stronger evidence that anxious individuals fixate threat-related stimuli more than non-anxious ones, and it is possible that this finding may extend to any emotional stimuli whether negative or positive in valence. It is disappointing that there is little or no experimental research on scanning patterns in anxious patients.

DISTRACTIBILITY

The distractibility of anxious and non-anxious groups has been compared in several studies. This issue is relevant to attention, because distractibility is in general terms likely to be inversely related to attentional control. Studies on distraction can be appropriately divided into those which used only non-threatening distractors and those which included threatening distractors. Theoretical predictions are more straightforward in the latter case. If the cognitive system of anxious individuals is hypervigilant to threatening stimuli, the obvious expectation is that anxious groups should be more distracted than non-anxious groups by the presence of threat-related distractors. However, it is assumed within hypervigilance theory that anxious individuals are more susceptible than non-anxious individuals to distraction with both threatening and non-threatening distractors.

There is a general limitation of most studies of distraction. Distraction is typically assessed by the degree of impairment of task performance when a task is performed in the presence of distracting stimuli rather than on its own. As Graydon and Eysenck (1989) pointed out, compensatory processing activities may prevent the adverse effects of distracting conditions from lowering the level of performance.

Non-threatening Distractors

Totally opposed views on the effects of anxiety on distractibility have been proposed by different theorists. Easterbrook (1959) argued that anxiety produces a narrowing of attention in which task stimuli increasingly become the focus of attention. Presumably this greater attention to task stimuli is associated with an increased ability to resist distraction. On the other hand, Wachtel (1967) argued that anxiety reduces attentional control, and thus increases susceptibility to distraction. According to the theoretical position argued for in this book, anxious individuals would generally be expected to be more distractible than non-anxious ones. Rapid detection of threatening stimuli in the environment requires diverting processing resources away from the current task to extraneous sources of stimulation.

Subjects high in trait anxiety have occasionally been found to be less distractible than those low in trait anxiety (e.g., Zaffy & Bruning, 1966). However, it has usually been the case that high trait anxiety is associated with a high level of distractibility (Dornic, 1977; Dornic & Fernaeus, 1981; Eysenck & Graydon, 1989; Pallak, Pittman, Heller, & Munson, 1975). In the study by Eysenck and Graydon (1989), subjects carried out a letter-transformation task in which strings of letters had to be transformed in a specified manner (e.g., JULI + 4 = ? [NYPM]). This task was performed on its own or in the presence of letter or meaningless blip distractors. Neurotic introverts (i.e., those high in trait anxiety) and stable extraverts (i.e., those low in trait anxiety) did not differ in their performance of the letter-transformation task under control or blip distractor conditions. However, the letter distractors impaired performance for the neurotic introverts but not for the stable extraverts. These findings suggest that anxious individuals are more distractible than non-anxious ones mainly when the distracting stimuli resemble the task stimuli.

In sum, high trait-anxious individuals have generally been found to be more distractible than low trait-anxious individuals in the presence of non-threatening distractors. Unfortunately, it is not possible to provide an unequivocal interpretation of the findings. The distractibility of high trait-anxious individuals may reflect environmental scanning for threatening stimuli, but there are other possible explanations. For example, Graydon and Eysenck (1989) found that distraction effects were consistently greater when the overall demands on processing capacity were high than when they were low. Since high trait-anxious individuals often have less available working memory capacity than low trait-anxious individuals, it is possible that they are more distractible because they have less processing capacity to prevent distracting stimuli from disrupting performance.

Threatening Distractors

As was pointed out earlier, anxious individuals are predicted to be more distractible than non-anxious individuals. The reason is that high distractibility occurs as a consequence of an attentional system geared to the rapid detection of threat. It follows that anxious individuals should be especially susceptible to distraction when the distracting stimuli are threatening rather than non-threatening in nature.

Beck and Emery (1985) have adopted a similar theoretical position as far as anxious patients are concerned. They argued that patients with anxiety disorders are highly distractible. This distractibility arises because anxious patients are continually scanning the environment for threatening stimuli.

The studies reported in this section, and several studies discussed later in this chapter, have involved the presentation of threat-related words. What types of threatening words would be most appropriate to present? As far as normals are concerned, Endler (1983) obtained evidence that those high and low in trait anxiety differ in their sensitivity to social evaluation and physical danger situations. Beck, Laude, and Bohnert (1974) and Hibbert (1984) reported the thoughts and images of patients with generalized anxiety disorder during anxiety attacks. The majority of those thoughts and images related to physical or psychological threat to the self. The implication of these findings is that anxious individuals are especially sensitive to social and physical threats. Accordingly, social (e.g., inept, stupid) and physical (e.g., paralysed, pain) threat words have been used in most of the studies.

The specific nature of the threatening stimuli has generally been found to have no systematic effect on performance. When there is no reference to the type of threat in the discussion of findings, the reason is that the effects were comparable with social and physical threat words.

There is some evidence that patients with generalized anxiety disorder are more distractible than normal controls with threatening distractors. Mathews and MacLeod (1986) asked their subjects to shadow (i.e., repeat back) the message presented to one ear, while ignoring occasional threatening and neutral words presented to the other ear. There was a marginally significant tendency for threatening words on the non-attended channel to disrupt shadowing performance more than neutral words for the anxious patients but not for the normal controls. Since there was no conscious awareness of the words on the unattended channel, it appears that pre-attentive processes can be involved in the production of distraction effects.

As we saw earlier, Broadbent et al. (1986) argued that there is an important distinction between focused attention, in which early selection is based on a simple physical attribute such as location, and search, in which selection is based on the category to which a stimulus belongs. According to Broadbent et al. (1986), the difference in detection times between tasks providing or not providing advance information of target location gives a measure of the advantage stemming from being able to use focused attention. Anxiety in normals interacted with cognitive failure (assessed by the Cognitive Failures Questionnaire) on this measure. In essence, an inability to focus attention was found mainly among those high in anxiety and high in cognitive failure.

Distraction was also considered by Broadbent et al. (1986), but did not relate to anxiety level.

Mathews, May, Mogg, and Eysenck (1990) used a similar method to Broadbent et al. (1986) in two experiments. In the first experiment, subjects had to detect a letter at a known (cued) or unknown (uncued) location and in the presence or absence of digit distractors. In the second experiment, words were used as targets, and the distractors consisted of threatening or non-threatening words. There were three groups of subjects in each experiment: current patients with generalized anxiety disorder; recovered patients who had suffered from generalized anxiety disorder; and normal controls.

The findings from the first experiment did not produce any interesting differences among the three groups. All groups showed a reasonable ability to focus attention, and the adverse effects of distraction on speed of target detection were comparable in all groups. In the second experiment, however, there was a highly significant interaction between group and distraction on target location cueing (cued vs. uncued). As can be seen in Fig. 4.1, the three groups performed equivalently in the absence of distractors, but the currently anxious and recovered anxious groups were more adversely affected than the normal controls by the presence of distractors. These group differences were due to performance when the target location was unknown.

There were group differences with respect to both threatening and non-threatening distractors, as can be seen in Figure 4.2. The currently anxious group differed significantly from the control group with both

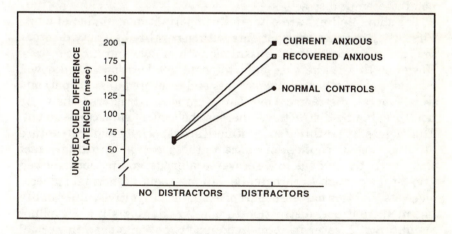

FIG. 4.1. Speed of target detection (uncued–cued) as a function of anxiety group, and distraction (present vs. absent). Data from Mathews, May, Mogg, and Eysenck (1990), Exp.2.

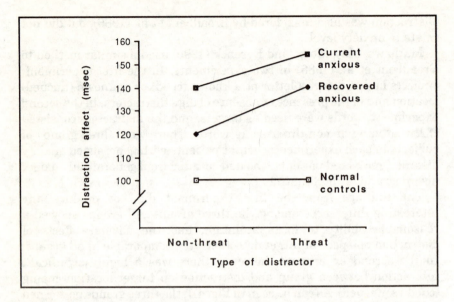

FIG. 4.2. Distraction effects (distraction–no distraction) as a function of anxiety group and distraction (threatening, non-threatening) on uncued trials only. Data from Mathews, May, Mogg, and Eysenck (1990), Exp.2.

types of distractor. The recovered anxious group resembled the currently anxious group in terms of the size of the distraction effect with threatening distractors, but they resembled the control group with non-threatening distractors.

The above findings are potentially important in a number of ways. First, they indicate that patients with generalized anxiety disorder are more susceptible to distraction than are normal controls. However, this is the case only when target location is unknown. Secondly, currently anxious patients and recovered anxious patients were more distracted by threatening distractors than by non-threatening distractors, whereas the control subjects were not. This suggests that threatening stimuli are especially likely to capture attention and disrupt performance for these groups. Thirdly, the fact that currently anxious and recovered anxious groups both showed greater distraction to threatening stimuli than did normal subjects suggests that this may form part of a manifest cognitive vulnerability factor. In contrast, distraction to non-threatening stimuli was not significantly greater in recovered anxious patients than in normal controls, and so distraction in this sense presumably either forms part of a latent cognitive vulnerability factor or reflects current clinically anxious mood state.

Unfortunately, some of the findings obtained by Mathews et al. (1990) in their second experiment were not replicated by Mathews, Mogg, Kentish, and Eysenck (in preparation). They carried out a longitudinal study in which patients with generalized anxiety disorder were tested while clinically anxious, during recovery, and at follow-up. When they were clinically anxious, they were slowed down significantly (compared to controls) in the detection of targets at unknown locations by threatening distractors. However, the two groups did not differ in their performance in the presence of non-threatening distractors. At the second time of testing, the recovered anxious patients did not differ from normal controls in any aspect of performance. Therefore, there was no evidence to support the involvement of a manifest cognitive vulnerability factor.

Eysenck and Byrne (in press) used a similar experimental design to that of Mathews et al. (1990) with normals high and low in trait anxiety. They discovered that those high in trait anxiety were more distracted than those medium or low in trait anxiety when physical threat distractors were used (see Fig. 4.3). However, the groups did not differ in distraction with social threat distractors or with neutral distractors. These findings are approximately in line with the predictions of hypervigilance theory (see Chapter 3). However, the failure to obtain group differences in distraction effects with social threat distractors is unexpected and difficult to interpret.

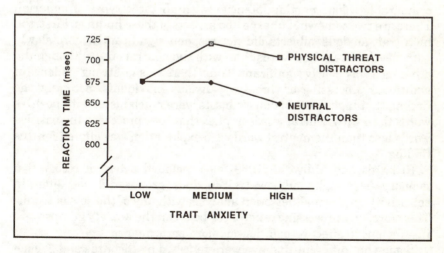

FIG. 4.3. Speed of target detection as a function of anxiety group and distraction (physical threat vs. neutral). Data from Eysenck and Byrne (in press).

Modified Stroop

One commonly used experimental paradigm which involves distraction is the modified Stroop. Stroop (1935) found that the speed of naming the colours in which words were printed was greatly slowed when the words were themselves colour names differing from their ink colour (e.g., the word 'RED' printed in blue). This paradigm has been modifed so that subjects are required to name the colours in which either threat-related or non-threatening words are printed. The general expectation is that anxious individuals will process the threat-related words to a greater extent than non-anxious individuals, and this should slow their colour naming. It should be noted that the processes involved in the modified Stroop may not resemble those in the original Stroop as much as is sometimes imagined. For example, response competition is presumably considerably more of a factor in the original than in the modified Stroop.

Non-clinical Studies

The modified Stroop has been used in some studies on non-clinical groups. Richards and Millwood (1989) compared groups high and low in trait anxiety on their colour naming of threatening, neutral, and emotionally positive words. There was a highly signficant interaction between group and emotional valence: The group high in trait anxiety responded fastest with the positive words and slowest with the threat-related words, whereas the group low in trait anxiety had comparable colour naming latencies with all three types of material. There are two somewhat unexpected aspects of these findings. First, the high trait-anxious subjects did not respond significantly more slowly with the threat-related words than with the neutral ones, although the difference was nearly significant. Thus, there was no strong evidence of additional processing of threat by anxious indviduals. Secondly, the finding that high trait-anxious subjects were much faster with positive words than with neutral words implies that they processed the positive words less than the neutral words. No explanation was offered for this finding.

Richards and Millwood (1989) also included a test of recognition memory. The high and low trait-anxious groups did not differ in sensitivity on a signal-detection analysis with any of the sets of words. Therefore, any processing differences between the anxiety groups were insufficient to affect recognition-memory performance.

Somewhat different findings were reported by Richards and French (1990). They found with the modified Stroop task that high trait-anxious subjects had significantly longer colour naming latencies for anxiety-related words than for neutral words. The same subjects did not have long latencies to happiness-related words, so the disruption effect was specific to anxiety-related words rather than to emotional words in general.

Mogg and Marden (1990) found that high trait-anxious subjects were relatively slower than low trait-anxious subjects in colour naming threat-related and emotionally positive words. As they concluded, these results, "suggest that anxiety is associated with selective processing of emotional stimuli in general, rather than threatening information in particular" [p. 228]. However, it should be pointed out that the findings of Richards and Millwood (1989) and of Richards and French (1990) are inconsistent with this conclusion.

Mogg, Mathews, Bird, and MacGregor-Morris (1990) compared the performance of high and low trait-anxious subjects on the modified Stroop task under stressful or non-stressful conditions. Some of the threatening words referred to physical and social dangers, and the remainder referred to failure and ineptitude. There was a significant interaction between group and threat versus non-threat content, which was largely due to the fact that only the high trait-anxious group was slowed in colour naming by threat-related words. However, this group difference was no longer significant when state anxiety levels were controlled for, which suggests that state rather than trait anxiety may have been the critical variable.

The pattern of results was rather different with the stress manipulation. High stress slowed colour naming for the threat words referring to failure and ineptitude, but not for threat words referring to social and physical dangers. State-anxiety scores were not significantly higher in high stress subjects than in low stress subjects, and a covariance analysis indicated that the effects of stress on colour naming were not mediated by state anxiety. Since stress was produced by a failure experience on an anagram task, it seems likely that this failure experience directly primed cognitive representations of achievement-related threats only.

MacLeod (1990) investigated colour naming on the modified Stroop task with subliminal presentation of threat-related and neutral words. The words were presented for only 20 msec, and the subjects had no ability to discriminate between words and non-words. State anxiety was manipulated by testing subjects either well before their examination or in the week beforehand. Increased state anxiety led to increased slowing on threat-related relative to neutral words by the high trait-anxious subjects, but to a relative speeding by the low trait-anxious subjects. In other words, trait anxiety and state anxiety jointly determined speed of colour naming to threatening words.

Martin, Williams, and Clark (1991) compared the modified Stroop performance of normal groups high, intermediate, and low in trait anxiety. The three groups did not differ in speed of colour naming with either threat-related or neutral words. There was no support for the predicted slowing of colour naming threat-related words by anxious subjects. Indeed, the high trait-anxious group responded faster than the other two groups with the threat-related words.

What can be concluded from these inconsistent findings? The studies by Richards and Millwood (1989), Richards and French (1990), and MacLeod (1990) are methodologically superior to the other three studies in one important respect. They assessed colour naming on a word-by-word basis, whereas Mogg and Marden (1990), Martin et al. (1991), and Mogg et al. (1990) simply measured the total time to colour name dozens of words on a sheet. It is clearly more difficult to interpret colour naming speed with the latter measurement technique.

In any case, there is reasonable evidence that those high in trait anxiety have slower colour naming with threat-related words than with neutral words, whereas those low in trait anxiety do not. The findings of MacLeod (1990) suggest that pre-attentive processes may be involved in producing this bias effect. At present, the relative contributions of trait and state anxiety to the bias effect are unclear. An important issue which requires more research is whether the bias in anxiety in normal groups is limited to threatening material or whether it applies generally to all emotional stimuli. In terms of biological utility, it is more likely that the bias is restricted to threat-related stimuli.

Clinical Studies

Even stronger evidence of the disruptive effects of anxiety on the modified Stroop has been obtained with anxious patients. For example, Mathews and MacLeod (1985) compared the performance of patients with generalized anxiety disorder and normal controls on the modified Stroop. The patients took longer to colour name the threatening words than the non-threatening ones, but the normal controls did not. In addition, there was some evidence of more specific interference effects: only those anxious patients with predominant physical worries had slowed colour naming with physical threat words.

Mogg, Mathews, and Weinman (1989) attempted to replicate the study of Mathews and MacLeod (1985). Anxious patients were slowed in their colour naming by threatening words relative to non-threatening words, whereas the normal controls performed equivalently with the two types of words. They also found that there was a considerably degree of specificity in the findings: Anxious patients with predominant physical concerns were slowed only on physical threat words, and patients with predominant social concerns were slowed only on social threat words.

There is one important difference between the findings of the two studies. Mathews and MacLeod (1985) reported that state anxiety was more important than trait anxiety in producing the general interference effect, whereas Mogg et al. (1989) found that trait anxiety was more predictive of this effect. In addition, of course, the existence of specific interference effects in both studies suggests the involvement of specific knowledge structures or schemata.

Martin et al. (1991) endeavoured to clarify the relationship between anxiety and modified Stroop performance. In one of their experiments, patients with generalized anxiety disorder were compared with normal controls having the same level of trait anxiety. This was done in order to determine whether slowed colour naming with threatening words is due to the level of anxiety or is more directly a function of patient status. There was a significant interaction between group and word valence: The patients were slower at colour naming threatening words than non-threatening words, whereas the normal controls exhibited the opposite tendency. The implication is that patient status is important, perhaps because patients are especially sensitive to environmental threats.

Martin et al. (1991) carried out another experiment in which they replicated the finding of a general slowing to threatening words by patients with generalized anxiety disorder. An additional finding of potential importance was that the anxious patients also showed significant slowing of colour naming with emotionally positive words (e.g., affectionate, joyful). This suggests that anxious patients engage in increased processing of all emotional stimuli regardless of whether they are emotionally negative or positive. If this finding were to be repeated with other paradigms, it would have far-reaching theoretical implications.

Mathews, MacLeod, and Tata (in press) have shed light on the mechanisms underlying the performance of clinically anxious subjects on the modified Stroop task. They compared the performance of patients with generalized anxiety disorder and normal controls with supraliminal and subliminal word presentation. The patients (but not the normal controls) were slower at colour naming with the threatening than with the non-threatening words regardless of whether the words were presented supraliminally or subliminally. The bias effect was slightly, but non-significantly, greater with subliminal presentation. This bias effect, like the one found in high trait-anxious normals, seems to involve pre-attentive processes.

Mathews et al. (in preparation) used the modified Stroop in their longitudinal study. They discovered that the colour naming of clinically anxious patients with generalized anxiety disorder was slowed down on threatening words more than on neutral words. However, the two groups did not differ in their naming time on emotionally positive words. The patients did not exhibit disrupted colour naming performance with threat-related words either during recovery or at follow-up.

In sum, there is considerable evidence that colour naming in patients, but not in normal controls, is disrupted with threatening words. There is also evidence for specificity of effects, with patients being slowed mainly with those threatening words relevant to their predominant concerns. The interpretation of these findings is not clear, mainly because the processes involved in producing interference on the modified Stroop have not been established. The findings probably reflect preferential processing of threat-related words by anxious patients. However, it is also possible that these words produce anxiety in these patients, and this anxiety disrupts performance. In essence, disruption on colour naming is at best a rather indirect measure of selective processing of the threat-related words.

The finding of specificity of disruptive effects suggests that the threatening words were thoroughly processed by the anxious patients. However, this finding may be of less theoretical signficance than it appears. This thorough processing may occur simply because each of the threatening words was re-presented several times.

SELECTIVE ATTENTIONAL BIAS

The research to be discussed in this section is concerned with attention to, and processing of, threatening stimuli. Of particular interest is the situation in which a threatening and a non-threatening stimulus are presented concurrently, and the allocation of processing resources to the two stimuli is assessed. According to the general theoretical framework adopted in this book, anxious individuals generally attempt to maximize the probability of threat detection. As a consequence, they should have a selective attentional bias favouring threat.

The concerns of this section clearly overlap with those of the preceding section. One important difference is that most of the studies reported in this section have measured the allocation of attention to threatening and non-threatening stimuli in a more direct fashion. It is thus generally easier to interpret the findings of these studies than of those on the modified Stroop and other tasks involving distraction.

Byrne's Hypothesis

Byrne (1964) proposed an interesting hypothesis relating his personality dimension of repression-sensitization to cognitive functioning. He argued that sensitizers approach threatening stimuli, whereas repressors tend to avoid such stimuli. Byrne (1964) denied that his Repression-Sensitization Scale was simply a measure of trait anxiety. However, the correlations between the Repression-Sensitization Scale and standard trait-anxiety questionnaires are so high (approximately +0.80 to +0.85; Watson & Clark, 1984) that it must be concluded that he was wrong. That is to say, sensitizers are individuals high in trait anxiety and repressors are individuals low in trait anxiety.

The evidence has been discussed in detail by Eysenck (1989 a), and so no more than a partial review will be provided here. One of the main lines of research has involved the phenomenon of perceptual defence. This occurs when emotionally threatening or taboo stimuli have higher perceptual recognition thresholds than neutral stimuli. If perceptual defence occurs because there is partial avoidance of the threatening stimuli, then perceptual defence effects should be especially large among repressors and non-existent (or even reversed) among sensitizers.

There were no differences between sensitizers and repressors in most of the studies of perceptual defence. In those cases where significant differences were obtained, it is not possible to rule out the possibility that individual differences in response bias rather than perceptual sensitivity were involved. It is noteworthy that there was no support for Byrne's (1964) hypothesis in the two studies (Van Egeren, 1968; Wagstaff, 1974) in which systematic attempts were made to assess perceptual sensitivity uncontaminated by response bias. Since the perceptual defence paradigm requires primarily relatively 'early' and low-level perceptual processes, it is possible that sensitizers and repressors might differ in their processing of threatening stimuli if the later stages of perceptual processing were involved. However, the evidence is against this possibility. When the duration of visual attention to threatening pictures of mutilated bodies and corpses and to neutral pictures was assessed in sensitizers and repressors, the two groups did not differ in duration of attention to either type of stimulus (Carroll, 1972; Lewinsohn, Berquist, & Brelje, 1972).

The above evidence was considered by Watson and Clark (1984). They argued that repression-sensitization and trait anxiety can both be regarded as measures of negative affectivity. Their conclusion concerning the relationship between negative affectivity and the processing of sexually provocative stimuli, of painful or gruesome stimuli, and of taboo words was as follows:

The results have been overwhelmingly negative. Taken together, they indicate that NA [i.e., negative affectivity] is unrelated to the approach/ avoidance of these types of threatening stimuli [p. 481].

Selective Processing: Non-clinical

It follows from Watson and Clark's (1984) pessimistic conclusion quoted above that individuals high and low in trait anxiety do not differ in their processing of threatening stimuli. This seems counter-intuitive, since it is generally assumed that those high in trait anxiety are considerably more sensitive to threat-related stimuli than those low in trait anxiety. A possible resolution of this apparent paradox was offered by Eysenck et al. (1987). They proposed that sensitizers (or those high in trait anxiety) differ from repressors (or those low in trait anxiety) in terms of a selective mechanism which operates when at least one threatening and one neutral stimulus are presented concurrently. In their own words, "the notion that those high in trait anxiety have a pre-attentive selective bias in favour of threat whereas those low in trait anxiety have the opposite bias is consistent with the data currently available" [p. 192].

The first empirical test of this selective bias hypothesis was reported by Eysenck et al. (1987; see Eysenck, 1991 a, for more details). They made use of a modified dichotic listening task in which pairs of words were presented concurrently, one to each ear. Every word presented to the attended ear had to be shadowed (i.e., repeated back aloud), but the words on the unattended ear were to be ignored. All of the words on the unattended ear were affectively neutral, whereas the words on the attended ear were a mixture of neutral and socially and physically threatening (e.g., grave, fail). In order to assess the allocation of processing resources, a tone was sometimes presented to either the attended or to the unattended ear very shortly after a pair of words had been presented, with the subjects being instructed to respond to this tone as rapidly as possible. It was assumed that the faster the speed of responding to the tone, the greater was the allocation of resources to the ear in question. The subjects all filled in the Facilitation-Inhibition Scale (Ullmann, 1962), which is a questionnaire correlating very highly with both the Repression-Sensitization Scale and measures of trait anxiety (facilitators = high trait anxiety; inhibitors = low trait anxiety).

The results are shown in Fig. 4.4. They correspond remarkably well to the predictions of the selective bias hypothesis. The facilitators tended to allocate processing resources to the ear to which a threatening word

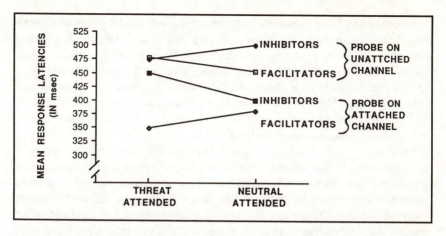

FIG. 4.4. Probe reaction time as a function of facilitation-inhibition, probe channel, and type of attended word (threat vs. neutral). Data from Halkiopoulos (see Eysenck, 1991 a).

had just been presented, as was indicated by their rapid responding to the tone when it followed a threatening word to the same ear, coupled with rather slow responding when it followed a threatening word in the other ear. Inhibitors demonstrated precisely the opposite pattern of responding, because they avoided allocating processing resources to the ear on which a threatening word had just been presented.

These findings have been replicated and extended in a number of recent studies using a visual analogue of the auditory task employed by Eysenck et al. (1987). In this task, two words are presented concurrently, one to an upper and the other to a lower location on a screen. On critical trials, one of these words is threat-related and the other is affectively neutral. The distribution of attention is measured by recording speed of detection of a dot which can replace either word. It is assumed that detection latencies are shorter in attended areas. MacLeod and Mathews (1988) discovered that the selective bias is affected by state anxiety as well as by trait anxiety. High and low trait-anxious students demonstrated no attentional bias towards or away from examination-relevant stress words a long time prior to an important examination. However, the results were quite different in the week before the examination, when the levels of state anxiety were elevated. At that time, the students high in trait anxiety showed attentional bias to the threat-related stimuli, whereas those low in trait anxiety showed bias away from the same stimuli. A rather similar performance pattern involving the interaction of trait and state anxiety was reported by D.E. Broadbent and M. Broadbent (1988).

Another study of selective bias was reported by Mogg et al. (1990) using the same task as MacLeod and Mathews (1988). Somewhat surprisingly in view of previous findings, they failed to discover any selective bias associated with high trait anxiety. However, there were effects attributable to a stress manipulation (success vs. failure on an anagram task). High and low trait-anxious subjects under high stress shifted their attention towards threat-related words, whereas subjects under low stress exhibited no bias.

MacLeod (1990) discussed an experiment using a modified version of the attentional deployment task. Word pairs were presented as prime displays. Each display was followed by a target word which had to be named. The naming latency for the target word was reduced if it had been included in the prime display, and it was assumed that attended primes would produce a greater reduction than unattended primes in naming latency. The word pair consisted of a threat-related and a neutral word on critical trials. High and low trait-anxious subjects performed this task when state anxiety was low (six weeks before their examination) and when it was high (in the week beforehand). Performance on the critical trials was determined interactively by trait and state anxiety. Those high in trait anxiety showed more attentional bias towards threat when stressed, whereas those low in trait anxiety showed more bias away from threat when stressed.

Mogg et al. (1991 b) made use of a somewhat different experimental task to assess attentional bias. This task involved the visual presentation of a series of word pairs differing in emotional valence. Each word pair was displaced by two bars of colour which were presented simultaneously. The subjects had to decide which colour bar had appeared first, and this decision was used as the index of which word in the word pair was receiving more attention.

The subjects were normals high and low in trait anxiety, and they were subjected to stressful (failure experience) or non-stressful conditions. Neither trait anxiety nor stress was associated with a bias favouring threat-related words. In a second experiment, the presentation time for the word pairs was changed from the 500 msec of the first experiment to 730 msec. In addition, there was no stress manipulation. There was some evidence that trait anxiety was associated with an attentional bias, but the effects of state anxiety appeared to be greater. In essence, individuals low in state anxiety had an attentional bias towards positive and away from negative words.

It is not easy to interpret the various findings obtained by Mogg et al. (1991 b). The colour perception task is limited in a number of ways. Several subjects commented that the two colour bars seemed to appear simultaneously (which they actually did), and this made them reluctant to guess. The need to make contrived decisions may have led the subjects to use various strategies unrelated to the actual deployment of attention.

In sum, there is reasonably strong evidence that normal individuals high in trait anxiety have a selective bias towards threatening stimuli. The relative contributions of trait anxiety and state anxiety have been difficult to assess, in part because they are normally highly correlated (up to approximately +0.7). However, there are a number of studies (D.E. Broadbent & M. Broadbent, 1988; MacLeod & Mathews, 1988; MacLeod, 1990) in which high state anxiety served to magnify the selective attentional biases shown by high and low trait-anxious individuals under non-stressed conditions.

Selective Processing: Clinical

MacLeod et al. (1986) compared the performance of generalized anxiety disorder patients and normal controls on the visual version of the attentional deployment task. The patients selectively allocated attention towards threat-related words (both social and physical threats), whereas the controls had a non-significant tendency to allocate attention away from threat. In other words, patients with generalized anxiety disorder have a selective bias which extends at least to social and physical threats.

Mogg, Mathews, and Eysenck (in press) used the same experimental task with generalized anxiety disorder patients, recovered generalized anxiety disorder patients, and normal controls. They replicated the key findings of MacLeod et al. (1986): The currently anxious patients allocated attention towards threat-related stimuli, whereas the controls had no attentional bias. This pattern of results was the same for social and physical threats, and so the attentional bias exhibited by anxious patients is reasonably general. However, there was some evidence of specificity. The attentional bias towards social threat words correlated significantly with the anxious patients' ratings of social worries, but not with their ratings of physical worries.

A group of recovered anxious patients was included in order to discover whether the attentional bias forms part of a cognitive vulnerability factor or whether it is a secondary consequence of clinically anxious mood state. In fact, the performance of the recovered patients resembled that of the control subjects more than that of the currently anxious patients. An implication is that the attentional bias probably does not form part of a manifest vulnerability factor, but may either form part of a latent vulnerability factor or be a consequence of anxious mood state.

MacLeod et al. (1986) failed to discover any relationships between attentional bias and either trait or state anxiey, and Mogg et al.'s (in press) study did not clarify the relationship between attentional bias and either state or trait anxiety. However, there was no attempt to manipulate the level of state anxiety, and it is possible that the introduction of situational stress might have increased the impact of state anxiety on attentional bias.

The above findings are consistent with the notion of a selective attentional bias. However, they do not provide definitive support for selectivity *per se*. What needs to be demonstrated is that anxious patients devote more attention than normal controls to a threatening stimulus when it is presented concurrently with a non-threatening stimulus, but that the two groups do not differ in their initial processing of a threatening stimulus presented on its own, i.e., when selective allocation of processing resources is not possible.

The selective attentional bias has been examined in the above direct fashion by MacLeod and Mathews (1991 b) and by Mogg, Mathews, Eysenck, and May (1991 a). The lexical decision task was used. In the standard version of this task, subjects are presented with a string of letters and have to decide as rapidly as possible whether or not it represents a word. Research on the standard lexical decision task by Hill and Kemp-Wheeler (1989) and by MacLeod (1990) has consistently failed to reveal relatively faster lexical decision latencies for threatening words by anxious than by non-anxious groups. The same finding (or non-finding) was reported by MacLeod and Mathews (1991 b) with generalized anxiety disorder patients when only one letter string was reported. However, they also used a double-string condition in which two letter strings were presented concurrently, with one string above and the other below the fixation point. They were either both non-words or one word and one non-word, and the task was to report as rapidly as possible whether or not a word had been presented. Under these conditions, patients with generalized anxiety disorder showed selective speeding in lexical decisions for threatening words compared to normal controls.

The findings of MacLeod and Mathews (1991 b) are precisely in line with the notion that anxious patients have a selective attentional bias towards threat. However, Mogg et al. (1991 a) obtained more complex findings with the same experimental paradigm. They pointed out that there was a potential confounding in the study of MacLeod and Mathews (1991 b), because their threatening words probably formed a more homogeneous category than did their non-threatening words. Accordingly, Mogg et al. (1991 a) included an additional set of neutral words drawn from the category of household terms.

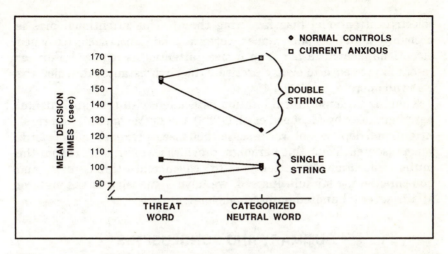

FIG. 4.5. Lexical decision times with single and double strings with the word below the fixation point. Data from Mogg, Mathews, Eysenck and May (1991 a).

Mogg et al. (1991 a) carried out an analysis of their data that was directly comparable to that conducted by MacLeod and Mathews (1991 b), i.e., omitting the data from the category of household terms. The generalized anxiety disorder patients did not differ from the normal controls in their lexical decision latencies with single or double letter strings, and so the findings of MacLeod and Mathews (1991 b) were not replicated. However, more detailed analyses revealed the existence of a more specific selective bias in anxious patients. They showed a bias towards threat in the double-string condition only when the threatening word was presented below the fixation point (see Fig. 4.5). It can also be seen in Fig. 4.5 that lexical decision latencies in the double-string condition were consistently faster when the word appeared above rather than below the fixation point. These results can be accounted for in a *post hoc* fashion. The anxious patients and the normal controls preferentially attended to stimuli in the upper position, and this preference prevented any selective attentional bias from manifesting itself. In other words, focused attention was involved. In contrast, fast lexical decision latencies to threatening words below the fixation point occurred only when there was a selective capture of attention by those words. Anxious patients showed this effect, whereas the normal controls exhibited the opposite effect because of their reluctance to shift attention to threatening words. Here, attentional search was presumably involved.

In sum, despite some complexities in the data, it seems reasonable to conclude that patients with generalized anxiety disorder possess a selective attentional bias favouring threat. This attentional bias is probably manifest only under certain conditions, such as when attentional search rather than focused attention is required. Further research is needed to clarify precisely the circumstances in which the bias will operate.

There is an important limitation associated with the experimental paradigm used by MacLeod et al. (1986) and by Mogg et al. (in press). Attentional deployment was assessed 500 msec after each pair of words was presented. Thus, this paradigm provides no information about the initial allocation of attention to concurrent threatening and non-threatening stimuli. Instead, we have a snapshot of the state of affairs several hundred milliseconds later.

SUMMARY AND CONCLUSIONS

We have now considered several different, but related, aspects of attentional functioning. These include breadth of attention, scanning, distractibility, and selective attentional bias. In an ideal world, there would be information available on all of these attentional characteristics under stressed and non-stressed conditions for normals high and low in trait anxiety, for current patients with generalized anxiety disorder, and for recovered patients who previously suffered from generalized anxiety disorder. As the reader has undoubtedly noticed, the reality is a long way removed from this ideal. That means that most of the conclusions drawn can be no more than tentative. This is especially the case with respect to two of the putative attentional phenomena associated with anxiety: one is broad attention prior to threat detection, and the other is visual scanning.

The findings so far as normals high in trait anxiety are concerned are reasonably straightforward. High trait anxiety has been found to be associated with a reduction in the breadth of attention in conditions permitting focused attention. High trait-anxious individuals appear to scan the visual environment more extensively than low trait-anxious individuals, and they are more distracted than low trait-anxious individuals by neutral distractors. Their performance is more disrupted than that of low trait-anxious individuals on the modified Stroop task with threat words, and they exhibit a selective attentional bias favouring threat. In sum, the available evidence has provided consistent support for the view that normals high in trait anxiety are characterized by hypervigilance.

Patients suffering from generalized anxiety disorder also seem to be characterized by hypervigilance. They exhibit a narrowing of attention in the presence of salient stimuli, and they are more distractible than normals with both threat-related and neutral stimuli. Furthermore, they have disrupted performance on the modified Stroop task when required to colour name threat-related words. Finally, they have a selective attentional bias favouring threat-related stimuli.

According to the theoretical position put forward in Chapter 3, one way of determining whether or not there is a cognitive vulnerability factor associated with generalized anxiety disorder is to compare the cognitive performance of patients with that of normals high in trait anxiety. Any aspects of non-normal cognitive functioning in generalized anxiety disorder patients which are also found in high trait-anxious normals may be involved in cognitive vulnerability. Thus, hypervigilance in its various manifestations may very well form part of a cognitive vulnerability factor for generalized anxiety disorder.

While the evidence available is not conclusive, it definitely points in the direction of hypervigilance being a latent vulnerability factor rather than a manifest one. Recovered anxious patients have been assessed on selective bias, on the modified Stroop task, and on distractibility to non-threatening and for threatening distractors (Mathews et al., 1989 a; Mogg et al., in press; Mathews et al., in press). Mathews et al. (1989 a) discovered that recovered anxious patients were more adversely affected than normal controls by threat-related distractors, but all of the other findings indicated that the cognitive performance of recovered anxious patients resembled that of normals. These findings suggest that the cognitive vulnerability factor is latent rather than manifest.

The notion that hypervigilance is a latent vulnerability factor is further supported by several studies on the selective attentional bias (D.E. Broadbent & M. Broadbent, 1988; MacLeod & Mathews, 1988; MacLeod, 1990). It was found in all of those studies that selective attentional bias is an interactive function of trait and state anxiety, i.e., both high trait anxiety and high state anxiety are required to produce a bias effect. In other words, high trait anxiety appears to be a necessary but not a sufficient condition for hypervigilance.

In sum, hypervigilance is found in generalized anxiety disorder patients and in normals high in trait anxiety, especially under stressful conditions. However, it is not found in patients who have recovered from generalized anxiety disorder. There are some lacunae in the evidence, but the position at present suggests that hypervigilance is a latent vulnerability factor for generalized anxiety disorder. Some of these issues are discussed further in Chapter 8.

CHAPTER FIVE

Comprehension, Memory, and Threat

INTRODUCTION

The theoretical approaches of Beck (e.g., Beck & Emery, 1985) and of Bower (1981, 1987) were discussed at some length in Chapter 2. However, a brief recapitulation of the essence of their theories will serve as a useful introduction to our discussion of the comprehension of, and memory for, threat-related material.

Beck (e.g., Beck & Emery, 1985; Beck & Clark, 1988) claimed that individuals who develop clinical anxiety are characterized by schemas relating to personal vulnerability and danger. These schemas remain in a latent state until they are activated by relevant stressful life events. After they have become activated, these schemas exert a pervasive influence on the processing of threat-related information. The processes allegedly affected include those involved in comprehension and in memory.

According to Bower's (1981, 1987) semantic network theory, experiencing an emotional state leads to activation of the corresponding emotion node within the semantic network. This produces activation of related nodes, most of which contain affect-congruent information. An implication of this theoretical approach is that the processing of any information which is congruent with the current mood state will tend to be facilitated. While Bower (1981, 1987) focused primarily on mood effects, his theory can readily be extended to encompass the effects of personality. If, for example, individuals high in trait anxiety have formed more associations between the anxiety node and other anxiety-congruent nodes than those low in trait anxiety, then mood-congruent effects should occur more often in high trait-anxious individuals.

In spite of the substantial differences between the theoretical positions of Beck and of Bower, both theorists predict that there should be wide-ranging mood-congruent effects throughout the cognitive system. It would thus be expected that anxious individuals (both high trait-anxious normals and patients with generalized anxiety disorder) should exhibit superior comprehension of, and long-term memory for, anxiety-relevant information than non-anxious individuals. If ambiguous stimuli having both a threatening and a non-threatening interpretation were presented, then it might be expected on both theories that anxious individuals would be more likely than non-anxious individuals to favour the threatening interpretation.

The theoretical position adopted in this book differs from those discussed above. According to hypervigilance theory, most of the cognitive differences between anxious and non-anxious individuals arise because anxiety has the specific function of facilitating the rapid detection of threat. Accordingly, anxiety affects the pre-attentive and attentional systems, and many of the effects of anxiety on memory may arise indirectly as consequences of the involvement of those systems.

More specifically, the extent to which information is remembered depends upon the precise pre-attentive, attentional, and perceptual processes occurring at the time of learning (Craik & Lockhart, 1972). In other words, memory traces are formed as by-products of attentional and perceptual processes, and so the level of memory can be predicted only if we understand the role played by those processes. For example, a relevant factor is whether or not the selective attentional bias is operative during encoding. Another relevant factor is the type of memory test employed. For example, there is strong evidence that the processes involved in tests of explicit and implicit memory are rather different (see Eysenck & Keane, 1990), and this may be important in determining the effects of anxiety on memory performance. An implication of these various considerations is that it is rather difficult to predict accurately the nature and extent of memory differences between high-anxious and low-anxious groups.

INTERPRETATION OF AMBIGUITY

The interpretation of ambiguous stimuli by normal groups varying in their level of trait anxiety or the related personality dimension of repression-sensitization has been investigated a number of times. Studies of repression-sensitization have mostly been designed to test Byrne's (1964) hypothesis, according to which sensitizers approach threatening stimuli, whereas repressors tend to avoid such stimuli. Since the theories of Byrne (1964), Beck (e.g., Beck & Clark, 1988), and Bower (1981) all make essentially the same predictions, the findings of studies on the interpretation of ambiguity cannot readily be used to compare the three theories.

Relevant studies on normal groups were reported by Blaylock (1963), Haney (1973), and Eysenck et al. (1987). Blaylock (1963) reported in one study that sensitizers were more likely than repressors to interpret homographs in a threatening fashion as indicated by associations to the homographs. However, she failed to replicate that finding in a second study. Haney (1973) discovered that sensitizers were significantly more likely than repressors to produce threatening interpretations of ambiguous sentences. Eysenck et al. (1987) made use of a simple task in which subjects were asked to write down the spellings of auditorily presented words. Some of the words were homophones having both a threat-related and a neutral interpretation (e.g., die, dye; pain, pane). There proved to be a significant correlation of +0.60 between trait anxiety and the number of threatening homophone interpretations. The interpretation of half of the homophones was socially threatening, whereas the other half had a physically threatening interpretation. However, the type of threat did not interact with the primary reported concerns of the subjects.

MacLeod (1990) discussed three studies on interpretation of ambiguity which he and his associates have carried out. In two of the studies, the homophone task was carried out under normal conditions or high-arousal conditions (following exercise). In both studies, there was an interaction between trait anxiety and arousal: High trait-anxious subjects showed an increased tendency to provide threatening interpretations of the homophones when aroused, whereas low trait-anxious subjects showed a decreased tendency. In the other study, ambiguous sentences having a threatening and a non-threatening interpretation were presented. Each sentence was followed by a word strongly associated with one of the possible interpretations, and the subject's task was to name this word as rapidly as possible. It was assumed that word naming would be faster when the word's meaning was congruent with the subject's interpretation of the preceding sentence. There was an interaction between trait and state anxiety. In this interaction, high trait-anxious subjects were faster to name words related to threatening interpretations and slower to name words related to non-threatening interpretations when they were high in state anxiety than when they were low, whereas low trait-anxious subjects showed the opposite pattern. Thus, all three of these studies indicate that an interpretive bias favouring threat depends on the conjoint influence of trait anxiety and state anxiety or arousal.

The homophone task has also been used with anxiety disordered patients. Mathews et al. (1989 b) used three groups of subjects: currently anxious patients with a diagnosis of generalized anxiety disorder, a recovered group of patients who had had generalized anxiety disorder, and normal controls. They also recorded skin conductance responses to the homophones. It was assumed that there would be a greater skin conductance response to homophones which were interpreted in a threatening fashion than to homophones which were interpreted in a non-threatening fashion. Response bias could be investigated, because subjects who interpreted homophones in a threatening fashion but nevertheless wrote down the neutral spelling would have unexpectedly large skin conductance responses. The skin conductance data failed to provide any evidence that the three groups differed in response bias.

Mathews et al. (1989 b) found that the currently anxious group produced significantly more threatening homophone interpretations than the normal controls. This suggests that patients with generalized anxiety disorder have an interpretive bias. The recovered anxious group was intermediate between the other two groups. Since the recovered group did not differ significantly from either of the other two groups, it is not clear whether the interpretive bias forms part of a manifest or latent vulnerability factor or whether it is simply a secondary consequence of clinically anxious mood state.

Mathews et al. (1989 b) also confirmed the importance of trait anxiety in the interpretation of ambiguous stimuli. Overall, there was a highly significant correlation of +0.49 between trait anxiety and the number of threatening interpretations. However, the correlation was 0.00 in the recovered anxious group.

How are we to account for the consistent finding that anxious groups are more likely than non-anxious groups to interpret ambiguous words in a threatening fashion? Research on the resolution of lexical ambiguity has generally supported the exhaustive access model, according to which all of the meanings of ambiguous words are activated automatically (Simpson, 1984). The particular meaning which reaches conscious awareness may then be determined in part by selective biases which either facilitate or inhibit further processing of the threatening interpretations of ambiguous words. Anxious groups may differ from non-anxious groups in the nature of such selective biases.

There are at least two other possibilities which need to be considered. It is well known that the interpretations of ambiguous words are strongly affected by word frequency (e.g., Eysenck et al., 1987). Probably the simplest explanation of the data from the homophone task is that anxious groups are more familiar with the threatening homophone interpretations than are non-anxious groups. However, this cannot account for all of the data. In particular, MacLeod's (1990) finding that high trait-anxious subjects show an interpretive bias only when aroused is not explicable in terms of word familiarity. The other possibility is that response bias is involved. In other words, non-anxious groups may be more reluctant than anxious groups to write down threatening homophone interpretations.

Some of the above issues were addressed by Eysenck et al. (1991). In the first experiment, they presented a mixture of ambiguous and neutral sentences to currently anxious patients with generalized anxiety disorder, recovered anxious patients who had suffered from generalized anxiety disorder, and normal controls. The ambiguous sentences could be interpreted in either a threatening or a non-threatening fashion (e.g., 'The two men watched as the chest was opened'). The presentation of these sentences was followed by an unexpected test of recognition memory, in which subjects had to decide whether each sentence corresponded in meaning to one of the sentences presented previously. The sentences used on the recognition test consisted of reworded versions of the ambiguous sentences, and were designed to capture either the threatening or the non-threatening interpretation of those sentences.

As can be seen in Fig. 5.1, the currently anxious patients showed evidence of an interpretive bias. They recognized more of the

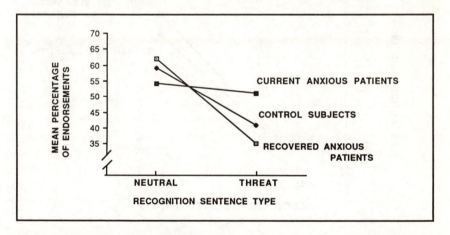

FIG. 5.1. Recognition-memory endorsements as a function of anxiety group and sentence threat value. Data from Eysenck, Mogg, May, Richards, and Mathews (1991), Exp.1.

threatening interpretations and fewer of the neutral interpretations than did the other two groups. On the basis of these data, it is not possible to decide whether the interpretive bias operates at the time of comprehension or at the time of retrieval.

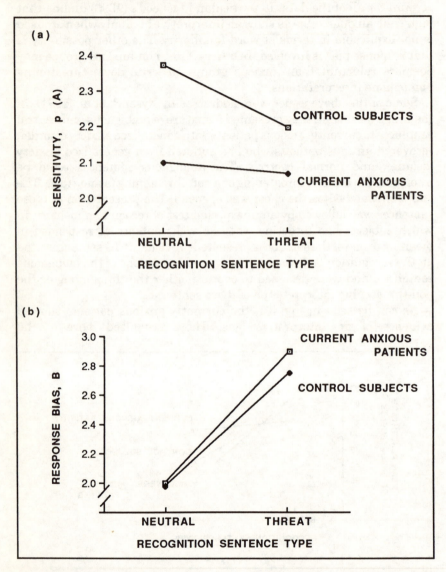

FIG. 5.2. Sensitivity (a) and response-bias measures (b) on recognition memory as a function of anxiety group and sentence threat value. Data from Eysenck, Mogg, May, Richards, and Mathews (1991), Exp.2.

Figure 5.1. also indicates that there was very little difference in the memory performance of the recovered anxious and normal control groups. This tends to rule out the possibility that the interpretive bias shown by clinically anxious patients forms part of a manifest cognitive vulnerability factor. Presumably the interpretive bias shown by the currently anxious patients is due either to their clinically anxious mood state or to a latent vulnerability factor.

The above experiment suffers from the limitation that the group differences in memory performance may simply reflect response bias. For example, anxious individuals may be more likely than non-anxious ones to endorse threatening responses regardless of the information which they have stored in memory. In their second experiment, Eysenck et al. (1991) examined this issue by means of signal-detection analyses designed to distinguish between sensitivity and response-bias effects. As can be seen in Fig. 5.2, they discovered that anxious patients and normal controls did not differ with respect to response bias. However, they did differ in sensitivity, indicating that anxious patients have an interpretive bias for ambiguous material.

In sum, it has been established that anxious individuals differ from non-anxious ones in terms of an interpretive bias with ambiguous stimuli. This is the case with both non-clinical and clinical anxious groups. The fact that recovered anxious patients do not show an interpretive bias indicates that a manifest vulnerability factor is not involved. The data are most consistent with the notion that the interpretive bias forms part of a latent vulnerability factor. The existence of a latent vulnerability factor is also suggested by the fact that an interpretive bias in normals is most readily demonstrated in high trait-anxious individuals who are also high in state anxiety.

NEGATIVE MEMORY BIAS: NON-CLINICAL STUDIES

The starting point for much of the research on retention of threatening material by anxious groups is a study by Rogers, Kuiper, and Kirker (1977). Subjects were asked to make judgements about words, using the following judgement tasks: self-referent judgements (i.e., describes you?); semantic judgements (i.e., means the same as?); and structural judgements (i.e., capital letters?). They discovered that subjects who made self-referent judgements showed much better recall on a subsequent unexpected memory test than did the other groups of subjects. Rogers et al. (1977) explained this finding by assuming that everyone possesses an extensive self-schema. This self-schema is activated when self-referent judgements are made, especially when the judgements are affirmative.

Activation of the self-schema may lead to the activation of a network of associations which assist the subsequent retrieval process.

Beck and Emery (1985) argued that anxious individuals possess schemas relating to vulnerability and to danger, whereas non-anxious individuals do not. The combined views of Rogers et al. (1977) and of Beck and Emery (1985) suggest that threatening material related to their negative self-schemas should be relatively better recalled by anxious than by non-anxious group, but the groups should not differ in their recall of positive or neutral material. This predicted pattern of findings is known as the negative memory bias.

A number of researchers have investigated memory for threatening and neutral material by anxious and non-anxious groups. O'Banion and Arkowitz (1977) presented subjects high and low in social anxiety with a mixture of positive and negative trait adjectives. They gave them all the same inaccurate information about which of the adjectives described them. On a subsequent unexpected test of recognition memory, the interaction between social anxiety and the emotional valence of the trait adjectives was not significant. As a consequence, the findings do not provide any support for the notion that anxious subjects have a negative memory bias.

The study by O'Banion and Arkowitz (1977) suffers from the deficiency that it is improbable that the subjects actually believed the misleading information that they were given about the trait adjectives which allegedly described them. A superior study from the methodological perspective was reported by Breck and Smith (1983). They used the same adjectives as O'Banion and Arkowitz (1977), but instructed their subjects to decide whether each adjective was self-descriptive. Their subjects were high or low in social anxiety, and they were informed that the experiment would or would not be followed by social interaction. On the subsequent unexpected test of recall, there was a highly significant interaction between social anxiety and trait adjective valence. A higher proportion of negative self-descriptive adjectives was recalled by the anxious than by the non-anxious subjects, but the opposite was the case for recall of the positive self-descriptive adjectives. Of importance, this interaction was significant only when the subjects had been informed that the experiment would be followed by social interaction. This pattern of findings led Breck and Smith (1983) to draw the following conclusion:

> The results of the current investigation suggest that socially anxious subjects do have a more negative self-schema than do non-anxious subjects and that the self-schema may be activated when anticipating social interactions [p. 75].

Kent (1985) studied memory for pain in high and low scorers on the Dental Anxiety Scale. The experienced pain they reported at the end of a dental session was compared with the amount of pain they recalled having experienced three months later. The dentally anxious subjects recalled much higher levels of pain than they had actually experienced, whereas the dentally non-anxious subjects recalled their experienced pain with reasonable accuracy. These findings are consistent with the existence of a negative memory bias in anxious individuals, but are not entirely convincing. Since Kent (1985) did not consider memory bias for positive events, we do not know that the memory bias he observed was specific to negative events.

Norton et al. (1988) presented a mixture of anxiety-related, anger-related, and neutral words to subjects who were either non-clinical panickers or non-panickers. The list was presented four times for recall, and the first presentation was preceded by a paragraph which described someone having a panic attack, becoming very angry, or becoming hungry. Only those panickers who had seen the paragraph about someone having a panic attack recalled significantly more anxiety-relevant words than the non-panickers, and then only on trials one and two. In other words, priming and/or induction of anxious mood state was needed to produce a negative memory bias in the panickers.

Kennedy and Craighead (1988) obtained estimates of the amount of positive and negative feedback received during a learning task from non-clinical anxious and non-anxious groups. The groups did not differ in their estimates of positive feedback. However, in the first of two experiments the anxious subjects gave higher estimates than non-anxious subjects of the amount of negative feedback. Since the level of depression was equated in the two groups, the findings of Kennedy and Craighead (1988) provide reasonable evidence of a negative memory bias in anxious subjects.

Claeys (1989) compared incidental recall in subjects high and low in dispositional social anxiety. High social-anxious subjects recalled more self-descriptive unlikeable trait words than low social-anxious subjects, but the two groups did not differ in their recall of likeable trait words.

Mayo (1983) asked his subjects to recall real-life personal experiences in response to a set of words. Neuroticism was significantly associated with the number of unpleasant memories retrieved, whether or not mood state at the time of testing was controlled statistically. Mayo (1989) used a similar paradigm, and found that high neuroticism was associated with reduced recall of happy memories. In addition, high trait anxiety was associated with the retrieval of fewer happy and more unhappy memories. Mood at the time of retrieval had very little effect on the emotional valence of what was retrieved.

There is at least one major problem with the studies by Mayo (1983, 1989). His findings may indicate that individuals high and low in neuroticism and trait anxiety differ in their memory processes. However, an alternative explanation is simply that the nature of the information stored in long-term memory differs in those high and low in neuroticism and trait anxiety. The data do not indicate which of these explanations should be preferred.

Interesting evidence for a negative bias for recall of trait words among those high in neuroticism was reported by Young and Martin (1981) and by Martin, Ward, and Clark (1983). A self-referent task was used in both studies. One cannot interpret the findings of Young and Martin (1981) in an unequivocal fashion, because it is possible that the negative trait words were recalled better by those high in neuroticism simply because they had greater familiarity with those words. However, Martin et al. (1983) replicated the findings of Young and Martin (1981), and they also discovered that there was no negative recall bias when the encoding task involved deciding whether the trait words described a 'typical undergraduate from your college'. These findings cannot be accounted for in terms of differential familiarity.

There is a moderate correlation between neuroticism and depression scores. Accordingly, it could be argued that the findings of Young and Martin (1981) and Martin et al. (1983) reflect the influence of depression rather than of neuroticism or anxiety. However, there is some counter-evidence. Martin et al. (1983) measured depression, and found that the negative memory bias was associated with neuroticism rather than with depression.

So far we have discussed evidence which is consistent with the notion that normals high in neuroticism or anxiety exhibit a negative memory bias. However, there are other studies which failed to find any evidence of a negative memory bias. MacLeod (1990) designed an experiment based on the evidence that anxious individuals show a processing bias in favour of threatening stimuli when it is necessary to select between a threatening and a neutral stimulus. He varied the importance of selectivity by presenting pairs of words differing in their affective valence either sequentially or concurrently to two different locations. A cue presented shortly after the words indicated which word was to be recalled, and the key measure was the latency of recall. The most interesting findings were obtained with concurrent presentation. Subjects high in trait anxiety had longer latencies to recall threatening than neutral words, with those low in trait anxiety having the opposite pattern of results. The results are totally inconsistent with the notion that individuals high in trait anxiety have a negative memory bias.

Watts, Trezise, and Sharrock (1986) carried out a rather unpleasant experiment in which subjects were presented with a number of large and small freeze-dried spiders mounted on cards. Spider phobics did not differ from controls in their recognition memory for small spiders, but spider phobics had significantly inferior recognition memory to the controls for large spiders. A methodological problem with this experiment is that subjects may not have attended fully to the whole of each stimulus.

In sum, there is a reasonable amount of evidence demonstrating the existence of a negative memory bias in non-clinical anxious groups. The evidence seems to be especially clear when there is priming of the relevant negative schema and/or induction of an anxious mood state (Breck & Smith, 1983; Norton et al., 1988). In other words, the activation of one or more negative schemas generally leads to a negative memory bias. When there is no induction of an anxious mood state, the findings are very inconsistent. Under those circumstances, the predicted negative memory bias was observed in four studies, the findings were non-significant in four studies, and the reverse negative memory bias was found in one study (Watts et al., 1986).

Evaluation

On the face of it, several of the studies which we have discussed appear to offer reasonable evidence for a negative memory bias in individuals high in trait anxiety or neuroticism. Such a state of affairs would conflict with the theoretical position of Williams et al. (1988), according to whom anxiety affects attentional rather than memorial functioning. However, it must be accepted that there are problems of interpretation with some of the findings. For example, measures of anxiety and of depression typically correlate reasonably highly with each other (Watson & Clark, 1984), and there is plentiful evidence of a negative memory bias associated with depression (see Blaney, 1986, for a review). Accordingly, it is extremely important to demonstrate that any obtained negative memory bias depends on individual differences in anxiety rather than in depression.

There are also more general problems related to the notion that memory performance on the self-referent task provides direct evidence about underlying self-schemas. One problem was identified by Klein and Kihlstrom (1986). They found that the self-referent task does not produce superior recall to other semantic tasks provided that the task used requires that the stimulus material be organized into categories. The implication is that self-referent encoding is confounded with categorical organization, and the latter factor may be of more consequence than the former one.

Another general problem is that it is generally assumed that schema-relevant information will be remembered better than information which is not schema-relevant. However, there are findings which do not square with that assumption. For example, Friedman (1979) discovered that recognition memory was much better for schema- or frame-inconsistent objects than for those that were consistent. In some ways, the presence of schema-relevant distortions and intrusions can provide more direct evidence concerning underlying schemas. Calvo (1986) presented his subjects with a text about a student who was placed in an evaluation situation. Subjects high in trait anxiety made more intrusion errors than those low in trait anxiety when they had previously received failure feedback, but the groups did not differ following success feedback or no feedback. Calvo (1986) interpreted his data by assuming that a negative schema was activated in individuals high in trait anxiety receiving negative feedback. However, an alternative interpretation is that the intrusions occurred because of response bias rather because of any direct effect on memory *per se*.

Perhaps the simplest explanation for the existence of a negative memory bias in non-clinical anxious individuals is based on word frequency or familiarity. Common words are generally recalled better than rare ones (Eysenck, 1977), and threatening words may well be more familiar to anxious individuals than to non-anxious ones. However, it is not possible to account for all of the findings in this way. It was found in a number of studies (e.g., Breck & Smith, 1983; Martin et al., 1983; Norton et al., 1988) that there was a negative memory bias in some conditions but not in others. This indicates clearly that additional factors must be involved.

The evidence reveals that negative memory bias is obtained most consistently when there is induction of an anxious mood state, or underlying danger or threat schemata are activated. Since an anxious mood state probably facilitates activation of danger schemata, it is reasonable to conclude that activation of such schemata may be a necessary precondition for a negative memory bias in non-clinical anxious groups. These schemata remain latent and do not affect memory performance directly unless they are activated.

IMPLICIT MEMORY BIAS: NON-CLINICAL STUDIES

According to Schachter (1987), "Implicit memory is revealed when previous experiences facilitate performance on a task that does not require conscious or intentional recollection of those experiences; explicit memory is revealed when performance on a task requires conscious recollection of previous experiences" [p. 501]. In terms of this definition, all of the studies we have considered thus far were concerned with explicit memory rather than implicit memory. There are good grounds for arguing that different processes underlie explicit and implicit memory. For example, amnesic patients are typically greatly impaired on tests of explicit memory, but often perform normally on tests of implicit memory (see Eysenck & Keane, 1990).

There are various views on the processes involved in explicit and implicit memory. According to Graf, Squire, and Mandler (1984), the presentation of a word leads to the automatic activation of its internal representation in memory. This activation may last for some considerable time, and it serves to facilitate performance on tests of implicit memory. Elaboration, in which there is processing of the meaning of the activated word and its connections with associated words, facilitates performance on tests of explicit memory, but not on those of implicit memory.

Roediger and Blaxton (1987) argued that the distinction between data-driven processes (i.e., those triggered off by external stimuli) and conceptually driven processes (i.e., those initiated by the subject) is of value in understanding what is involved in explicit and implicit memory. In essence, they proposed that implicit memory typically depends on data-driven processes, whereas explicit memory depends on conceptually driven processes.

Even though the processes involved remain unclear, it is of theoretical interest to study the effects of anxiety on implicit memory. It seems likely that implicit memory is less affected than explicit memory by strategic processes at the time of encoding and at the time of test. Thus, tests of implicit memory may offer a way of assessing memory which is relatively uncontaminated by strategic factors.

Richards and French (1991) presented their subjects with a list of words under reading or self-referenced imagery conditions. This was followed by a word-fragment completion task in which they wrote down the first word they thought of which was consistent with the presented fragment. The measure of implicit memory was the tendency to complete the word fragments with list words. Subjects high in trait anxiety (but not those low in trait anxiety) demonstrated a negative memory bias on this test of implicit memory when it followed self-referenced imagery but not when it followed simply reading the list words. However, there was no memory bias on a test of explicit memory.

Mathews et al. (1989 a) also used a word-completion task as their measure of implicit memory. There were three groups of subjects (currently anxious patients, recovered anxious patients, and normal controls) in their study, which is described in more detail below. Unlike

Richards and French (1991), they failed to uncover any relationship between trait anxiety and negative memory bias in implicit memory.

Mathews et al. (in preparation) carried out a longitudinal study. They compared implicit memory in normal controls with that of generalized anxiety disorder patients during the course of recovery. There was no negative memory bias in implicit memory associated with trait anxiety in either group. More studies are planned, but at present the circumstances in which non-clinical anxious groups have a negative memory bias in implicit memory remain unclear.

NEGATIVE EXPLICIT MEMORY BIAS: CLINICAL STUDIES

The existence of a negative memory bias in explicit memory is predicted by various theories, including those of Beck and Emery (1985) and Bower (1981). Furthermore, as we saw in Chapter 4, anxious patients attend selectively to threatening rather than non-threatening stimuli, and this selective bias might lead to superior encoding and retrieval of threatening material by anxious patients. Some of the relevant issues are discussed by Eysenck and Mogg (1990, 1991).

Mogg, Mathews, and Weinman (1987) presented a mixture of positive, threatening negative (e.g., humiliated), and non-threatening negative (e.g., bored) adjectives to patients with generalized anxiety disorder and to normals. The subjects had to decide whether or not some of the words described them, and for the other words to decide whether they described a certain well-known television performer. The surprising finding on subsequent tests of both recall and recognition was that anxious patients had poorer retention of threat-related words than did the control subjects. In other words, the findings were in precisely the opposite direction to that predicted by schema theory.

Mogg (1988) reported five additional experiments in which the retention of threatening and neutral stimulus material in generalized anxiety disorder patients and in normal controls was compared. The typical finding was a complete absence of a negative memory bias in the anxious patients, a finding which was obtained in four separate experiments using recall as the measure of retention. In the remaining experiment, anxious patients showed a negative memory bias with recall, but failed to do so with recognition memory.

Mathews et al. (1989 a) carried out a study on current patients with generalized anxiety disorder, recovered patients who had suffered from generalized anxiety disorder, and normal controls. These groups were presented with a series of threatening and non-threatening words. They were told to imagine themselves in a scene involving themselves and the referent of each word. This was followed by a test of cued recall. None of the groups exhibited a negative memory bias on the test of cued recall, which is in line with previous non-significant findings.

Mogg and Mathews (1990) investigated explicit memory in anxious patients with generalized anxiety disorder and in normal controls. There were self-referent and other-referent tasks, and memory was assessed by free recall. The anxious patients showed some tendency to recall relatively more threat-related words. However, the anxious patients also produced relatively more threat-related intrusion errors, and the recall bias was obtained in the other-reference condition as well as the self-reference condition. Overall, the pattern of findings suggests that the apparent negative memory bias may actually have been due to response bias.

Apparently striking evidence of a negative memory bias in anxious patients was reported by Greenberg and Beck (1989). Subjects had to decide whether depression-relevant and anxiety-relevant adjectives described them, described the world, or described the future. There was then a test of free recall. The key finding for present purposes was that the anxious patients recalled considerably more negative than positive anxiety-relevant adjectives, whereas the control subjects recalled the same number of negative and positive adjectives. While this seems to indicate the existence of a negative memory bias in these anxious patients, that is not actually the case. The anxious patients responded 'yes' to far more negative anxiety-relevant adjectives than did the controls on the encoding task, and the free recall data were simply analysed in terms of raw scores. In other words, the apparent negative memory bias occurred simply because the anxious patients had a much larger pool of words from which to recall.

In sum, it has proved remarkably difficult to obtain good evidence for the existence of a negative explicit memory bias in anxious patients, in spite of the strong evidence that depressed patients have such a memory bias. The theoretical implications of the non-existence of this memory bias in anxious patients will be discussed later in this chapter. However, there are two obvious points to be made here. First, it is clear that the cognitive processes and mechanisms in anxious patients are not the same as those in depressed patients. Second, affect-congruent processing is clearly less prevalent than has been assumed by theorists such as Beck and Emery (1985) and Bower (1981).

NEGATIVE IMPLICIT MEMORY BIAS: CLINICAL STUDIES

In the preceding section, we discussed the study by Mathews et al. (1989 a), in which they failed to demonstrate the existence of a negative memory bias on an explicit memory test of cued recall. However, they also used a word completion task. The extent to which word completions were affected by the previous presentation of list was used as the measure of implicit memory. As can be seen in Fig. 5.3, the currently anxious patients produced more word completions corresponding to list words than did the normal controls, but they produced fewer word completions corresponding to non-threatening list words. Thus, the currently anxious patients showed a negative implicit memory bias.

The performance of recovered anxious patients is also shown in Fig. 5.3. Their implicit memory performance resembled that of the normal controls rather than that of the currently anxious patients. Thus, a negative implicit memory bias does not constitute a manifest cognitive vulnerability factor. It remains to be established whether this memory bias depends on a clinically anxious mood state, or whether it involves a latent cognitive vulnerability factor.

Mathews et al. (in preparation) also assessed implicit memory by means of a word-completion task in their longitudinal study. They found no evidence for an implicit memory bias in their generalized anxiety disorder patients either when they were clinically anxious or during recovery. It is not at all clear why their results differ so much from those of Mathews et al. (1989 a).

MacLeod (1990) used a task in which the colours in which threat-related and neutral words were printed had to be named. Recognition memory was used to assess explicit memory and lowered perceptual thresholds for previously presented words were used to

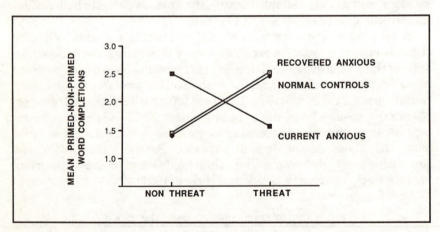

FIG. 5.3. Word completion performance (primed–non-primed) as a function of anxiety group and list word type (threatening vs. non-threatening). Data from Mathews, Mogg, May, and Eysenck (1989 a).

assess implicit memory. Neither group showed a memory bias in explicit memory, but the anxious patients had a significant negative memory bias in implicit memory. This study differed from those of Mathews et al. (1989 a) and Mathews et al. (in preparation) in that there was probably more opportunity for selective processing of the threatening stimuli.

In sum, the limited available evidence suggests that currently anxious patients may have a negative implicit memory bias, in spite of the fact that they do not have a negative explicit memory bias. Theoretically, it is reasonable to assume that this negative implicit memory bias can be demonstrated more reliably if conditions at the time of learning permit selective allocation of processing resources to threat (e.g., MacLeod, 1990). If anxious patients do have a negative implicit memory bias, there are important theoretical implications. These implications are discussed in the next section.

SUMMARY AND THEORETICAL INTEGRATION

We have seen that non-clinical anxious groups often exhibit a negative memory bias in explicit memory, particularly when the underlying schemas are activated via priming or mood induction. These groups may or may not also have a negative memory bias in implicit memory, although most of the evidence suggests that they do not. In contrast, anxious patients definitely do not have a negative memory bias in explicit memory, but there are indications that they may possess a negative implicit memory bias.

According to the theories proposed by Bower (1981) and Beck and Emery (1985), affect-congruent processing occurs throughout the cognitive system. It appears to follow that anxious patients and non-clinical anxious groups should both exhibit negative memory biases in explicit and implicit memory. There is no obvious way in which either theory could account for the actual pattern of findings.

The most surprising finding from most theoretical perspectives is the absence of a negative bias in explicit memory for patients with generalized anxiety disorder. It is all the more surprising because there is substantial evidence of the existence of such a bias in depressed patients (see Blaney, 1986), and there are also several demonstrations of a negative explicit memory bias in high trait-anxious normals. A possible theoretical interpretation of the various findings was proposed in similar terms by Williams et al. (1988) and by Mathews et al. (1989 a). According to Williams et al. (1988), the encoding of threat-related and neutral information involves integration or priming and elaboration.

Anxious individuals differ from non-anxious ones mainly in terms of priming rather than elaboration, and so threat-related stimuli may receive more integration or priming from anxious individuals (see Chapter 2). In general terms, explicit memory involves elaboration, whereas implicit memory depends mainly on integration. According to Mathews et al. (1989 b), anxious patients may find prolonged processing of threatening material to be so aversive that they have developed strategies which restrict the elaboration of processing. Cognitive avoidance (Foa & Kozak, 1986), which may involve attempts at distraction, is an example of such a strategy. These avoidance strategies are sometimes so effective that anxious patients remember less threat-related material than normal controls (e. g., Mogg et al., 1987).

It follows from the theoretical views of Williams et al. (1988) and of Mathews et al. (1989 a) that clinically anxious groups should have a negative bias in implicit memory but not in explicit memory. Thus, we have here a potential explanation for the findings from patients with generalized anxiety disorder. The possible existence of a negative memory bias in implicit memory for non-clinical anxious groups can also be accounted for.

What is less clear from the theoretical perspectives of Williams et al. (1988) and Mathews et al. (1989 a) is why non-clinical anxious groups often exhibit a negative memory bias in explicit memory. If anxiety does not affect elaboration, and explicit memory depends on elaboration, it seems to follow that high trait-anxious normals should not have a negative explicit memory bias. Indeed, MacLeod (1990), when discussing the theory of Williams et al. (1988), argues that, "since anxiety does not influence elaborative processing [of threat-related information], recall for this information will be unaffected" [p. 46].

It is also not entirely clear from the above theoretical perspectives why it has proved relatively difficult to obtain convincing evidence of a negative implicit memory bias in non-clinical anxious groups. There is allegedly more integration of the representations of threat-related stimuli in anxious individuals than in non-anxious ones, and integration is of central importance in determining implicit memory performance. From these assumptions, the natural prediction seems to be that high trait-anxious individuals should have a negative implicit memory bias.

The limited data currently available make it difficult to provide a definitive account of the effects of anxiety on explicit and implicit memory biases. However, for what it is worth, it is possible to offer a few speculations.

First, it is assumed that a negative explicit memory bias depends on the activation of underlying danger or other threat-related schemas. High trait-anxious individuals possess such schemas but low trait-anxious individuals do not, and so it is only those normals high in trait anxiety who have a negative explicit memory bias. Since the bias requires schema activation, it is more readily demonstrated in high trait-anxious subjects when the conditions (e.g., priming, high state anxiety) facilitate such activation.

Second, as Williams et al. (1988), Mathews et al. (1989 a), and others have suggested, clinically anxious patients tend to respond to highly threatening stimuli and situations by adopting a strategy of cognitive avoidance. If some such assumption is not made, it is difficult to account for the absence of a negative explicit memory bias in patients with generalized anxiety disorder. The main problem with making this assumption is that there is no direct evidence in any of the published memory research that anxious patients are actually adopting a cognitive avoidance strategy. As a consequence, it must be an important research objective to obtain stronger evidence for cognitive avoidance.

Third, it is assumed that the negative implicit memory bias is most likely to occur in individuals with well-integrated representations of threatening information who are high in state anxiety. Patients with generalized anxiety disorder and normals high in trait anxiety are generally characterized by such well-integrated representations. High state anxiety is relevant because it enhances the integration or activation of threatening representations. It follows that patients with generalized disorder, who typically have high state anxiety, should show an implicit memory bias. Recovered anxious patients should not, because their level of state anxiety is generally insufficiently high. Normals high in trait anxiety will often not show an implicit memory bias under normal testing conditions, but should do under stressful conditions. These predictions are consistent with virtually all of the findings on anxiety and implicit memory bias. However, the view that negative implicit memory bias forms part of a latent cognitive vulnerability factor would be much more convincing if it were to be demonstrated that high trait-anxious normals and recovered anxious patients show the bias when high in state anxiety.

In sum, it is proposed that the explicit and implicit memory biases both depend on internal structures associated with high trait anxiety (negative schemas and well-integrated representations of threat, respectively), combined with high state anxiety. This formulation is consistent with most of the evidence, apart from the failure of generalized anxiety disorder patients to show an explicit memory bias. In order to explain this failure, it is necessary to invoke the notion of cognitive avoidance or some similar strategy which prevents the bias from manifesting itself.

CHAPTER SIX

Worry

INTRODUCTION

Worry is clearly an important phenomenon. Indeed, it is the most commonly reported symptom by patients with psychological problems who consult their doctors (Goldberg, Bridges, Duncan-Jones, & Grayson, 1987). It is also of obvious relevance to anxiety. However, while there has been an enormous amount of research on anxiety, relatively little work has been specifically directed at worry. There are probably two main reasons for this neglect. First, there have been major disagreements about its appropriate definition. Second, worry is an internal mental event, and so it is rather difficult to measure or to assess.

In spite of the fact that worry is an inaccessible process, its importance means that it merits investigation with whatever techniques are available. As far as the definition of worry is concerned, there is perhaps a greater consensus than is often believed to be the case. For example, Borkovec, Robinson, Pruzinsky, and DePree (1983 a) proposed the following reasonable definition:

> Worry is a chain of thoughts and images, negatively affect-laden and relatively uncontrollable. The worry process represents an attempt to engage in mental problem-solving on an issue whose outcome is uncertain but contains the possibility of one or more negative outcomes. Consequently, worry relates closely to fear process [p.9].

O'Neill (1985) argued that Borkovec et al. (1983 a) had failed to demonstrate that worry differs in any important respect from anxiety. According to him: "Worry and anxiety are two referents of the same thing—worry indicating only the cognitive component, anxiety including the autonomic component." As Tallis, Eysenck, and Mathews (1992) pointed out, O'Neill's (1985) argument is illogical. If worry is the cognitive component of anxiety, then manifestly worry is not the same thing as anxiety! In fact, the view that worry is the cognitive component of anxiety is entirely reasonable, and that view is the one adopted here.

There is reasonably strong evidence that worry is an important component of trait anxiety or neuroticism. Steptoe and Kearsley (1990) administered three inventories (the Cognitive-Somatic Anxiety Questionnaire; the Worry-Emotionality Scale; and the Lehrer-Woolfolk Anxiety Symptom Questionnaire), all of which are designed to assess the cognitive and somatic components of anxiety. In addition, they administered the neuroticism scale of the Eysenck Personality Inventory. Neuroticism correlated more highly with the cognitive component than with the somatic component of all three questionnaires. For example, neuroticism correlated +0.59 with the cognitive scale of the Cognitive-Somatic Anxiety Questionnaire, but only +0.33 with its somatic scale.

Borkovec et al. (1983 a) correlated trait anxiety with the amount of time which people spend worrying. They reported a correlation of +0.67 between these two variables. Tallis, Eysenck, and Mathews (1992) developed the Worry Domains Questionnaire, which provides both a global assessment of worry and of domain-specific worry. Trait anxiety was correlated with two slightly modified versions of the Worry Domains Questionnaire. The correlations were +0.78 and +0.84. Therefore, it is reasonable to propose that worry is the principal component of trait anxiety.

How important is worry as a characteristic of generalized anxiety disorder? One strong indication of its significance is provided by DSM-IIIR (1987), which is the current diagnostic and statistical manual of the American Psychiatric Association. According to DSM-IIIR, the presence of prolonged (more than six months), unrealistic, and excessive worry is found in generalized anxiety disorder. Such worry, provided that it relates to concerns in at least two areas of life, and "the person has been bothered by these concerns more days than not", is a central defining feature of generalized anxiety disorder.

Evidence supporting the view that worry is especially closely associated with generalized anxiety disorder was reported by Barlow (1988) and by Gross and Eifert (1990). Barlow (1988) discovered with small samples that 100% of patients with generalized anxiety disorder, but only 50% of patients with other anxiety disorders, reported unrealistic worry over minor concerns. Sanderson and Barlow (1990) compared the percentages of patients from each of five anxiety disorder categories who responded "Yes" to the following question: "Do you worry excessively about minor things?" It was 91% for patients with generalized anxiety disorder, compared to 59% for obsessive-compulsives, 41% for panic disorder patients with agoraphobia, and 32% for both simple phobics and social phobics.

Gross and Eifert (discussed by Gross, Oei, & Evans, 1989) identified orthogonal panic and generalized anxiety dimensions in both anxious patients and students on the basis of their reports of anxiety state symptoms. Worry was the symptom which was most strongly associated with the generalized anxiety dimension. Gross et al. (1989) carried out a similar study on various groups of anxious patients, and came to the following conclusion:

Worry is the cardinal feature of generalized anxiety [p. 159].

In sum, it has been found consistently that individuals who are high in trait anxiety report worrying considerably more than those who are low in trait anxiety. It has also been found that patients with generalized anxiety disorder worry much of the time, significantly more so than patients suffering from other anxiety disorders. It is noteworthy that the above effects are very strong. This suggests that worry may be the central ingredient in both trait anxiety and generalized anxiety disorder.

DOMAINS OF WORRY

Not surprisingly, the content of worries reflects those areas of life which are of major importance to the worrier. As a first approximation, one may assume that worries occur in response to the actual or potential non-achievement of goals associated with major sources of life satisfaction. According to Argyle (1987), these sources include the domestic, social, and work areas.

The fact that many worries relate to potential frustrative non-reward helps to account for the wide range of worries which individuals experience. There is obviously an almost limitless number of events which might happen in the future which would serve to thwart or frustrate one or other of an individual's life goals. There are really two factors at work here. First, the anxiety-producing events experienced by most people involve frustrative non-reward far more often than they involve actual aversive stimulation (Borkovec, Metzger, & Pruzinsky, 1986). Secondly, contemplation of the future (as happens with worry) is often a much richer source of possible frustrating events than is contemplation of the past.

Various theoretical positions can be identified with respect to individual differences in the content of worries. If the amount that a person worries is solely a function of his or her personality (e.g., a 'born worrier', high trait anxiety), then individuals might be consistent in their levels of worry across the major areas of life. As a consequence, areas or domains of worry would correlate highly with each other, and there would be a single major worry factor. However, it is also reasonable to argue that individuals with different personalities attach different levels of importance to life's major areas (e.g., social, work). If that is the case, then the pattern of worry would vary from individual to individual, and a number of worry domains would be identifiable. A further possibility is that the amount an individual worries depends primarily on his or her experiences, in which case the domains of worry would correlate modestly or not at all with each other. Finally, and most plausibly, personality and experiences may interact to determine an individual's level of worrying in each area of life.

There have been various recent attempts to provide structural accounts of worry and to identify the major worry domains. The approaches of Meyer, Miller, Metzger, and Borkovec (1990), Tallis et al. (1992), Eysenck and van Berkum (in press), and Barlow (1988) are all considered below.

Meyer, Miller, Metzger, and Borkovec (1990)

Meyer et al. (1990) developed the Penn State Worry Questionnaire. Items were selected primarily on the basis of their apparent relevance to worry in patients with generalized anxiety disorder. These items were administered to college students, and the resultant data analysed by means of a principal components factor analysis with oblique rotation. There was a general factor acccounting for 22.6% of the variance, and five smaller factors each of which acccounted for less than 5% of the variance. Progressive refinements led to the final version of the Penn Sate Worry Questionnaire. It contains 16 items and measures only the general factor.

The findings of Meyer et al. (1990) appear to indicate that there is a single general worry factor. However, most of the items on the Penn State Worry Questionnaire have a very general focus and do not refer to any specific worry domain (e.g., 'My worries overwhelm me', 'I have been a worrier all my life'). Specific domains of worry are unlikely to be discovered with such items.

Performance on the Penn State Worry Questionnaire by college students was correlated with a number of personality measures. The highest correlation was with trait anxiety (+0.64), but there were also interesting correlations with self-esteem (-0.34), various measures of self-consciousness (+0.26 to 0.38), and depression (+0.36). The closeness of the association between trait anxiety and worry score confirms the view that a crucial difference between individuals high and low in trait anxiety is in terms of the amount of worrying they do.

Meyer et al. (1990) also provided additional evidence of the importance of worry in generalized anxiety disorder. Patients with generalized anxiety disorder had a mean worry score of 68 on the Penn State Worry Questionnaire, which is considerably higher than the mean score of 49 found in a large normal sample. Worry scores in these patients decreased more if they received coping desensitization plus cognitive therapy than if they received non-directive therapy.

In sum, Meyer et al. (1990) found that a general factor of worry is of great importance to trait anxiety in normals and to generalized anxiety disorder. However, they did not demonstrate that all worry factors other than the general factor are of little consequence.

Tallis, Eysenck, and Mathews (1992)

Tallis et al. (1992) made use of the worries listed by 71 individuals to construct a 155-item General Worry Questionnaire containing both frequency and intensity scales. This questionnaire was completed by 95 subjects, and the data analysed by means of an agglomerative method of cluster analysis. Six clusters were identified in both the frequency and intensity data, and were also judged to be highly coherent in terms of an underlying unitary theme. These clusters or domains were as follows: relationships; lack of confidence; aimless future; work incompetence; financial concerns; and socio-political concerns.

The above clusters formed the basis of a 30-item Worry Domains Questionnaire which was administered to 100 subjects. The interrelationships among the six worry domains were calculated. The four domains of relationships, lack of confidence, aimless future, and work incompetence were all fairly highly inter-correlated, whereas the domain of socio-political concerns was quite separate from all of the other domains. Subjects reported more worry about socio-political concerns than about any other domain, but it appears improbable that most people actually worry more about issues such as the starving millions in the Third World or violations of human rights than about themselves and their future. It seems likely that social desirability bias affected responding within the socio-political domain.

It would obviously be desirable to have independent evidence that there are actually distinct worry domains. Tallis, Eysenck, and Mathews (1991 b) made a start in that direction. Two groups of subjects were selected in part on the basis of their scores on an earlier version of the Worry Domains Questionnaire: One group consisted of high scorers on lack of confidence and low scores on physical threat (a domain not included in the Worry Domains Questionnaire), whereas the other group scored low on both domains. Subjects were presented with words one at a time belonging to the four categories of physical threat, social threat (relevant to lack of confidence), neutral, and positive. They were instructed to imagine a 'real-life' future situation involving themselves relevant to each word within a 10 second period. The two groups did not differ in terms of the number of images formed in response to the physical threat, neutral, or positive words. However, the subjects reporting more worries in the domain of lack of confidence formed significantly more images to social threat words than low worriers within 10 seconds. These findings suggest that the two groups differed specifically with respect to worries in the domain of lack of confidence or social threat rather than simply a global tendency to worry.

Rather similar findings were obtained in a second experiment by Tallis et al. (1991 b). Subjects who were high scorers on the domains of lack of confidence and aimless future but low scorers on the physical domain were compared with low scorers on all three domains. All of the subjects were instructed to imagine as quickly as possible a future scene

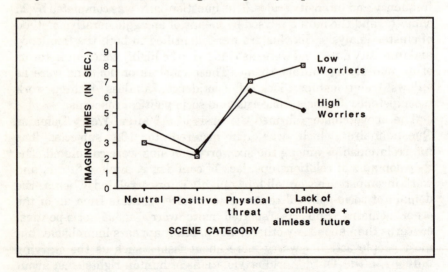

FIG. 6.1. Imaging times as a function of worry group and type of scene imagined. Data from Tallis, Eysenck, and Mathews (1991 b), Exp.2.

relevant to each of a series of phrases drawn from the physical threat domain, the combined lack of confidence and aimless future domains, positive life events, and neutral life events. As can be seen in Fig. 6.1, the two groups differed significantly only with respect to imaging times in the lack of confidence/aimless future domains. These data provide further support for the psychological reality of worry domains.

In sum, Tallis et al. (1991 b) have provided good evidence that there are a number of worry domains, perhaps as many as five or six. However, the fact that there are reasonably high inter-correlations among some of the proposed worry domains suggests that it might be preferable to postulate fewer domains.

Eysenck and van Berkum (in press)

Eysenck and van Berkum (in press) adopted a similar approach to that of Tallis et al. (1992). They devised a questionnaire consisting of 109 items based on worries which had been listed by 60 individuals. This questionnaire was administered to 98 normal individuals. The resultant data were cluster analysed using the inter-item correlations as the similarity measure, and the group average linkage procedure as the hierarchical clustering method. This produced nine clusters which appeared to have psychological reality, to which were added items from two more areas of concern (physical danger worries and worries about panicking and loss of control in stressful situations).

Five items were selected from all of the above 11 clusters to form the Worry Questionnaire. This was administered to 113 normals, along with the trait anxiety scale of the Spielberger State-Trait Anxiety Inventory and the Marlowe–Crowne Social Desirability Scale as a measure of defensiveness. Those who scored low on trait anxiety but high on social desirability or defensiveness were regarded as repressors. Repressors are susceptible to stress in various ways (e.g., at the physiological level), but they deny this at the level of conscious report (cf. Weinberger, Schwartz, & Davidson, 1979). It was thus anticipated that repressors would report consistently low levels of worry across the various clusters or domains.

Ten major clusters or domains were identified statistically within the Worry Questionnaire. They were as follows: physical health; general social-evaluative; personal relationships; financial; personal fulfilment; nuclear–international concerns; society and environment; health of close ones; physical appearance; panic and loss of control. The matrix of correlations among these scales, computed over the 113 subjects, was submitted to a principal components analysis. The two resulting factors were varimax-rotated. The first factor accounted for 52.3% of the variance. As can be seen in Fig. 6.2, the general social-evaluative, personal relationships, financial, personal fulfilment, and appearance scales all loaded highly on this factor. The pattern of loadings suggests that this factor essentially reflects worries related to one's social-evaluative self-concept. The second factor accounted for 11.4% of the variance. It had high loadings from physical health, nuclear–international concerns, society and environment, and health of close ones. This factor appears to reflect worries about physical threat to oneself and to others.

A striking feature of this analysis of the Worry Questionnaire is the extent to which the factors identified correspond to those obtained from analysing anxiety questionnaires. For example, Endler, Magnusson, Ekehammar, and Okada (1976) factor analysed data from Spielberger's State-Trait Anxiety Inventory, the Behavioural Reactions Questionnaire, and the S-R Inventory of Anxiousness. They obtained two major factors which they labelled interpersonal threat and physical danger, which bear obvious similarities to the two major factors extracted from the Worry Questionnaire. They found that trait anxiety as assessed by the State-Trait Anxiety Inventory loaded 0.80 on the interpersonal threat factor but only 0.25 on the physical danger factor.

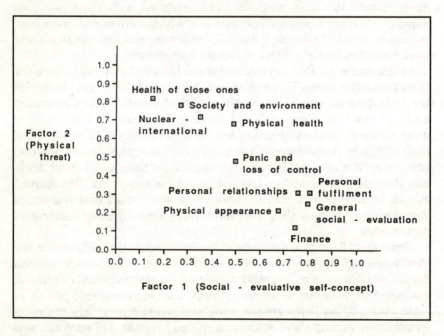

FIG. 6.2. Loadings of worry domains on major worry factors. Data from Eysenck and van Berkum (in press).

In similar fashion, Eysenck and van Berkum (in press) discovered that the social-evaluative factor was much more important than the physical danger factor in accounting for worry data. The implication is that the underlying structure of worry is very similar to that of anxiety.

The notion that worry and anxiety are closely related was also supported by the finding that mean worry frequency across all of the scales correlated +0.65 with trait anxiety. There was also a highly significant correlation of −0.26 between mean worry frequency and defensiveness as assessed by the Marlow–Crowne Scale. Individual differences were considered further by identifying groups of subjects who were high-anxious (high trait anxiety), truly low-anxious (low trait anxiety and low defensiveness), and repressors (low trait anxiety and high defensiveness). The mean worry frequency of the high-anxious group of subjects was considerably higher than that of the other two groups, who did not differ from each other. The three groups were also compared with respect to their pattern of worries by means of a discriminant analysis involving all 10 scales. The truly low-anxious and repressor groups did not differ in their pattern, but there were interesting differences between the high-anxious group on the one hand and the other two groups on the other hand. In essence, there were large differences on those scales relevant to the major factor of social-evaluative self-concept (especially the general social-evaluative, personal relationships, personal fulfilment, and appearance scales). However, there were relatively small group differences with respect to some of the scales (e.g., society and environment, health of close ones) relevant to the major factor of physical threat. These findings support the view (e.g., Endler et al., 1976) that social-evaluative concerns are of central importance to individual differences in trait anxiety.

The factor structure of worry proposed by Eysenck and van Berkum (in press) differs in a number of ways from that advocated by Tallis et al. (1992). However, there is agreement that several specific worry factors in the social-evaluative area are quite highly inter-correlated. Eysenck and van Berkum (in press) used these findings as evidence that there is a general social-evaluative worry factor, whereas Tallis et al. (1992) chose to remain at a more specific level of analysis. If one postulates a hierarchical worry structure, then the apparently conflicting views can be reconciled by proposing that Eysenck and van Berkum (in press) and Tallis et al. (1992) are simply focusing on different levels within the hierarchy.

In spite of the above arguments, there may be some advantages in proposing a general social-evaluative worry factor. For example, high and low trait-anxious individuals differ crucially in terms of a very general factor of perceived personal vulnerability or susceptibility to interpersonal threat (Endler et al., 1976). It seems reasonable that a comparably general factor might account for many of the differences between high and low worriers.

Barlow (1988)

Barlow (1988) argued that the excessive and/or unrealistic worries reported by generalized anxiety disorder patients fell into the four domains of family, finances, work, and personal illness. Detailed evidence to support this contention was reported by Sanderson and Barlow (1990), who administered the Anxiety Disorders Interview Schedule-Revised to patients with generalized anxiety disorder. They discovered that 79% of the patients had unrealistic worries about their families, 57% about finances, 43% about work, and only 14% about personal illness.

It would obviously be useful to know whether the four worry domains or spheres are also applicable to normal groups. Preliminary information on this was reported by Craske, Rapee, Jackel, and Barlow (1989). They asked generalized anxiety disorder patients and normal controls to fill in a questionnaire whenever they noticed themselves worrying. The two groups had comparable proportions of their worries in the work sphere, and the same was true for the family sphere. However, there were pronounced group differences in the other two spheres. The anxious patients had 31% of their worries in the area of personal illness compared to only 2% for the normal controls. In the sphere of finances, the percentages were 3% for the anxious patients and 26% for the normal controls.

It has proved relatively straightforward to categorize the worries of generalized anxiety disorder patients and normals according to the four spheres identified by Barlow (1988). However, this approach is limited because it focuses on the external source of worries at the expense of the internal psychological factors. For example, an individual might have worries in the spheres of family and work, with both sets of worries reflecting an underlying lack of confidence or undue sensitivity to social evaluation.

Summary and Conclusions

So far as the structure of worry in normals is concerned, there are grounds for arguing that there is a major social-evaluative factor and a smaller physical threat factor (Eysenck & van Berkum, in press). If it is preferred to operate at a more specific level, then it is possible to identify various components of the social-evaluative factor (e.g., relationships, lack of confidence, aimless future; Tallis et al., 1992). It is not clear whether this structural analysis is applicable to generalized anxiety disorder patients as well as normals. It seems likely that there is a reasonable correspondence between the two groups in the structure of worry, but patients may have a more diversified structure in the physical threat domain (cf., Craske et al., 1989).

While normals high and low in trait anxiety have the same worry structure, there are indications that there are qualitative as well as quantitative differences in their patterns of worry. High trait-anxious individuals differ markedly from low trait-anxious individuals with respect to the social-evaluative worry factor, but the difference is much smaller with the physical threat worry factor.

THEORETICAL APPROACHES

The growing interest in the phenomenon of worry has led to a number of recent theoretical developments. For example, Borkovec et al. (1986), Borkovec, Shadick, and Hopkins (1990), Barlow (1988), and Tallis and Eysenck (submitted) have all proposed theoretical accounts of worry. The theoretical position adopted in this book represents a modification of the one proposed by Tallis and Eysenck (submitted). It is useful, however, to consider this new theoretical position in the context of recent theories of worry which have appeared in the literature.

Borkovec et al. (1986)

According to Borkovec et al. (1986), worry can be understood within a complex theoretical formulation including elements of learning theory, cognitive processes, and self-theory. Mowrer's (1947) two-stage theory of fear provided the starting point. In this theory, neutral stimuli present at the time of an aversive event become feared via classical conditioning. These conditioned aversive stimuli are subsequently avoided, and avoidance responses are rewarded by fear reduction. Mowrer's (1947) theory offers a potential explanation of the origins of anxiety (through classical conditioning) and of its maintenance over time (through avoidance of the anxiety-provoking situation).

There are various problems involved in using Mowrer's (1947) theoretical model to understand the development of clinical anxiety. It is typically the case that no highly aversive or traumatic events can be identified in the lives of anxious patients. Borkovec et al. (1986) proposed instead that neutral stimuli may become conditioned to situations of frustrative non-reward in which the attainment of valued goals is thwarted. The limitations of Mowrer's stimulus-response conditioning approach led Borkovec et al. (1986) to propose a cognitive processing model of worry in which worry "can be viewed as a cognitive attempt to anticipate and thus avoid a myriad of possible, future outcomes" [p. 240]. It was proposed that memory mechanisms are involved in producing worry in at least two different ways. First, "there exists in memory a set of verbal and visual patterns related to the worry event. If this content area were to remain primed even during other cognitive activities, an alerting worry-related stimulus (a representation of the primed area) would be given a priority for processing and a worrisome intrusion would occur in awareness" [p. 243]. Second, worry occurs when a situation occurs for which there is no appropriate course of action stored in production memory.

The final aspect of Borkovec et al.'s (1986) theory is self-theory. In essence, frustrative non-reward can produce a self-evaluative state, leading in turn to a perceived discrepancy between the present self and the future or goal self. Such a discrepancy is likely to be threatening and to generate worry.

The complexity of Borkovec's theory, combined with the dearth of relevant empirical evidence, make it extremely difficult to evaluate. However, the learning theory, cognitive processing, and self-theory components of the overall theory do not seem to cohere very well. The self-theory adds little to the theory, and the proposed links between the learning theory and the cognitive processing theory are somewhat forced. In particular, it is not clear that worry in the cognitive processing theory is analogous to behavioural avoidance in the learning theory, although worry may lead to cognitive avoidance. Worry is generally associated with increased anxiety, whereas behavioural avoidance is associated with decreased anxiety. As a consequence, it is difficult to regard the consequences of worrying as rewarding in the same way as behavioural avoidance.

Borkovec et al. (1990)

Borkovec et al. (1990) developed some of the theoretical ideas of Borkovec et al. (1986), especially the notion that worry can be regarded as a form of cognitive avoidance. The essence of Borkovec et al.'s (1990) theory was expressed by them in the following terms:

> Worry is primarily a conceptual, verbal-linguistic activity ... Worry may be directly, immediately, and negatively reinforced by the avoidance of imagery and, therefore, ... of peripheral physiological activations. GADs [generalized anxiety disordered patients] fear negative somatic arousal and affect. In response to perceived threat, the shifting of attention to

conceptual activity at the very least reduces the generation of imagery and/or other routes to accessing memory structures that might otherwise issue efferent command into the autonomic/affective systems. We are positing an actual suppression of physiological/affective process as a direct consequence of worrisome conceptual activity. One worries in order to avoid imagery/efferent command in order to avoid negative affect at the somatic level. There is a consequential increase in cortical activity and decrease in somatic activity [p.453].

There are at least three testable hypotheses which emerge from this theoretical framework:

1. worry involves thought of a mainly linguistic kind;
2. worry reduces or actually inhibits imagery activity; and
3. worry reduces or inhibits somatic physiological activity.

Borkovec and Inz (1990) investigated generalized anxiety disorder patients and normal controls during a self-relaxation period and while worrying about a topic of current concern. The amount of thinking increased from 15% during relaxation to 26% during worrying for the control subjects, and it increased from 33% to 38% for the anxious patients. In contrast, imagery decreased from 56% during relaxation to 44% during worrying for the controls, and for the anxious patients it decreased from 36% to 20%. Thus, worry altered the balance between thought and imagery in the predicted fashion. However, the control subjects reported much more imagery than thought during the worry period, which appears to be inconsistent with the notion that worry primarily involves verbal-linguistic activity.

Since language is predominantly a left-hemisphere function, it might be expected that there would be increased left-hemisphere activation during worry. Carter, Johnson, and Borkovec (1986) discovered that worry led to increased EEG beta activity in the frontal lobes. Of particular interest, there was a greater relative shift towards left frontal activation during worry.

So far as peripheral physiological activation is concerned, most of the evidence indicates that worry has little or no effect (e.g., Deffenbacher, 1980; Karterolitis & Gill, 1987). In similar fashion, Borkovec et al. (1983 a) discovered that there were marginal differences between worriers and non-worriers during either rest or worry periods. Of course, these findings do not really support the hypothesis that worry actually inhibits somatic physiological activity. However, Hoehn-Saric, McLeod, and Zimmerli (1988) discovered that female generalized anxiety disorder patients had smaller skin conductance responses and reduced variability of skin conductance and heart rate than non-anxious controls during cognitive stress tests. During rest, the two groups differed physiologically only with respect to elevated muscle tension in the patients. A limitation of this study is that it is not clear that the physiological differences during stress were due to group differences in the amount of worry.

What is apparently the strongest evidence that worry can reduce physiological activity was reported by Borkovec and Hu (1990). They used a situation in which groups of subjects with a phobia of public speaking were required to form an image of a scene involving public speaking on several occasions with short intervals in between each image formation. These intervals were devoted to relaxed, neutral, or worrisome thinking about public speaking, with heart rate being unaffected by the nature of these thoughts. Heart rate during imagery of the phobic situation increased most for subjects who had been having relaxing thoughts, an intermediate amount for subjects who had neutral thoughts, and did not increase at all for subjects who had been experiencing worrisome thoughts. The mechanism involved is not clear, but it is possible that worry served in some way to inhibit the increase in heart rate that would normally be elicited by phobic imagery.

The theoretical formulation of Borkovec et al. (1990) has a number of attractive features. For example, the view that worry primarily involves verbal-linguistic activity is probably correct and deserves emphasis. In addition, the mystery of why it is that some people devote a considerable proportion of the day to an apparently almost fruitless activity like worry is addressed more directly by Borkovec et al. (1990) than by almost anyone else. However, there are at least two major problems with their theory. First, if worry is rewarding in the way proposed by Borkovec et al. (1990), then it is difficult to account for the fact that it is generally regarded as aversive. It is also difficult to explain why many people spend very little time worrying. Second, the evidence is by no means all supportive of the view that worry is associated with reduced somatic physiological activity. For example, worry has been found to produce a significant increase in cardio-vascular activity and in reported somatic symptoms (York, Borkovec, Vasey, & Stern, 1987). Worry generally has rather small effects on somatic physiological activity, and does not consistently reduce such activity.

Barlow (1988)

Barlow (1988) has proposed that intense worry occurs as a consequence of a complex chain of events:

1. Certain situations or unexplained arousal lead to the evocation of anxious propositions stored in memory and produce a state of negative affect.
2. Negative affect causes an attentional shift from the external environment to an internal self-evaluative focus.
3. Self-evaluative focus leads to a state of increased arousal.
4. Increased arousal activates an apprehensive hypervalent cognitive schema. This produces a perceived inability to predict and/or to control current or future situations, hypervigilance, and attentional narrowing. Attentional narrowing is especially important, because it prevents attention being directed to ongoing events unrelated to worry.
5. Activation of the apprehensive hypervalent cognitive schema produces worry.
6. Worry leads to dysfunctional performance; this can increase negative affect and thus activate the above sequence of events in a more severe form.

There is empirical evidence for at least some of the above events. For example, a link between arousal and self-focused attention was demonstrated by Wegner and Guiliano (1980). Subjects lay down and relaxed, sat in a chair, or ran on the spot in order to induce different levels of arousal. After that, they were given sentences with words missing, and instructed to complete the sentences. The most aroused subjects (i.e., those who had run on the spot) used the greatest number of self-relevant words, and the least aroused subjects (i.e., those who had relaxed) used the smallest number.

Much research points to the importance of perceived uncontrollability and unpredictability as factors involved in anxiety. For example, Mineka and Kihlstrom (1978) reviewed the animal literature with its many paradigms for creating anxiety. They concluded that anxiety is caused in every paradigm because "environmental events of vital importance to the organism become unpredictable, uncontrollable, or both" [p. 257].

Barlow (1988) argued that Easterbrook's (1959) hypothesis provides support for his contention that arousal leads to attentional narrowing and worry. However, as we saw in Chapter 4, Easterbrook's hypothesis is no more than partially correct. Furthermore, Barlow (1988) misinterprets Easterbrook (1959), claiming that Easterbrook, "suggested that narrowing of attention is a preoccupation with mood-congruent material during emotional reactivity that varies as a function of the emotion ... one becomes preoccupied with the central mood-congruent cues as intensity of mood increases, at the expense of concurrent attention to external stimuli" [p. 58]. In fact, Easterbrook's (1959) hypothesis is not concerned at all with mood-congruent effects!

Barlow's (1988) theory is an impressive attempt to identify some of the major cognitive processes involved in the initiation and maintenance of worry. He is surely correct that memory and attention both play crucial roles in worrying. In addition, the theory provides a persuasive explanation of why intense worry is so difficult to control: An internal focus on oneself and one's worries combined with a narrowing of attention mean that attention cannot be re-directed to external stimuli. Barlow (1988) focused on the intense worries experienced by anxious patients, and so his theory may not be entirely relevant to worry in normals. For example, he contends that high arousal is an antecedent of worry, and that worry is always dysfunctional. These contentions may be largely correct when applied to clinical worries, but seem implausible with respect to the everyday worries of normal individuals.

New Theoretical Framework

Tallis and Eysenck (submitted) used the theoretical formulations of Borkovec and Barlow as the basis for developing a somewhat new theoretical approach (see Fig. 6.3). Many of the ideas put forward by Tallis and Eysenck (submitted) are incorporated in the new theoretical framework proposed here, together with some additional theoretical speculations. The starting point of this new theoretical framework is that an adequate theory of worry needs to account for several characteristics of worry. First, there is the function (if any) served by worry. Second, the factors responsible for the onset, maintenance, and cessation of worry need to be identified. Third, a comprehensive theory of worry would need to explain why it is that some people consistently worry more than others.

It is often assumed that worry serves no useful function. Common expressions such as, "I am worried sick about", or "Don't worry, it may never happen", are consistent with this view, as is the theoretical position of Barlow (1988). In contrast, Tallis and Eysenck (submitted) argued that worry actually fulfils at least three major functions:

1. An alarm function, introducing information about a threat into conscious awareness.
2. A prompt function, re-presenting threat-related thoughts and images into awareness.
3. A preparation function, permitting the worrier to anticipate a future situation and so possibly reduce its aversiveness via a process of habituation.

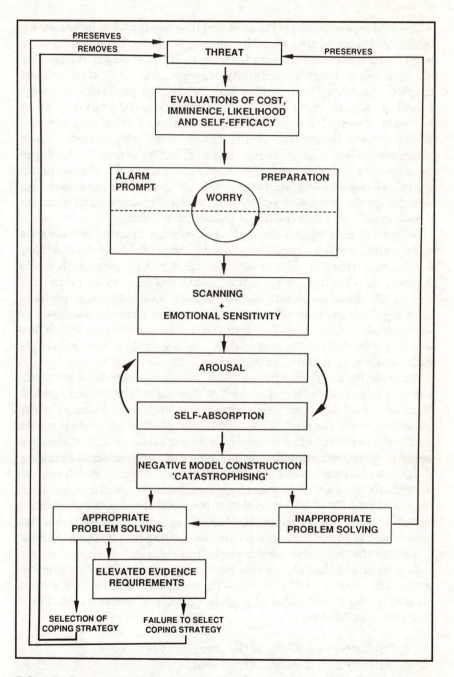

FIG. 6.3. Some of the key constructs and their interrelationships from the theory proposed by Tallis and Eysenck (submitted).

The evidence with respect to the third function is rather inconsistent. Janis (1958) argued that there is a strong tendency for people to deny danger, and for them "to bolster their sense of perceived invulnerability by developing blanket immunity expectations and thus almost completely ward off anticipatory fear" [p. 360]. A preferable strategy, according to Janis (1958), is for individuals to address the facts and allow the "work of worry" to reduce anxiety. He discovered that patients who were informed beforehand of the effects of surgery reported more pre-operative fear than those not informed, but less anger on the day of the operation and less disturbance when recalling the operation. In contrast, Ridgeway and Mathews (1982) discovered that pre-operative information about surgery and its effects actually increased the number of days of pain and also the use of pain-relieving drugs.

In spite of ambiguities about the preparation function of worry, its alarm and prompt functions ensure that it has evolutionary significance. There is obvious survival value in a process which forces the individual to attend to potential threats and dangers. Of course, the worry process becomes dysfunctional in some individuals, e.g., patients suffering from generalized anxiety disorder. In such individuals, the worry process is frequently activated by minor threats which are objectively improbable to materialize, and worrying severely disrupts their ability to function effectively.

According to the theory proposed by Tallis and Eysenck (submitted), worry is triggered by threat, which is defined in the *Oxford English Dictionary* as "an indication of something undesirable coming". The threat may be in the form of an environmental stimulus or it may be in the form of activated information in long-term memory. Most of the time worry is probably initiated at least in part by some external stimulus. Craske et al. (1989) found that 88% of the occasions on which normal individuals were worrying there was a recognizable specific precipitant, compared to 64% of worry occasions for generalized anxiety disorder patients. Since these percentage figures are based on retrospective reports and required conscious awareness of the precipitating stimulus, it is likely that they represent underestimates.

It is assumed that threat value is a major determinant of whether worry will occur, and if it does, of its duration. At least four factors determine the threat value of a given possible negative event. These factors are as follows:

1. Subjective probability of the aversive event occurring.
2. Subjective imminence of the event.
3. Perceived aversiveness of the event.
4. Perceived post-event coping strategies.

In general terms, a future aversive event which is regarded subjectively as highly likely is much more threatening than one which is regarded as improbable. For example, flying by plane is very threatening if the probability of a fatal crash is perceived as high, but not if the subjective probability corresponds to the objective probability of approximately one in 500,000. In support of this position, it has been found in self-report data that subjective probabilities correlate very highly with the extent of worry (see Mathews, 1990). However, studies in which the impact of the probability of an aversive event occurring was assessed by psychophysiological measures provide surprisingly little support for the predicted positive relation between probability of an aversive event and anticipatory stress (see Paterson & Neufeld, 1987, for a review). This may be due to reliance on objective rather than subjective probabilities. Another possibility is that worry or anticipatory stress is determined by the degree of uncertainty about occurrence of the threatened event, i.e., aversive events with a 50% probability of occurrence are most threatening (Epstein & Roupenian, 1970). At present, there is insufficient evidence to be confident of the function relating subjective probability to threat.

One of the determinants of subjective probability is an individual's anxiety or stress level. It has been found that heightened anxiety or stress can have a surprisingly widespread or global effect on probability estimates. Bower (1983) discovered that induction of an unhappy mood by hypnotic suggestion led to an increase in the subjective probabilities of several disasters. Harrison (1984) found that negative events were rated as more probable during an unhappy or anxious mood, even when there was a minimal relationship between the event and the situation used for hypnotic mood induction. Johnson and Tversky (1983) reported that subjects who read a detailed account of an individual's death exhibited global increases in risk estimation across all causes of death. In contrast, Butler and Mathews (1987) reported that the stress of an impending examination had the greatest effect on the subjective probabilities of self-relevant, negative examination-related events, and had only small or non-existent effects on the subjective probabilities of other negative events.

A future aversive event which is imminent is generally more threatening than one which lies further in the future. For example, Monat (1976) instructed subjects that electric shock would be presented after 1, 3, or 12 minutes. Heart rate, galvanic skin response, and self-reported anxiety were all highest in subjects faced with the most imminent threat and lowest in those subjects with the least imminent threat. In similar fashion, Butler and Mathews (1987) discovered that state anxiety levels were higher one day before an examination than one month before. Spiegler, Morris, and Liebert (1968) assessed worry and emotionality, and discovered that only worry scores were elevated five days before an examination.

It might be argued that one of the reasons why greater imminence of a threatening event causes increased worry is because it is associated with heightened subjective probability. This may be the case if the threatened event is uncontrollable (e.g., having a plane crash). However, with a threatened event over which individuals have some control (examination failure), it was found that worry increased with greater imminence, but the perceived probability of negative outcomes was unaffected (Kent & Jamburathan, 1989). In contrast, as we have just seen, Butler and Mathews (1987) found elevated estimates of examination failure in students shortly before an examination.

It is almost tautological to argue that the threat posed by a situation depends on the perceived aversiveness associated with the threatened event happening. However, it is important to note that the cost or severity of a threatened event typically depends on the individual's motivations or goals. As Paterson and Neufeld (1987) expressed it, "stressor severity can be considered as being made up of three dimensions: the importance of the desires or goals likely to be blocked by event occurrence, the number of goals blocked, and the intensity of the deprivation" [p. 406].

Evidence that the importance of the threatened goals is a relevant factor was obtained by Vogel, Raymond, and Lazarus (1959). They selected two groups, one consisting of boys high in achievement motivation and low in affiliation motivation, and the other consisting of boys high in affiliation motivation and low in achievement motivation. They discovered that the level of physiological arousal was higher when the more rather than the less valued goal was threatened.

One reason why more time is spent worrying about threats to major than to minor goals is the fact that there is likely to be a considerably richer network of information in long-term memory relevant to major goals. As a consequence, there are far more environmental stimuli which can trigger worrying about major than minor goals.

There is very little evidence directly investigating the notion that worry is affected by the extent to which the individual perceives that he or she possesses appropriate post-event coping strategies. However, there is substantial evidence that coping strategies and control generally are effective in reducing stress (e.g., Neufeld & Paterson, 1989).

Borkovec et al. (1986) argued that most worry concerns potential frustrative non-reward of important goals. One of the implications of that position is that those individuals having the least confidence in their ability to control themselves and the environment in order to achieve their goals should be most vulnerable to worry. There are various personality dimensions which are of relevance. Tallis and Eysenck (submitted) emphasized the dimension of self-efficacy (Bandura, 1989), and trait anxiety is also highly relevant. High trait-anxious individuals characteristically lack confidence at an interpersonal level and are very sensitive to social evaluation. Since other people are of great importance in the achievement of most major goals, it follows that the characteristics of high trait-anxious individuals make them highly susceptible to worry. This issue is disscussed at greater length later in the chapter.

One of the factors determining whether or not a given threat will initiate worry is the nature of the ongoing cognitive activities when threat is presented. According to Borkovec et al. (1986), "as nonworry activity increases, the likelihood of worry intrusions declines" [p. 244]. In other words, there is competition between threat cues and other sources of information for limited processing resources. A more detailed conceptualization was proposed by Eysenck (1979 a, 1982, 1983) and elaborated by Eysenck and Calvo (in press). In essence, it is assumed that worry involves the resources of the working memory system (Baddeley, 1986), which is a system for the transient storage and active processing of information. Worry primarily uses the resources of the attention-like central executive component of working memory, plus some of the resources of the articulatory loop (a system involved in rote rehearsal). The fact that worrying is associated with an increase in verbal-linguistic activity (Borkovec & Inz, 1990) is clearly consistent with the notion that the articulatory loop is involved in worry.

Probably the most important factor determining the cessation of a worry episode is the salience of environmental demands. If worry utilizes the resources of the central executive of the working memory system, then pressing external demands which also involve the use of the central executive will tend to lead to a reduction in worry activity. Occasionally, worry will produce appropriate problem-solving. If the worry process leads to an acceptable way of handling the concern which is the central focus of worry, then that can cause a cessation of worry.

It has been argued that there are four factors (subjective probability; subjective imminence; perceived aversiveness; and perceived post-event coping strategies) which determine the extent to which a given concern will be worried about. However, it is very likely that there are complex interactions among these factors. For example, greater imminence may be associated with higher subjective probability. This could happen because subjective probability is affected by the availability of information about the aversive event, and more information is available as the event becomes more imminent. More research is needed in order to clarify the interrelationships of the four factors determining worry.

The theoretical framework proposed here has some definite implications for interventions designed to reduce an individual's level of worry. In essence, what is required is to reduce subjective probability, subjective imminence, or perceived aversiveness, or increase perceived post-event coping strategies. A worry episode will generally need to last for some time in order to provide the opportunity for such changes to occur. There is no evidence directly relevant to these aspects of the theoretical framework. However, it is interesting to note that Borkovec, Wilkinson, Folensbee, and Lerman (1983 b) found that worry could be greatly reduced by an intervention in which the subjects established a 30 minute daily worry period.

INDIVIDUAL DIFFERENCES

Individual differences in amount of worrying could occur for a variety of reasons within the theoretical framework proposed by Tallis and Eysenck (submitted). *Inter alia*, high worriers may detect more threats than low worriers, they may regard threatening events as more threatening because of greater subjective probability, perceived aversiveness, or perceived imminence, they may have fewer perceived post-event coping strategies, they may be less likely to adopt an appropriate problem-solving approach, and they may have elevated evidence requirements for accepting that they have discovered solutions to their worries.

There are relatively few studies in which high and low worriers were compared directly. However, as we saw earlier in the chapter, individual differences in amount of worrying correlate highly with trait anxiety. Trait anxiety has cognitive and somatic components, and worry can be regarded as the cognitive component of trait anxiety. With that in mind, one can assume that normals high and low in trait anxiety differ substantially in the amount they worry. So far as clinical groups are concerned, patients with generalized anxiety disorder suffer (by definition) from unrealistic or excessive worry.

Initiation of Worry

If one regards normals high in trait anxiety and patients with generalized anxiety disorder as groups of high worriers, then there is convincing evidence that high worriers selectively allocate processing resources to threatening stimuli. This evidence, which is discussed at length in Chapter 4, has revealed the existence of an attentional bias towards threat in both high-trait anxious normals and generalized anxiety disorder patients. Another reason why these groups of high worriers detect more threats than low worriers is because they are more likely to interpret ambiguous stimuli in a threatening fashion (see Chapter 5).

It is reasonably clear that high worriers are more stressed than low worriers by many threatening events. For example, consider the increase in state anxiety produced by failure feedback. It has been found fairly consistently that this increase is much greater in high trait-anxious individuals (Saltz, 1970). While the greater aversiveness of threat cues in high worriers could be due to higher subjective probability, higher perceived aversiveness of the event, fewer perceived post-event coping strategies, or imminence of the threatened event, most of the relevant research has focussed on subjective probability. There is good evidence that anxious and worried groups have elevated subjective probability judgements when deciding on the likelihood of negative events happening to them. This has been found to be the case in high trait-anxious subjects (Butler & Mathews, 1987; MacLeod, Williams, & Bekerian, 1991), in generalized anxiety disorder patients (Butler & Mathews, 1983), and in chronic worriers (MacLeod, 1990; MacLeod et al., 1991).

MacLeod et al. (1991) shed some light on why it is that high worriers show these elevated subjective probability judgements. They discovered that high worriers showed evidence of increased accessibility of reasons why a negative event would happen to them relative to the accessibility of reasons why it would not. When high worriers were instructed to think of reasons why negative events would not happen to them, they showed a substantial reduction in subjective probabilities. In contrast, this manipulation had no effect on low worriers. An implication is that worriers may often have elevated subjective probabilities because they do not spontaneously generate many reasons why the threatened event will not happen.

The probability that a threatening stimulus in the environment will initiate worry activity in an individual almost certainly depends in part on the prevailing level of state anxiety. In other words, worry activity may be an interactive function of stored worry structures, current emotional state, and environmental threat. It is likely that high trait-anxious normals have more, and more elaborate, worry structures than low trait-anxious normals. Since they are also more often in an anxious mood state and are more sensitive to environmental threat, it is not surprising that high trait-anxious individuals worry considerably more than low trait-anxious ones.

The main focus has been on the ways in which high trait-anxious normals differ in their worry activity from low trait-anxious normals. However, it is assumed that generalized anxiety disorder patients differ from normals in their worrying similarly to the ways in which normals high in trait anxiety differ from those low in trait anxiety.

Maintenance and Cessation of Worry

One reason why worry episodes may be longer for high worriers than low worriers is because they require more evidence before making a decision. The notion that high worriers have elevated evidence requirements was investigated by Tallis, Eysenck, and Mathews (1991). They used a task in which subjects had to decide whether a target letter was present or absent. They found that worriers took significantly longer than non-worriers to made decisions on target-absent trials. Metzger et al. (1983) found that worriers took longer than non-worriers to respond, especially when the task stimuli were ambiguous. Elevated evidence requirements in worriers may prevent them from implementing solutions to their worries that non-worriers would accept.

Eysenck (1984 b) proposed a structural theory based on the notion of 'worry clusters'. These clusters consist of tightly organized anxiety- or worry-related information stored in long-term memory. The repetitive and uncontrolled nature of worry stems in part from the highly structured nature of these worry clusters. According to Eysenck (1984 b), "there are major differences between individuals high and low in trait anxiety in the number and structure of worry clusters they possess" [p. 548]. Worry clusters are of particular importance in maintaining the worry process once it has been initiated.

Eysenck (1984 b) investigated the impact of trait anxiety and of induced anxious mood on the amount of worrying when subjects were cued with one of their current worries. Induced anxious mood was found to facilitate the initiation of the worry process, but its subsequent maintenance was far more a function of trait anxiety. Of particular importance, induced anxious mood had only a transient effect on worrying in low trait-anxious individuals. This was attributed to their relatively small number of worry clusters.

There are probably various other reasons why individuals high in trait anxiety tend to worry for longer periods of time than those low in trait anxiety. For example, as we saw in Chapter 5, anxiety tends to disrupt complex cognitive processing. This might prevent the high trait-anxious individual from thinking in an organized fashion about the worries in his or her life. Another possibility is that the existence of attentional and interpretive biases in high trait-anxious individuals reduces the probability of non-threatening stimuli capturing their attention and thus bringing a worry episode to a close. Similar considerations presumably apply in the case of patients suffering from generalized anxiety disorder.

SUMMARY AND CONCLUSIONS

The evidence suggests that worry is of central significance to trait anxiety in normals and to generalized anxiety disorder in clinical patients. It is thus extremely important for worry to be better understood in order to enhance our understanding of anxiety.

There are different views on the issue of the number of different worry domains which should be postulated. There is some evidence (Tallis et al., 1992) for the existence of six domains, consisting of relationships, work incompetence, lack of confidence, financial concerns, aimless future, and socio-political concerns. However, the fact that many of these domains correlate fairly highly with each other suggests that there is a smaller number of central worry domains. According to Eysenck and van Berkum, these central worry domains concern social-evaluative self-concept and physical threat to oneself and to others. Many of the apparent inconsistencies in the literature can be accommodated by assuming that worries possess a hierarchical structure, with different theorists focusing on different levels within that structure.

According to the theory of worry presented in this chapter, worry serves three major functions: an alarm function, a prompt function, and a preparation function. Worry is determined by the threat value of a given possible negative event, with threat value itself being determined by subjective probability of the event occurring, subjective imminence of the event, perceived aversiveness of the event, and perceived post-event coping strategies. There are several reasons why high trait-anxious normals worry more than low trait-anxious normals. The threat value of environmental stimuli will tend to be greater for them because of attentional and interpretive biases, they may have more structured worry clusters, they may perceive themselves as possessing poorer post-event coping strategies, and their elevated evidence requirements may lead them to reject reasonable solutions to their current concerns. The same or similar factors probably account for the much greater proportion of the time that generalized anxiety disorder patients spend worrying than do normals.

CHAPTER SEVEN

Processing and Performance

INTRODUCTION

This chapter deals with the effects of anxiety on general aspects of cognitive functioning. It is widely accepted that high trait-anxious individuals tend to perform cognitive and motor tasks at an inferior level to low trait-anxious individuals. This inferior performance is especially likely to occur when the task is difficult or complex and when it is performed under stressful conditions. Our primary focus will be on attempts to account for the effects of anxiety on performance, and more specifically to identify which components of the information processing system are most affected by anxiety. The approach taken in this chapter can be contrasted with the one taken in Chapter 4, where the emphasis was on the effects of *threatening* stimulation on the cognitive functioning of individuals varying in their level of anxiety.

Not surprisingly, performance on almost any task is affected adversely at extreme levels of stress or state anxiety. For example, over 200 of the muzzle-loading rifles used in one of the battles during the American Civil War were loaded at least five times without being fired at all (Walker & Burkhardt, 1965). Under laboratory conditions, Patrick (1934 a, b) made use of an apparently simple task, in which subjects had to discover which of four doors was locked. Since the same door was never unlocked on two successive trials, the optimal strategy was to try each of the other three doors in turn. When the conditions were non-stressful, approximately 60% of the solutions were optimal. However, this figure dropped to only 20% when the subjects had cold water streams directed at them, or had their ears blasted by a car horn, or were given continuous electric shocks until they found the right door.

The fact that very high levels of state anxiety cause a general impairment in virtually all aspects of information processing means that the findings are of only modest theoretical relevance. It is far more informative (and probably more realistic) to consider less stressful conditions, where it is possible to distinguish between those tasks which are and are not impaired by anxiety. One is then able to identify those aspects of information processing which are especially vulnerable to heightened levels of anxiety.

It would be possible to proceed by considering all of the specific performance effects associated with high anxiety. However, such an approach would be relatively incoherent and theoretically uninteresting. As a consequence, the approach actually adopted involves considering cognitive effects of anxiety from the perspective of some of the theoretical formulations which have been put forward in this area.

SARASON'S (1984, 1988) COGNITIVE INTERFERENCE THEORY

Several theorists who have attempted to account for the adverse effects of anxiety on performance have argued that worry and other cognitive forms of anxiety play a major role. These theorists include Mandler and Sarason (1952), Deffenbacher (1980), and Morris, Davis, and Hutchings (1981). A representative theory of this type was proposed by Sarason (e.g., 1984, 1988). According to Sarason (1988), "Proneness to self-preoccupation and, most specifically, to worry over evaluation is a powerful component of what is referred to as test anxiety" [p.5]. Since self-preoccupation and worry over evaluation impair performance, it is predicted that high test-anxious individuals are most likely to perform below the level of low test-anxious individuals when evaluative instructions are given, and when the task itself is relatively complex. Since worry allegedly interferes with attention to the current task, it follows that the adverse effects of worry on task performance should be greatest on those tasks requiring the most attention (i.e., relatively difficult tasks). These predictions have generally been supported (cf., Sarason, 1988).

The basic problem with Sarason's theoretical approach is that it exaggerates the importance of self-preoccupation and worry. For example, high-anxious individuals should perform a task less well than low-anxious individuals if they engage in significantly more self-preoccupation and worry. In fact, there are several studies in which that did not happen. Calvo and Ramos (1989) and Calvo, Alamo, and Ramos (1990) discovered that their high-anxious subjects had much higher worry scores than their low-anxious subjects on difficult tasks, but the two groups did not differ in their performance. Blankstein, Toner, and Flett (1989) and Blankstein, Flett, Boase, and Toner (1990) discovered that high test-anxious subjects had more negative thoughts about themselves than did low test-anxious subjects, but the two groups did not differ in their anagram performance.

Another problem with Sarason's (1984, 1988) theoretical approach is its over-simplified account of interactions between anxiety and task difficulty. In particular, task difficulty appears to be equated with the amount of attentional resources required by a task. This has the undesirable consequence that transformational and storage processes are ignored.

HUMPHREYS AND REVELLE'S (1984) INFORMATION PROCESSING THEORY

Humphreys and Revelle (1984) proposed a complex theory relating personality, motivation, and performance. They argued that in order to understand the effects of any personality dimension on cognitive performance it is necessary to consider the following factors: situational moderators; personality states; motivational direction and intensity; information processing resources; and the cognitive tasks themselves. The overall picture so far as trait anxiety is concerned is shown in Fig. 7.1.

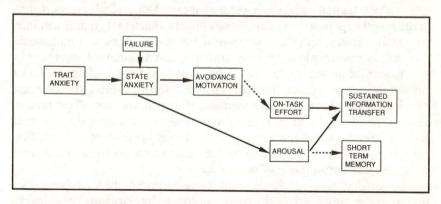

FIG. 7.1. Factors determining the effects of anxiety on performance. Based on Humphreys and Revelle (1984).

It can be seen that the relevant personality state associated with trait anxiety is state anxiety. State anxiety is determined interactively by trait anxiety and by various situational moderators such as success or failure experiences and ego threat.

State anxiety increases the level of avoidance motivation, largely because of worry and other self-concerned thoughts (it is "possible to equate the worry or cognitive component of anxiety with avoidance motivation", Humphreys & Revelle, 1984, p. 176). On-task effort and arousal both increase sustained information transfer. Information-transfer tasks are those in which "the subject is required to process a stimulus, associate an arbitrary response ... to the stimulus, and execute the response. Furthermore, there is no appreciable retention of information required nor is there an appreciable amount of distraction" [p. 161].

Another assumption built into the theoretical account of trait anxiety and cognitive performance provided by Humphreys and Revelle (1984) is the notion that arousal reduces short-term memory. Short-term memory tasks "require subjects to either maintain information in an available state through rehearsal or other processes or retrieve information that has not been attended to for a short time" [p. 164]. All cognitive tasks involve sustained information transfer, but they differ in terms of the degree of involvement of short-term memory. Accordingly, the effects of trait anxiety vary from task to task primarily because those tasks with a substantial short-term memory component are relatively much more adversely affected than tasks with minimal involvement of short-term memory.

The theoretical approach proposed by Humphreys and Revelle (1984) represents an interesting attempt to consider the effects of anxiety on performance in information processing terms (i.e., sustained information transfer and short-term memory). Of particular importance is the novel explanation of curvilinear effects of arousal on performance which the theory provides. As arousal increases, there is a monotonic increase in sustained information transfer, and a monotonic decrease in short-term memory. Arousal will have a curvilinear effect on tasks involving both sustained information transfer and short-term memory, provided that the respective monotonic functions are of particular shapes. In general terms, it is more plausible to assume that arousal has different monotonic effects on two components of information processing than it is to assume that arousal has a curvilinear effect on a single information processing component.

The theory of Humphreys and Revelle (1984) has at least two apparent advantages over the theory proposed by Sarason (1984, 1988). First, the notion that anxiety affects arousal means that the effects of anxiety on performance do not depend exclusively on cognitive processes (e.g., worry). Second, tasks can be categorized in terms of the two factors of short-term memory and sustained information transfer instead of simply their dependence on attentional resources.

In spite of the above-mentioned advantages, the theory suffers from a number of significant limitations. There is a definite problem so far as testability is concerned. Since anxiety allegedly increases sustained information transfer via heightened arousal, but decreases sustained information transfer via increased avoidance motivation, it is obviously very difficult to predict *a priori* whether anxiety will facilitate or impair performance on tasks involving sustained information transfer.

Some of the theoretical constructs incorporated into the model are either imprecisely defined, or else defined in ways which conflict with contemporary usage. The two clearest examples are 'arousal' and 'short-term memory'. 'Arousal' is regarded as a general, uni-dimensional construct, and the level of arousal is allegedly unaffected by effort. In view of the evidence that there are several qualitatively different activation states (e.g., Hockey, 1986), most theorists have rejected the notion of a single arousal continuum. The view that effort expenditure does not affect arousal in the sense used by Humphreys and Revelle (1984) is also inconsistent with most of the available evidence (e.g., Eysenck, 1982).

The problem with the short-term memory construct is that it is not related to contemporary theorizing. There is a consensus that the notion of a unitary short-term storage system is inadequate (e.g., Crowder, 1982), and that it should be replaced by more complex conceptualizations. As is discussed in some detail below, Baddeley and Hitch (1974) and Baddeley (1986) have argued that the unitary short-term memory store should be replaced by a much more complex, three-component, working memory system. A theoretical change of this kind seems necessitated by the evidence.

It seems likely that the role of arousal is exaggerated within the theory. For example, Holroyd, Westbrook, Wolf, and Badhorn (1978) did not find any differences in the psychophysiological responses of high- and low-anxiety subjects to the stress of a testing situation. In a review of the literature on psychophysiological correlates of trait anxiety and neuroticism, Fahrenberg (1987) concluded that there did not appear to be any such correlates.

The most important objection to the theory, however, is that it fails to include a control system which monitors and adjusts the functioning of the information processing system. Suppose, for the sake of argument, that anxiety actually has the theoretically specified effects on sustained information transfer and short-term memory during initial performance of a complex task. When the anxious person monitors his or her performance, and discovers that it is relatively inadequate, it is probable that attempts will be made to compensate for this by changes in the processing resources applied to the task. It may be impossible to provide a complete account of the effects of anxiety on task performance without specifying some such monitoring system, together with compensatory processes to be used when the monitoring system signals that performance is being impaired by anxiety. In other words, anxiety does not generally produce task-avoidance motivation, as Humphreys and Revelle (1984) argued, but rather motivation to avoid aversive consequences by compensatory effort. The theoretical issues involved are discussed in more detail later in the next section of the chapter.

PROCESSING EFFICIENCY THEORY

Despite its limitations, the theoretical approach adopted by Humphreys and Revelle (1984) has much to recommend it. In particular, if one is to understand the effects of anxiety on performance in information processing terms, it is essential to consider the pattern of anxiety-induced performance changes across a wide range of different cognitive tasks.

A generalization which is applicable to most studies which have investigated the effects of anxiety on two or more tasks is that anxiety has a greater detrimental effect on difficult or complex tasks than it does on simple ones. For example, Mayer (1977) considered the effects of trait anxiety on various simple problems such as visual search and easy mathematical operations, as well as on much more complex cognitive tasks such as water-jar problems and anagrams. There was no effect of trait anxiety on performance of the simple problems, but high anxiety reduced the percentage of complex cognitive tasks solved correctly from approximately 80% to just over 40%.

Some theorists have attempted to account for the interaction between anxiety and task difficulty by means of a single explanatory principle. For example, J.T. Spence and K.W. Spence (1966) argued that anxiety acts as a drive, making it more likely that the strongest response will be produced. This can be advantageous with very simple tasks, where the strongest response will often be the correct one, but will be disadvantageous with more complex tasks, in which the strongest response will initially be incorrect.

The interaction between anxiety and task difficulty can also be accounted for by the theory proposed by Humphreys and Revelle (1984). They argued that high levels of state anxiety reduce short-term memory. Since difficult tasks generally make more demands on short-term memory than easy tasks, it follows that anxiety will typically have a greater adverse effect on more complex tasks.

A rather different theoretical position was advocated by Eysenck (1979 a, 1982, 1983), and subsequently developed and expanded by Eysenck and Calvo (in press) into the processing efficiency theory. According to the theory, it is state rather than trait anxiety which determines the level of performance. State anxiety is basically determined by trait anxiety and by situational stress. While there is a clear conceptual distinction between trait and state anxiety, it can be less easy to distinguish between their effects at an empirical level. The reason for this is that trait and state anxiety generally correlate highly with each other.

As with Sarason's (1984, 1988) theory, it is assumed that worry and self-concern have an important influence on performance. Worry about task performance pre-empts some of the resources of the working memory system. It is assumed that a working memory system is one which permits concurrent transient storage of information and ongoing processing of task information. Baddeley (1986) has described the possible components of a working memory system. He distinguished three components, consisting of a modality-free central executive, an articulatory loop used for rote rehearsal, and a visuo-spatial sketch pad. Worry primarily uses the resources of the central executive component of the working memory system, which resembles attention. In addition, worry probably makes use of the resources of the articulatory loop. As a consequence, the effects of anxiety on performance are determined in part by the demands which the task makes on the central executive and on the articulatory loop. Difficult tasks often impose greater demands on these components than do easy tasks, and so we have here a potential explanation for the typical interaction between anxiety and task difficulty.

Evidence which may be relevant to the notion that worry primarily uses the resources of the central executive has been obtained by Teasdale, Proctor, and Baddeley (1990). They studied some of the factors determining the incidence of stimulus-independent thoughts, i.e., worry and other thoughts essentially unrelated to the immediate sensory input. In essence, while there was some indication that the articulatory loop and the visuo-spatial sketch pad might be involved in the production of stimulus-independent thoughts, there was much stronger evidence of the involvement of the central executive. For example, it had previously been established that the ability to generate random letters or numbers depends on the involvement of the central executive (Baddeley, 1986). It would thus be expected that worry and other stimulus-independent thoughts would be less likely to occur at times when subjects were successfully generating random sequences of digits than when the sequences were non-random. That is precisely what Teasdale et al. (1990) reported. They also found that stimulus-independent thoughts were considerably less frequent when the subjects were consciously aware of the digits they were generating. This finding is relevant because it seems reasonable to assume that conscious awareness is one of the characteristic features of the central executive.

Worry serves a second, motivational function. The presence of worry about task performance typically leads to the allocation of extra processing resources to the task, in an attempt to improve performance and thus reduce or eliminate worry. There is a control or executive system involved here. This control system reacts to information indicating that the level of task performance is below that desired by the subject by applying extra effort or processing resources to the task. Hockey (1986) has provided some interesting ideas as to how a control system of this sort might operate.

There are various reasons why high-anxious individuals are more likely than low-anxious individuals to apply additional processing resources or effort to an ongoing task. The fact that anxious individuals tend to worry more than non-anxious individuals means that they are more concerned to improve performance in order to reduce threat and worry. Another reason is that the 'natural' level of performance of anxious individuals is lower than that of non-anxious individuals, because of the resources which they devote to worry, self-concern, and so on. This increases the likelihood of detecting a mismatch between expected and actual performance, which in turn activates additional processing resources. There are other reasons, such as the possibility that anxious individuals may be more likely than non-anxious individuals to have an unrealistically high level of aspiration so far as performance is concerned.

According to the processing efficiency theory, there is an important theoretical distinction between performance effectiveness and processing efficiency. Performance effectiveness refers to the quality of task performance, and processing efficiency refers to the relationship between the effectiveness of performance and the effort or processing resources invested in performance. In approximate terms, processing efficiency can be defined as performance effectiveness divided by effort. This distinction has not been incorporated into other theories of anxiety and performance, presumably because it is assumed that anxiety has comparable effects on internal efficiency and external performance, and that processing efficiency can be inferred directly from performance effectiveness. The assumptions of processing efficiency theory are very different. According to processing efficiency theory, it is entirely possible for anxiety to have different effects on performance effectiveness and processing efficiency. More specifically, since anxious individuals generally make more use of the control system and so exert more effort, it follows that anxiety will typically impair processing efficiency more than performance effectiveness.

It should be emphasized that processing efficiency theory is still at a relatively early stage of development. As a consequence, much more is known about some aspects of the theory than about others. Those components of the theory which receive little discussion in this chapter are those about which our ignorance is greatest.

In sum, there is some overlap between processing efficiency theory and other theories in that there is an emphasis on the role played by worry and other cognitions in affecting performance. However, processing efficiency theory differs from other theories in at least two important ways. First, it is assumed that worry, self-concern, and so on, all affect the working memory system by pre-empting some of its resources. As a consequence, the general expectation is that adverse effects of anxiety on task performance will increase in line with increasing task demands for the resources of working memory, especially those of the central executive. Second, it is assumed that any adverse effects of anxiety will generally be greater on processing efficiency than on performance effectiveness. The evidence relating to these two major predictions is considered below.

Working Memory

Some of the earliest work to implicate the working memory system in mediating the effects of anxiety on performance was carried out on the digit span task. This task primarily involves the articulatory loop of the working memory system, but also has some involvement of the central executive. Eysenck (1982) discussed the findings from 14 studies in which digit span was assessed in groups high and low in trait anxiety under non-stressed conditions. There were non-significant effects of trait anxiety on digit span performance in nine studies. In the five remaining studies, trait anxiety was negatively related to digit span in three studies, but positively related in the other two. In contrast, there were seven experiments in which stress significantly reduced digit span performance, and four more in which high state anxiety was associated with significantly lowered digit span (see Eysenck, 1979 a, for details). In more recent research, Darke (1988 a) found that high test anxiety impaired digit span performance under ego-threat conditions, but Calvo, Ramos, and Estevez (submitted) found that test anxiety had no effect on letter span under either evaluative or non-evaluative conditions. In spite of some inconsistencies, it is primarily under conditions of high state anxiety or stress that there are adverse effects of anxiety on digit span performance. This is as predicted by the processing efficiency theory.

Digit span studies can provide no more than partially relevant evidence about the viability of the processing efficiency hypothesis, because the digit span task does not fully engage the resources of the central executive. A more appropriate task is the reading span task used by Darke (1988 a). He used a version of the task in which up to six sentences were presented for comprehension, and there was also a test of recall for the last word in each sentence. This task makes considerable use of working memory, because the storage demands of the last words in each sentence are combined with the demands on the central executive of the comprehension task. It would thus be predicted that any adverse effects of anxiety would be greater on the reading span task than on the digit span task. This was exactly what Darke (1988 a) found. The performance of low test-anxious subjects was 68% higher than high test-anxious subjects on the reading span task, but only approximately 20% higher on digit span.

Calvo et al. (submitted) extended the findings of Darke (1988 a), who only studied performance under ego-threatening conditions. They investigated letter span and reading span under both evaluative and non-evaluative testing conditions. Test anxiety had no effect on letter span, but there was a very significant interaction between test anxiety and testing conditions on reading span. There was no effect of test anxiety on reading span under non-evaluative testing conditions, but the low test-anxious subjects performed 64% better than the high test-anxious subjects under evaluative testing conditions. These findings suggest that it is a transitory working memory deficit associated with high state anxiety which causes impaired reading span in high test-anxious individuals.

Eysenck (1985) used a letter transformation task with subjects high and low in trait anxiety. In this task, subjects must work through the alphabet a specified distance with between one and four initial letters. For example, the problem, 'B + 4 = ?', requires subjects to decide which letter is four on from 'B' (the answer is 'F'), and the answer to 'JULI + 4 = ?' is 'NYPM'. The subjects were required to transform all of the letters in the problem before providing an answer. The letter transformation task is very suitable for testing the prediction from the processing efficiency theory, because the demands on working memory escalate dramatically as the number of letters increases (due to greater storage and organizational demands).

Eysenck (1985) discovered that there was a highly significant interaction between trait anxiety and the number of letters in the

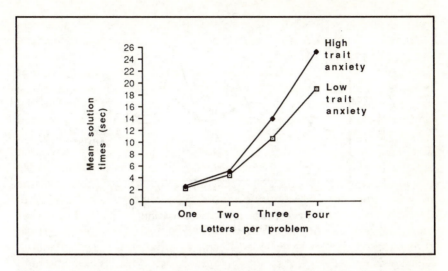

FIG. 7.2. Solution times on the letter transformation task as a function of trait anxiety and number of letters in the problem. Data from Eysenck (1985).

problem in determining solution time (see Fig. 7.2). High trait anxiety did not affect solution speed with one- and two-letter problems, but had a marked slowing effect with three- and four-letter problems. While these findings are precisely in line with processing efficiency theory, they are limited in that it is not clear which processing component or components of the more complex problems were adversely affected by anxiety. At least three processing components can be identified for each letter:

1. access to the alphabet in long-term memory;
2. performance of the transformation; and
3. rehearsal and storage of the accumulating answer.

Thus, a four-letter problem has 12 processing components, and anxiety might affect any (or all) of them.

In order to clarify matters, Eysenck (1985) carried out a further experiment with four-letter problems in which it was possible to analyse performance at the level of individual processing components. According to processing efficiency theory, anxiety mainly affects complex processing involving the central executive. The greatest demands on the central executive occur during rehearsal and storage of the accumulating answer, especially towards the end of each problem. As expected, the adverse effects of anxiety were greatest towards the end of the problem (see Fig. 7.3). It was only the rehearsal and storage

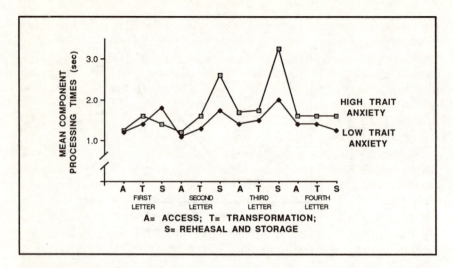

FIG. 7.3. Solution times on the components of the letter transformation task with four letters. Data from Eysenck (1985).

phases which were affected by anxiety, indicating that it was specifically the increased rehearsal and storage demands which led to the detrimental effects of anxiety on four-letter problems.

A rather different way to test processing efficiency theory is to investigate the effects of anxiety on tasks which do not involve the working memory system. Since, according to the theory, adverse effects of anxiety on performance occur because worry and other cognitions use some of the resources of working memory, it follows that anxiety should not have a detrimental effect on any task which does not depend on working memory. This prediction was tested by Darke (1988 b). He discovered that comprehension speed on a task which involved drawing necessary inferences was unaffected by test anxiety, and he claimed that this finding occurred because the task involves only automatic processes. He also found that high test-anxious subjects took much longer than low test-anxious subjects on a task which involved drawing unnecessary inferences, because the task required working memory. Darke (1988 b) summarized his findings as follows: "High anxiety subjects are disadvantaged *vis-à-vis* low anxiety subjects in their ability to infer implicit facts from explicit text only when the processing involved in such inferential reasoning relies on the working memory" [p. 504]. In fact, however, it is probable that even drawing necessary inferences involves some use of working memory resources.

More evidence that anxiety has no effect on tasks making minimal use of the working memory system was obtained by Eysenck (1989 b).

He compared subjects high and low in trait anxiety on the one-letter version of the letter transformation task; the over-learned skill of working a short distance through the alphabet is required for this specific task. There was no effect of anxiety on performance. There was also no effect of anxiety on performance of a concurrent probe task which was used to measure spare processing capacity, suggesting that the two groups allocated the same small amount of processing resources to the letter transformation task.

Most of the available research supports the notion that the working memory system is involved in determining the effects of anxiety on performance. However, findings apparently less favourable to the theory were reported by Leon and Revelle (1985). They investigated the effects of trait and state anxiety on analogical reasoning problems varying in their demands on working memory. The problems were given under either relaxed or stressed conditions, with stress consisting of ego threat and time pressure. There were no significant effects of trait anxiety on performance, and state anxiety did not interact as expected with task complexity in terms of either the number of task cues or demands on working memory. This led Leon and Revelle (1985) to conclude:

Neither cue utilization theory nor working memory capacity theory received any support whatsoever in our study [p. 1313].

The findings of Leon and Revelle (1985) are clearly anomalous, in view of the numerous studies which have obtained highly significant interactions between anxiety and task complexity. An obvious problem with their study is that state anxiety affected both speed and accuracy of performance. Under stressed conditions, more anxious subjects generally responded faster but less accurately than less anxious subjects, so that it is virtually impossible to decide whether or not the overall effectiveness of performance was affected by anxiety. Under relaxed conditions, subjects high in state anxiety tended to be slower and less accurate than those low in state anxiety, and therefore performed less effectively. However, the separate analyses of the speed and accuracy data provide an underestimate of the reduced efficiency associated with high state anxiety.

Why does high anxiety reduce the available capacity of working memory? According to processing efficiency theory, the major reason is that being anxious tends to lead to worry and to other task-irrelevant thoughts. The impact of anxiety on other aspects of the information processing system may also be relevant (see especially Chapter 4). For example, Beck and Emery (1985) argued as follows:

Because the [anxious] patient 'uses up' a large part of his cognitive capacity by scanning for threatening stimuli, the amount available for attending to other demands is severely restricted [p. 31].

In other words, anxious individuals may allocate more processing resources than non-anxious individuals to monitoring and attending to the environment, and this would impair processing efficiency on a task. It is entirely possible that the selective attentional bias shown by anxious individuals (see Chapter 4) reduces the working memory capacity available to them during task performance.

Processing Efficiency

One of the central predictions of processing efficiency theory is that anxiety typically impairs processing efficiency more than performance effectiveness. There are some difficulties with testing this prediction. While it is usually reasonably straightforward to assess performance effectiveness, the same is not true of processing efficiency. It is difficult to measure effort (which is relevant to processing efficiency), and the notion that efficiency is simply performance effectiveness divided by effort cannot be taken literally. One approach is to concentrate on those tasks where there are no effects of anxiety on performance effectiveness. In such situations, high-anxious subjects should generally exert more effort and thus have lower processing efficiency than low-anxious subjects.

There are several different methods which have been used to assess processing efficiency (see Eysenck & Calvo, in press, for a more detailed discussion). These methods include at least the following:

- psychophysiological measures;
- assessment of subjective effort;
- motivational manipulations;
- use of a secondary task;
- probe-latency assessment of spare processing capacity;
- the loading paradigm;
- assessment of processing time.

Psychophysiological measures were used in research by Weinberg and Hunt (1976) on a throwing task. They discovered that there was no effect of trait anxiety on performance effectiveness prior to the introduction of feedback. However, they also assessed efficiency by means of electromyography, and the resultant measures of muscle activity during the throwing task revealed clear evidence that high anxiety had impaired efficiency:

> High-anxious individuals anticipated significantly longer with the agonists and shorter with the antagonists than did the low-anxious group. Therefore, they were preparing for the throw in all of the muscles while low-anxious subjects were preparing mostly with the antagonist muscles. This implies that high-anxious subjects were using more energy than necessary, and expending it over a greater period of time, than were low-anxious subjects [p. 223].

Very similar findings with the same task were obtained by Weinberg (1978), with high trait anxiety having no effect on throwing performance but reducing the efficiency of muscle activity. The differences in muscle activity were so great that it was possible solely on the basis of electromyographic data to classify correctly 83% of the subjects as being high or low in anxiety.

The studies by Weinberg and Hunt (1976) and Weinberg (1978) provide good support for the notion that anxiety can impair efficiency without affecting performance effectiveness. The same conclusion follows from an important study by Dornic (1977), in which he assessed subjective effort. Different versions of a closed-system thinking task varying in the level of complexity were used. There were two groups of subjects, stable extraverts and neurotic introverts. Extensive evidence (see H.J. Eysenck and M.W. Eysenck, 1985) indicates that stable extraverts are low in trait anxiety, whereas neurotic introverts are high in trait anxiety. The two groups did not differ significantly in performance effectiveness on any of the versions of the thinking task. However, the position was quite different with respect to processing efficiency. Self-ratings of perceived effort indicated that the high-anxiety subjects (i.e., the neurotic introverts) expended much more effort than the low-anxiety subjects (i.e., the stable extraverts), especially when the thinking task was especially demanding. Since processing efficiency is defined by the relationship between performance effectiveness and expended effort, the implication is that the high-anxiety subjects had lower processing efficiency than the low-anxiety subjects.

Dornic (1980) subsequently conducted further experiments in which performance effectiveness and expended effort were both assessed. However, instead of a thinking task, subjects were required to perform either a visual search or a counting backwards task. As before, high-anxiety subjects exhibited comparable levels of performance to the low-anxiety subjects, but their greater level of perceived effort indicated that their processing efficiency was impaired.

The evidence of Dornic (1977, 1980) is consistent with the notion that individuals high in trait anxiety attempt to compensate for the adverse effects of anxiety by means of increased effort or investment of resources. They should, therefore, tend to be closer to maximum resource allocation than individuals low in trait anxiety. As a consequence, those high in trait anxiety should benefit less than those low in trait anxiety from a motivational manipulation designed to increase effort.

A motivational manipulation that was used in a number of studies involved using ego-involving or challenging instructions indicating, for example, that the task was a good measure of intelligence. Such instructions were found to improve the performance of low-anxious subjects, but to impair that of high-anxious subjects (e.g., Calvo & Alamo, 1987; Nicholson, 1958; Sarason, 1956, 1957, 1972). The main limitation of such studies is that the motivational manipulation may very well have had effects on worry as well as on effort.

Providing incentives is a way of increasing motivation without necessarily producing worry. The effects of incentives on the performance of high- and low-anxious groups were considered by Calvo (1985) and by Eysenck (1985). Calvo (1985) administered a test of non-verbal inductive reasoning containing items varying in their difficulty level, and monetary incentive for good performance was introduced in order to manipulate effort. There was a significant interaction between trait anxiety and incentive conditions: Incentive enhanced performance for those subjects low in trait anxiety but tended to impair performance for those subjects high in trait anxiety. This is consistent with the notion that those high in trait anxiety typically employ more effort than those low in trait anxiety. A similar pattern of findings was obtained by Eysenck (1985). He used the letter transformation task described earlier, and introduced monetary incentive. This monetary incentive had no effect on state anxiety. Only the subjects low in trait anxiety benefited from the introduction of incentive.

There are other ways in which effort expenditure and processing efficiency can be assessed. For example, according to Kahneman (1973), spare processing capacity is inversely related to the effort or processing resources invested in a primary task. It is possible to measure this spare processing capacity by considering the performance level on a secondary task which is performed concurrently with the primary task.

The relevant evidence was reviewed by Eysenck (1982). There were a total of 16 experiments in which anxiety (whether assessed by questionnaire or by the presentation of a stressor) had no effect on the performance of the primary task. In 11 of those experiments, anxiety nevertheless had a significantly adverse effect on the performance of the secondary task; the effects of anxiety were non-significant in the remaining studies. One interpretation of these findings is that the anxious subjects invested more effort and processing resources than non-anxious subjects in the performance of the primary task, and thus had less spare processing capacity for processing the secondary task. However, the findings can also be interpreted in line with the notion that high levels of anxiety produce a narrowing of attention (Easterbrook, 1959). There is a further possibility. The secondary task used in many of the studies involved incidental recall of words presented in the periphery of vision, and so the subjects were not aware that their memory for these stimuli was going to be tested. As a consequence, the anxious subjects may have performed poorly on this task because they chose not to attend to the secondary task stimuli rather than because they did not have sufficient resources to process them.

There is a rather different way of assessing spare processing capacity which is methodologically superior to the approach just described. This alternative method is sometimes known as the probe technique, because the secondary task involves making a simple motor response to an occasional probe stimulus. The instructions emphasize that the central task must be performed as well as possible, with any capacity that is left over being used to respond to the probe. The use of such instructions and the on-line assessment of spare processing capacity mean that a reasonably direct measure of spare processing capacity can be obtained.

Hamilton (1978) used the probe technique in conjunction with a digit span task. The probe was interpolated between the presentation of the digit string and its subsequent recall. The analysis of the probe data was confined to those trials on which the high- and low-anxious subjects recalled all of the digits correctly, so that performance effectiveness on the central task was equated. In the most difficult condition of the digit span task (seven digits presented), the high-anxious subjects had significantly slower probe response latencies than low-anxious subjects. In other words, performing the digit span task left high-anxious subjects with less spare processing capacity than low-anxious subjects.

Calvo and Ramos (1989) employed the probe technique on a number of different motor tasks which had varying attentional demands and muscular requirements. High- and low-anxious subjects did not differ in their probe reaction times on any of the tasks, which is inconsistent with the prediction of the processing efficiency theory. However, probe latencies were not affected by the attentional demands or muscular requirments of the tasks either, suggesting that probe latency was not a sensitive measure of spare processing capacity.

Eysenck (1989 b) used the probe technique with one- and two-letter problems of the letter transformation task. Trait anxiety did not affect performance effectiveness on these problems. On the secondary task, the high trait-anxious subjects had significantly longer probe response latencies than the low trait-anxious subjects on two-letter problems. This led Eysenck (1989 b) to draw the following conclusion:

> While the high- and low-anxious groups exhibited equal performance effectiveness on two-letter problems, the high-anxious group was actually performing with lower processing efficiency [p. 532].

A further way of assessing processing efficiency is to make use of a loading design. In essence, a task is selected on which groups high and low in trait anxiety exhibit comparable levels of performance when that task is performed on its own. If this comparability of performance effectiveness camouflages reduced processing efficiency by the high-anxiety group, then this may become manifest if the task has to be performed concurrently with a second task or load. The second task has to be performed to a given standard so that evidence of impaired efficiency will be present in performance of the primary task.

This strategy was followed by Eliatamby (1984). In the key conditions subjects solved anagrams either as the sole task or in conjunction with paced counting backwards by threes from a three-digit number. Groups high and low in trait anxiety did not differ in their performance of the anagram task when it was the only task, but the high-anxiety group was markedly inferior to the low-anxiety group when the concurrent task of counting backwards was introduced.

The loading paradigm was also used by Calvo and Ramos (1989) in a study on motor learning. Each of four motor tasks was performed on a practice trial followed by a transfer trial. Trait anxiety had no effect on transfer-trial performance when there was no load on the practice trial. However, the high trait-anxious subjects performed significantly less well than the low trait-anxious subjects on the transfer trial when there was a load on the practice trial. An implication is that the high trait-anxious subjects were using more of their available processing capacity than the low trait-anxious subjects to perform the motor tasks in the absence of an additional load.

A final way of assessing processing efficiency was used by Calvo and Carreiras (in press). Various texts were read, and were followed by tests of comprehension. Performance effectiveness as measured by comprehension scores did not differ between high and low test-anxious subjects. However, the high test-anxious subjects had slower reading times than low test-anxious subjects, especially for the more complex texts. This lengthened processing time was taken to reflect processing inefficiency on the part of the high test-anxious subjects.

Related research was reported by Calvo et al. (submitted). They replicated the findings that comprehension performance was unaffected by test anxiety, but that there was an adverse effect of test anxiety on processing efficiency when account was taken of reading time. In order to decide whether this effect on efficiency was due to reduced working memory capacity, Calvo et al. (submitted) re-analysed the efficiency data with reading span under evaluative conditions (a measure of working memory capacity) as the covariate. Since this reduced somewhat the effects of test anxiety on efficiency, it appeared to be the case that reduced working memory capacity was partially responsible for the poor processing efficiency of the high test-anxious subjects.

Finally, Calvo et al. (submitted) investigated the effects of word knowledge on comprehension efficiency. They discovered that using word-knowledge scores based on words used in the texts as a covariate reduced the effects of test anxiety on comprehension efficiency. More strikingly, there was no effect of test anxiety on efficiency when general vocabulary scores were used as a covariate. In other words, a knowledge deficit was responsible for most of the effects of test anxiety on processing efficiency.

Summary and Conclusions

In sum, several different techniques have been used to investigate the hypotheses that there are differential effects of anxiety on performance effectiveness and on processing efficiency. and that anxiety typically impairs processing efficiency more than performance effectiveness. The techniques which have been used include psychophysiological measures, assessment of subjective effort, secondary tasks, the probe technique, incentive and other motivational manipulations, loading paradigms, and assessment of processing time. All of these different lines of research indicate that performance effectiveness often provides an inadequate measure of internal processing activities. More specifically, high levels of anxiety frequently have a greater adverse effect on processing efficiency than on performance effectiveness. What is particularly impressive is the way in which converging evidence has been obtained from very different paradigms and techniques.

There is no doubt that the processing efficiency theory as presently formulated is over-simplified in a number of ways. In particular, it is assumed within the theory that the response of the control system to inadequate performance leads to increased effort and the allocation of additional processing resources. While this quantitative shift in the use of processing resources may well be a common reaction to inadequate performance, it is improbable that it is the only reaction. In many cases, there will be a qualitative shift from the current (and relatively unsuccessful) processing strategy to a different strategy. As a consequence, it will be necessary to carry out considerably more fine-grained analyses in order to ascertain more precisely why the effects of anxiety on performance effectiveness and processing efficiency are as they are.

Some evidence that compensatory activities can be relatively specific in nature was obtained by Calvo and Ramos (submitted). They discovered that anxious subjects tended to have longer reading times than non-anxious subjects when examining texts which needed to be read and comprehended. When reading time was controlled, anxious subjects showed more regressions in the text than non-anxious subjects. When reading time and regressions were controlled, the anxious subjects had more articulatory rehearsal than the non-anxious subjects.

Another possible over-simplification in the theory is the notion that worry primarily affects the central executive component of the working memory system. While there is considerable evidence that worry does pre-empt some of the resources of the central executive, it remains to be established whether or not worry also uses the resources of the other components of working memory. It has been found (Borkovec & Inz, 1990) that worry induction produces a shift towards predominance of thought over imagery, which suggests that worry is more likely to affect the workings of the articulatory loop than of the visuo-spatial sketch pad. In any case, it would clearly be useful to have additional information concerning the processing mechanisms involved in worry.

According to processing efficiency theory, reduced processing efficiency is due to high state anxiety rather than trait anxiety *per se*. While this prediction is supported by much of the evidence discussed in this chapter, the possibility remains that the processing inefficiency of high trait-anxious individuals may also be due in part to long-term, basic deficits. For example, Calvo et al. (submitted) discovered that the processing inefficiency (i.e., lengthened reading time) displayed by high test-anxious subjects performing a reading task was largely attributable to their knowledge deficit in terms of vocabulary. Culler and Holahan (1980) discovered that high-anxious students had poorer study habits than low-anxious students, which suggests the existence of another long-term deficit.

ANXIETY AND DEPRESSION

The evidence discussed in this chapter and in Chapter 4 has served to identify several general aspects of cognitive functioning which are associated with high anxiety. It is possible to construct a profile of such effects, which would include at least the following: low available working memory capacity; high distractibility; broad attention when the location of salient stimuli is unknown; narrow attention when the location of salient stimuli is known; and a generally high level of expenditure of effort or processing resources combined with poor processing efficiency. An issue of theoretical interest for which these findings have relevance concerns the relationship between anxiety and depression in general aspects of processing. Much of the available evidence suggests that anxiety and depression in normals resemble each other. For example, trait anxiety and depression correlate approximately +0.60 in normal groups (Watson & Clark, 1984). So far as clinical groups are concerned, patients with clinical depression typically also suffer from anxiety, and patients with a diagnosis of generalized anxiety disorder frequently have symptoms of depression as well.

Cognitive Differences

There are various practical difficulties involved in comparing the profiles of cognitive effects associated with anxiety and depression. The major obstacle is that the same experimental paradigms have only rarely been used with anxious and depressed groups. As a consequence, direct comparisons are typically impossible. However, there is suggestive evidence that the effects of anxiety and depression differ in important respects, and these will be considered in some detail. It should be noted that some of the studies of depression used normal groups, whereas others used clinical groups with varying severity of depression. The paucity of relevant data precludes use of stringent criteria in deciding which studies to include.

We saw earlier in the chapter that anxiety seems to be associated with excessive use of an executive or control system responding to a mismatch between the actual and required cognitive states with enhanced effort expenditure. The position is quite different with respect to depression. Consider, for example, the work of Seligman (1975) on learned helplessness. He demonstrated that an initial learning situation in which aversive events are independent of the response made often leads subsequently to very poor performance in a situation in which aversive events can be avoided by making appropriate responses. According to Seligman (1975), this poor performance is due to learned helplessness, which closely resembles reactive depression. While many of Seligman's (1975) theoretical arguments have been criticized (see Miller and Morley, 1986), it is nevertheless of interest that reduced motivation is one of the major characteristics of the learned helplessness state.

Ellis and Ashbrook (1987) agreed with Seligman (1975) that depression is associated with reduced motivation, although they referred to cognitive effort or allocation of capacity to the task in hand. Their evidence is rather limited, however. In a typical study (Ellis, Thomas, & Rodriguez, 1984), induction of a depressed mood state was found to reduce recall when the acquisition task required high effort, but not when it did not. This finding is consistent with the notion that depressed mood state reduces effort expenditure, but there are obviously other possible reasons why mood state interacted with task complexity. For example, this interaction would be expected on the additional assumption of Ellis and Ashbrook (1987) that depression reduces available processing capacity.

Although the evidence is by no means complete, Williams et al. (1988) came to the following conclusion:

> Increased effort seems much less likely to apply in depression [than in anxiety]. Indeed, the motivational deficit often assumed to be associated with depression would lead to the view that reductions in available capacity are exacerbated by poor allocation of even such resources as are available. Though direct assessments of this are difficult, the prediction would be that the kind of evidence Eysenck cites for increased effort in anxiety could not be paralleled in depression [p. 48].

Another important difference between anxiety and depression concerns the characteristic speed of performance on a range of simple tasks. Psychomotor retardation is a very common feature of depression (especially of severe depression), with depressed patients being slower than normal controls on several speed measures (Miller, 1975). One of the most popular measures is 'speech pause time' (SPT), which is defined as the mean time interval between successive phonations on a simple task such as counting from one to ten. It has consistently been found that depressed patients have longer SPTs than controls, but that after recovery they do not differ from normal controls (Greden & Carroll, 1980; Greden, Azbala, Smokler, Gardner, & Carroll, 1981; Szabadi, Bradshaw, & Besson, 1976). Similar findings under more naturalistic conditions were obtained by Hinchliffe, Lancashire, and Roberts (1971). They discovered from analyses of 5-minute samples of speech that depressed subjects had lower rates of speech than controls.

Anxiety seems to have rather different effects on speech rate, according to a literature review by Murray (1982). He concluded that neither trait anxiety nor state anxiety was signficantly related to the rate of speaking. This suggests that anxiety does not typically produce psychomotor retardation, but it would be useful to have information concerning the effects of anxiety on SPTs.

The evidence reviewed earlier in this chapter indicated convincingly that anxiety is usually associated with high distractibility. There are intriguing suggestions in the literature that the same may not be true of depression. Foulds (1952) found that a distracting task (repeating digits spoken by the experimenter) actually increased performance speed on the Porteus Maze Test for depressed patients. However, the distracting task led to more errors on the maze task, so that it is unclear whether distraction really improved overall performance effectiveness. Campbell (1957) essentially replicated these findings, and also discovered that repeating digits did not speed up the performance of normal controls. Shapiro, Campbell, Harris, and Dewsberry (1958) also obtained evidence of a beneficial effect of distraction on the performance of depressed patients. Blackburn (1975) discovered that listening to a pre-recorded news item tended to increase the performance of bipolar depressives on a concurrent maze task, but to decrease that of unipolar depressives.

All in all, there is very little evidence that depressed patients are more distractible than normals, and they may even be less distractible. It is not known why this is the case. However, it may occur because demanding tasks reduce the frequency of distracting thoughts (Fennell, Teasdale, Jones, & Damle, 1987).

Anxiety and depression differ in their effects on effort expenditure, psychomotor speed, and susceptibility to distraction. It is also possible that anxious and depressed individuals differ in terms of attentional selectivity to salient stimuli. Anxious individuals exhibit greater attentional selectivity than non-anxious individuals to salient stimuli, but depression may not affect attentional selectivity in the same way. In a study by Hemsley and Zawada (1976), subjects were presented with a series of digits, some of which were spoken in a male voice and some in a female voice. Normals have better digit recall when they are instructed which set of digits to recall before rather than after the digits have been presented. Depressed patients were unaffected by the timing of the recall instructions, presumably because of their inability to focus attention selectively. A finding which may be related to this was reported by MacLeod et al. (1986). Patients with generalized anxiety disorder selectively allocated processing resources to threat-related rather than neutral stimuli, whereas depressed patients did not differentially allocate processing resources to the two types of stimuli.

A further instance of non-selectivity in depression which may not, however, depend specifically on poor attentional selectivity was reported by Watts and Sharrock (1987). They studied memory for a prose passage. Depressed patients had less of a bias than control subjects in favour of recalling those parts of a story which were thematically central.

Cognitive Similarities

A theoretical account of the above differences in cognitive functioning between anxiety and depression will be proposed after the similarities have been discussed briefly. One of the main similarities is in terms of reduced available processing capacity. Eysenck (1979 a, 1982, 1983, 1988 b, 1991 d) argued that anxiety reduces available working memory capacity, perhaps because some capacity is taken up with worry, self-concern, and other task-irrelevant processes. Ellis and Ashbrook (1987) have put forward a very similar theory for depression, claiming that depression produces a reduction in the capacity available for task performance as a result of extra-task processing (e.g., negative thoughts about the self) and other task-irrelevant processing.

According to these theoretical formulations, depression and anxiety should both interact with task complexity. There are numerous studies in which anxiety was found to interact with task complexity (see Eysenck, 1982, for details), and there are various studies in which depression interacted with task complexity. For example, Roy-Byrne et al. (1986) found that normals put into a depressed mood state performed as well as normals on a relatively 'automatic' memory test, but showed impaired performance on recall. As we saw earlier, Ellis et al. (1984) discovered that normals put into a depressed mood state were at a disadvantage in recall when the encoding task was demanding but not when it was relatively undemanding. Although anxiety and depression both seem to interact with task complexity in a similar fashion, it is obviously possible that the factors producing the interactions may differ in the two cases.

Both anxiety and depression are associated with impaired long-term memory (see Eysenck, 1981, for a review of the anxiety literature). Mueller (e.g., 1976) has found several times that individuals high in test anxiety have poorer long-term memory than those low in test anxiety. Ray, Katahn, and Snyder (1971) reported that subjects high in test anxiety forgot more of a complex verbal task over a two day retention interval. Several studies have demonstrated that depression leads to poor long-term memory (e.g., Cronholm & Ottosson, 1961; Sternberg & Jarvik, 1976). In general terms, reduced semantic processing typically leads to impaired long-term memory (Craik & Lockhart, 1972). However, the evidence indicates that neither anxiety nor depression produces a change from semantic to non-semantic processing (e.g., Mueller, 1976, for anxiety; and Russell & Beekhuis, 1976, for depression). More promising is the notion that anxiety (Mueller, 1976) and depression (Ellis et al., 1984) both lead to reduced elaboration or extensiveness of processing. It is likely that this reduced elaboration occurs as a consequence of reduced available processing capacity.

Theoretical Speculations

We have seen that depressed individuals typically have psychomotor retardation, rather low effort expenditure, low distractibility, and possibly a lack of attentional selectivity to salient stimuli. This pattern of effects appears to reflect a *passive disengagement* from the external environment. If attention is likened to a beam of light, then it is as if depressed individuals have a broad, weak beam which is relatively unresponsive to environmental changes.

This lack of involvement with the environment is probably related to the depressed individual's focus on past losses. Finlay-Jones and Brown (1981) found that 65% of depressed patients had experienced at least one severe loss in the three months before onset, against only 8% of those with anxiety disorders. Eysenck and Adams (in preparation) asked normal subjects to think of times in the past when they had been either depressed or anxious. For depressed episodes, 41.7% were caused by events from the past, against only 8.3% for anxious episodes.

The notion that depression is associated with a passive disengagement from the external environment is not a new one. However, what has not been emphasized sufficiently hitherto is the fact that there are converging lines of evidence from very different sources which point to the same conclusion. For example, Beck, Shaw, Bush, and Emery (1979) obtained evidence of passive disengagement in depression from clinical interviews. Barlow (1988) also relied on clinical data. He concluded that depressed patients feel responsibility for negative events, and as a consequence have lost all hope of being able to cope.

In contrast to depressed individuals, anxious individuals typically exhibit high effort expenditure, no psychomotor retardation, high distractibility, and high attentional selectivity to salient stimuli. In addition, as we saw in Chapter 4, they selectively allocate processing resources to threatening stimuli. This pattern can be regarded as reflecting a very *active engagement* with the external environment. This active engagement may well be related to the future time perspective associated with anxiety, and to the fact that the future is usually somewhat uncertain and may contain dangers. Evidence for a future orientation was obtained by Eysenck and Adams (in preparation). They discovered that 59.1% of anxious episodes were caused by future dangers, whereas only 6.7% of anxious episodes were so caused.

In sum, the evidence indicates that anxious individuals have an active engagement with the environment, whereas depressed individuals have a passive disengagement. Evidence consistent with the general theoretical orientation presented here was reported by Schwarzer, Jerusalem, and Stiksrud (1984). They used a task in which subjects repeatedly experienced failure. The primary reaction to initial failure was challenge. As the number of failures increased, challenge was replaced by feelings of threat and anxiety, with the subjects persisting with the task (i.e., active engagement). Eventually, as failure continued, the subjects' dominant reactions were of loss of control, helplessness, and depression, and they gave up trying (i.e., passive disengagement).

SUMMARY AND CONCLUSIONS

There have been several attempts to provide theoretical accounts of the predominantly negative effects of anxiety on performance. Several theorists (e.g., Sarason, 1984, 1988) have proposed that anxious individuals are more prone to worry than non-anxious individuals, and that it is the disruptive effects of worry and self-preoccupation on attention to the task which causes decrements in performance. This approach is rather limited. Worry is not always associated with impaired performance, and it is difficult to account for beneficial effects of anxiety on performance within this approach.

A more complex theory was proposed by Humphreys and Revelle (1984). They argued that state anxiety increases avoidance motivation and arousal, with consequent effects on sustained information transfer and short-term memory. Their theory accounts for many findings, but there are problems with some of the theoretical constructs employed (e.g., short-term memory; arousal). Probably the greatest weakness of their theory is the absence of a control system which monitors performance.

Eysenck and Calvo (in press) have proposed processing efficiency theory. It is claimed within this theory that worry uses some of the resources of working memory, especially those of the central executive component. Emphasis is also laid on the existence of a control system which is designed to monitor and evaluate performance and also to plan and regulate the use of processing resources. The central theoretical distinction is between performance effectiveness and processing efficiency. The key prediction that anxiety is more likely to impair processing efficiency than performance effectiveness has been tested using at least seven different methods. Evidence from all of the methods provides support for the prediction.

There are important differences between the effects of anxiety and depression on general aspects of performance. The control system of anxious individuals seems to be used excessively in order to compensate for processing inefficiency, whereas the control system of depressed individuals is used very little in spite of their processing inefficiency. In essence, anxiety is associated with active engagement in the environment, whereas depression is associated with passive disengagement.

CHAPTER EIGHT

OVERVIEW

COGNITIVE VULNERABILITY FOR GENERALIZED ANXIETY DISORDER

It was argued in Chapter 3 that there are at least three possible interpretations that can be made with respect to any cognitive bias which is discovered in patients suffering from generalized anxiety disorder. First, the bias might simply reflect, or be a secondary consequence of, the patient being in a clinically anxious mood state. In that case, the bias would not be present either before or after the period during which the patient was clinically anxious, and it would not be present in normals high in trait anxiety. Second, the bias might involve manifest vulnerability. In that case, the bias would be present before and after a period of clinical anxiety, and it would also probably be found in normals high in trait anxiety under both stressed and non-stressed conditions. Third, the bias might involve latent vulnerability. In that case, the bias would be present before and after a period of clinical anxiety only when the patient was under conditions of stress or high state anxiety. The bias would also be present in high trait-anxious normals, but would be especially clear in such individuals under stressed conditions or when high in state anxiety.

There is a substantial amount of evidence discussed in this book (mainly in Chapters 4 and 5) which is of relevance in deciding among these three alternatives. For convenience, the overall findings are

	TRAIT ANXIETY	TRAIT X STATE	CURRENT G.A.D. PATIENTS	RECOVERED G.A.D. PATIENTS
1. SELECTIVE ATTENTIONAL BIAS	√	√	√	X
2. MODIFIED STROOP	√	√	√	X
3. DISTRACTABILITY GENERAL	√	?	√	X
4. DISTRACTABILITY THREAT	√	?	√	√ ?
5. SCANNING	√ ?	?	?	?
6. ATTENTIONAL BROADENING	?	?	?	?
7. ATTENTIONAL NARROWING	√ ?	?	?	?
8. INTERPRETIVE BIAS	√	√	√	X
9. EXPLICIT MEMORY BIAS	√	√	X	X
10. IMPLICIT MEMORY BIAS	√ ?	?	√	X

FIG. 8.1. Cognitive effects in various normal and clinical anxiety groups.

shown in Fig. 8.1. As can be seen in Fig. 8.1, there are some cases in which there is little or no relevant evidence (indicated by a ?). However, it would appear that there is now sufficient evidence to arrive at tentative conclusions concerning the interpretation of most of these cognitive biases.

The notion that the cognitive biases exhibited by currently anxious patients with generalized anxiety disorder reflect clinically anxious mood state is supported by the almost complete absence of cognitive biases in recovered patients. However, the fact that normals high in trait anxiety show all, or nearly all, of the biases is difficult to account for if clinically anxious mood state is required to produce each of the biases. It must thus be concluded that the various cognitive biases are probably not merely a secondary consequence of being clinically anxious.

The next possibility to be considered is that the cognitive biases are due to a manifest vulnerability factor. This is poorly supported by the data, except for the presence of several cognitive biases in normals high in trait anxiety. The fact that recovered anxious patients have practically no cognitive biases is inconsistent with the notion of a manifest vulnerability factor. In addition, manifest vulnerability is inconsistent with the finding that at least four cognitive biases (selective attentional bias; modified Stroop bias; interpretive bias; and explicit memory bias) are more pronounced in high trait-anxious normals when stressed or high in state anxiety than when non-stressed or low in state anxiety.

The final possibility to be considered is that the biases involve a latent vulnerability factor. Most of the available data are consistent with this possibility. The fact that recovered anxious patients do not display cognitive biases can be accounted for on the grounds that they are not stressed or high in state anxiety. However, the main support for a latent vulnerability factor comes from the interactions between trait anxiety and state anxiety or stress which have been found with four of the cognitive biases. In other words, it appears that cognitive biases in information processing can be obtained most readily in individuals who possess a cognitive vulnerability factor and who are also in stressed conditions or high in state anxiety.

The available evidence is consistent with a diathesis-stress model of generalized anxiety disorder, with cognitive vulnerability forming at least part of the diathesis or predisposition. If subsequent research confirms the existence of a latent cognitive vulnerability factor for generalized anxiety disorder, then considerable progress has been made at an explanatory level. The importance of this entire issue was emphasized by Clark (1989):

> Support or disconfirmation of the vulnerability hypothesis will determine the fate of cognitive models. If cognitive mechanisms prove to be no more than symptoms of clinical states, then the explanatory value of these models is greatly restricted. If, on the other hand, cognitive mechanisms can be found which place individuals at risk for certain clinical disorders, then the theoretical and clinical value of these mechanisms is readily apparent. Thus, research into cognitive vulnerability will play a very significant role in future evaluations of cognitive-clinical theories [p. 692].

HYPERVIGILANCE THEORY

The information contained in Fig. 8.1 is also of relevance in connection with the hypervigilance theory discussed in Chapter 3. Most of the available evidence is consistent with the view that hypervigilance forms an important part of a latent cognitive vulnerability factor for generalized anxiety disorder. However, there are clearly significant lacunae in that evidence. For example, very little is known concerning the effects of anxiety on visual scanning, on attentional broadening prior to the detection of a salient stimulus, or on attentional narrowing after the detection of a salient stimulus. Indeed, these phenomena have not as yet been investigated at all in patients with generalized anxiety disorder.

It is difficult to relate the findings on explicit and implicit memory biases to hypervigilance theory. However, there are two relevant points which need to be made.

First, as was noted in Chapter 5, the complexities of the findings appear to require a number of different explanatory principles. Examples are the presence of an explicit memory bias in anxious normals but not in clinical patients with generalized anxiety disorder and the presence of an implicit (but not an explicit) memory bias in generalized anxiety disorder patients.

Second, hypervigilance theory is potentially relevant only to certain aspects of the effects of anxiety on memory performance. More specifically, effects of anxiety on processes occurring at input are more readily addressed by hypervigilance theory than are effects on processes occurring at output during information retrieval. However, it is not clear in most studies whether the effects of anxiety on performance are attributable to processes occurring at input or at output.

There is some overlap between the predictions of hypervigilance theory and those generated by the theory of Williams et al. (1988). However, the theory of Williams et al. (1988) does not specifically include any cognitive effects based on the processing of non-threatening stimuli. As a consequence, their theory does not account for the existence of a general distractibility effect in generalized anxiety disorder patients and normals high in trait anxiety, nor does it make predictions about visual scanning in the absence of threatening stimuli or about the broadening or narrowing of attention.

It is not possible at present to come to any definitive conclusions concerning the ultimate value of hypervigilance theory. One of the characteristics which most clearly distinguishes it from other theories is the notion that the attentional processes of anxious individuals can differ from those of non-anxious individuals even in the absence of threatening stimuli. Accordingly, a considerable increase in research in which attentional processes are examined in conditions of potential (but not actual) threat is required.

ANXIETY DISORDERS AND
COGNITIVE BIASES

According to the classificatory system contained in DSM-IIIR, there are various different anxiety disorders, including panic disorder, agoraphobia, social phobia, simple phobia, obsessive-compulsive disorder, post-traumatic stress disorder, and generalized anxiety disorder. If it were possible to establish different patterns of cognitive biases for each anxiety disorder, then this would probably enhance our understanding of the nature of each disorder. On the other hand, an inability to differentiate among the various anxiety disorders on the basis of cognitive measures would suggest that such measures are relatively insensitive.

Before moving on to a discussion of the available evidence, it should be noted that most of the research on cognitive biases has focused on three of the anxiety disorders: generalized anxiety disorder; panic disorder; and post-traumatic stress disorder. Accordingly, the other anxiety disorders will not be considered. It should also be noted that many (or even most) patients exhibit symptoms associated with more than one anxiety disorder. For example, Sanderson, DiNardo, Rapee, and Barlow (1990) discovered a co-morbidity rate of 70% in a group of anxiety disorder patients. Their findings led them to the following conclusion:

> Key features of various anxiety disorders such as panic attacks, intrusive thoughts, social fears, and excessive worry seem to exist in most patients presenting with a principal diagnosis of almost any of the anxiety disorders [p. 311].

It might seem that the high incidence of co-morbidity means that it would be extremely difficult to establish differences in cognitive biases among patients belonging to different diagnostic categories. However, there is in fact reasonable evidence that the various anxiety disorders are separate. For example, panic disorder differs from generalized anxiety disorder in having a greater genetic component (see Torgersen, 1990). In addition, the incidence of generalized anxiety disorder is not greater among the first-degree relatives of panic probands (= persons taken as the starting points in familial studies of disease) than among normal controls, and the incidence of panic disorder is comparable among the close relatives of generalized anxiety disorder probands and normal controls (see Weissman, 1990). Such findings indicate that panic disorder and generalized anxiety disorder are clearly distinguishable.

Panic Disorder

McNally (1990) has published a very good review of the evidence relating to cognitive biases in patients suffering from panic disorder. Accordingly, only a rather brief description of the main findings will be given here.

Attentional biases have been investigated in a number of studies of patients with panic disorder. Research with the modified Stroop paradigm has consistently indicated that panic disordered patients have slower colour naming of threat-related words than do normal or other controls (Ehlers, Margraf, Davies, & Roth, 1988; Hope, Rapee, Heimberg, & Dombeck, 1990; McNally, Riemann, & Kim, 1991). It remains unclear whether this bias effect is general or specific to the main concerns of panic patients. Ehlers et al. (1988) found a general attentional bias which extended to physical threat, separation threat, and embarrassment threat. In contrast, Hope et al. (1990) found that the colour naming of panic patients was slowed to physical threat words but not to social threat words.

A rather different paradigm for the detection of attentional biases was used by Burgess et al. (1981). Two prose passages were presented concurrently, with the passage on the attended channel being shadowed and the other passage being presented on the unattended channel. The subjects were instructed to detect specific threat-related and neutral words presented on either channel. Agoraphobics (many of whom suffer from panic attacks) detected more threat-related than neutral words in the unattended passage. This suggests that panic patients have a selective attentional bias in favour of threat-related stimuli.

There is reasonably strong evidence that panic patients often interpret ambiguous stimuli in a threatening fashion. McNally and Foa (1987) discovered that agoraphobic patients were more likely than either former agoraphobics or normal controls to interpret in a threatening way ambiguous scenarios involving either internal or external stimuli. Clark (1988) reported that panic patients interpreted ambiguous bodily sensations as threatening, but not scenarios involving general events, social events, or symptoms not having a sudden onset. Clark et al. (1988) presented ambiguous sentence stems followed by a word which produced a threatening or a non-threatening interpretation for the sentence as a whole. The subjects' task was simply to read the final word out loud as rapidly as possible. Words producing a threatening interpretation were read faster than words producing a non-threatening interpretation by panic patients but not by normal controls. This suggests that panic patients were more likely than normal controls to interpret the sentence stem in a threatening way.

Various studies have indicated that panic patients have an explicit memory bias for threatening stimuli. Some of the most convincing evidence was obtained by McNally, Foa, and Donnell (1989) and Cloitre and Liebowitz (1989). It was found in both studies that anxiety-related words were recalled better than non-threatening words by panic patients, but this was not the case for normals.

Post-traumatic Stress Disorder

One of the earliest studies on cognitive biases in patients with post-traumatic stress disorder was carried out by Trandel and McNally (1987). They used a dichotic listening task in which threat words were sometimes presented on the unattended channel. It was assumed that processing of these threat words would produce concurrent errors on the shadowing task for attended channel material. In fact, there were only minor differences between panic patients, alcoholics, and controls in shadowing performance, suggesting that panic patients do not have a selective processing bias in favour of threat.

More impressive results were obtained by McNally, Kaspi, Riemann, and Zeitlin (1990) using the modified Stroop task. Vietnam combat veterans with post-traumatic stress disorder showed slowed colour naming with words relevant to their traumatic experiences, whereas veterans without post-traumatic stress disorder did not. Cassiday, McNally, and Zeitlin (submitted) also used the modified Stroop task. They found that rape victims with post-traumatic stress disorder showed slowing of colour naming of specific rape words, whereas rape victims without post-traumatic stress disorder did not. The former group also exhibited some interference of colour naming with general rape words.

Memory biases were examined by Zeitlin and McNally (submitted). They discovered that Vietnam combat veterans with or without post-traumatic stress disorder had an explicit memory bias for combat words. They also considered implicit memory bias on a word-completion test. Only the veterans with post-traumatic stress disorder had an implicit memory bias for combat words. However, this bias was present for both primed and unprimed words, which suggests that it may simply be a familiarity effect.

Comparisons
The present state of play with respect to our knowledge of cognitive biases in patients suffering from generalized anxiety disorder, panic disorder, and post-traumatic stress disorder is shown in Fig. 8.2. It should be borne in mind that some of the ticks and crosses are based on

	CURRENT G.A.D. PATIENTS	PANIC DISORDER	POST-TRAUMATIC STRESS DISORDER
1. SELECTIVE ATTENTIONAL BIAS	✓	✓	X?
2. MODIFIED STROOP	✓	✓	✓
3. DISTRACTABILITY GENERAL	✓	?	?
4. DISTRACTABILITY THREAT	✓	?	?
5. INTERPRETIVE BIAS	✓	✓	?
6. EXPLICIT MEMORY BIAS	X	✓	✓
7. IMPLICIT MEMORY BIAS	✓	?	✓ ?

FIG. 8.2. Cognitive effects in generalized anxiety disorder, panic disorder, and post-traumatic stress disorder.

the findings from no more than one or two studies. In addition, there are a number of gaps in the figure which need to be filled in by future research. In the light of the available evidence, the most obvious difference among the three anxiety disorders is in an explicit memory bias; this has been found with panic patients and patients with post-traumatic stress disorder but not with generalized anxiety disorder patients.

There are at least two speculative ways in which one might attempt to account for the above findings on explicit memory bias.

First, it is argued within DSM-IIIR that panic disorder and post-traumatic stress disorder are more severe disorders than generalized anxiety disorder in terms of symptom intensity and impairment in social and occupational functioning. This could have implications for the processing and storage of threat-related information. According to Williams et al. (1988), the reason why patients with generalized anxiety disorder do not exhibit an explicit memory bias is because they have developed a strategy of cognitive avoidance for threatening material. If panic disorder and post-traumatic stress disorder are more severe disorders, it is possible that it is more difficult for sufferers from those anxiety disorders to use an avoidance strategy. As a consequence, both clinical groups exhibit an explicit memory bias.

Second, there are differences among the three anxiety disorders in terms of their experiences of anxiety. Patients with generalized anxiety disorder experience high levels of anxiety in a wide range of situations; indeed, they are sometimes said to exhibit 'free-floating anxiety'. In contrast, there is a greater degree of specificity associated with the other two anxiety disorders. There are specific external stimuli which are of great relevance to the development of post-traumatic stress disorder, and there are specific internal stimuli associated with the (usually relative infrequent) experience of panic by panic disordered patients. This specificity may mean that threat-related words produce more distinctive memory encodings for panic and post-traumatic patients than for generalized anxiety disorder patients, and it is known that distinctive encodings are often better remembered than non-distinctive ones (Eysenck, 1979 b).

On the basis of the argument put forward above, it would be expected that the various biases could be produced with a wider range of threat-related words for generalized anxiety disorder patients than for panic disorder patients or post-traumatic stress disorder patients. There is some evidence for this, but more research is needed to clarify the situation.

FUTURE DIRECTIONS

All programmes of research are inevitably limited in some ways, and the one discussed in this book is no exception. The main emphasis in this book has been on research designed to decide whether there is a cognitive vulnerability factor for generalized anxiety disorder, and, if so, to identify the various biases involved. While there has been considerable progress in achieving these aims, there may be other forms of vulnerability which are not specifically cognitive in nature. For example, anxious normals may be vulnerable in part because of their ineffective and inappropriate behaviour, or they may be vulnerable because of their deficient or maladaptive coping strategies when confronted by difficulties. It is not currently known whether ineffective social behaviour and deficient coping strategies are involved in vulnerability to generalized anxiety disorder, but some of the relvant evidence will be discussed below.

One of the ultimate aims of research on cognitive vulnerability is to facilitate the prevention of clinical anxiety and the successful treatment of clinically anxious patients. Research in this area appears to be relatively lacking in direct implications for therapy. The present position and suggestions for the future are dealt with below.

Social Cognitions and Behaviour

Research on vulnerability has focused on intra-individual cognitive processes rather than on the inter-individual social processes which are of major importance in everyday life. There is no doubt that the social-evaluative area is of particular significance. As Sanderson and Barlow (1990) reported, the great majority of generalized anxiety disorder patients have unrealistic social-evaluative worries. In similar fashion, most of the worries of high trait-anxious normals are social-evaluative in nature (Eysenck & van Berkum, submitted).

There is evidence that individuals differ in terms of their perceptions of how others regard them in social situations. For example, Campbell and Fehr (1990) investigated perceptions of actual social interactions in individuals high and low in negative affectivity, a personality dimension which is closely related to trait anxiety (Watson & Clark, 1984). They discovered that those high in negative affectivity believed that the person with whom they interacted viewed them less positively than did those low in negative affectivity. In actual fact, there were no differences in the ratings of the two groups of subjects.

If high trait-anxious normals believe that others regard them rather negatively, this may have consequences for their social behaviour. It was found in one study (Farina, Allen, & Saul, 1968) that people who were told that they were about to interact with someone who perceived them in a stigmatized way (e.g., thought they were psychiatric patients), then they behaved in ways which confirmed the stigma and produced the feared rejection. With anxious individuals, their attentional and interpretive biases may lead them to regard other people's social behaviour towards them as more threatening that it actually is. As a consequence, they may behave aggressively or defensively or in other ways which actually elicit threatening behaviour from others.

A related phenomenon was discussed by Swann (1987). He reviewed a considerable body of evidence which indicates that people in social situations endeavour to obtain evidence which confirms their own view of themselves. Since high trait-anxious individuals tend to have a rather negative view of themselves (e.g., Endler et al., 1976), it follows that they adopt interaction strategies which elicit negative responses from others.

It has been argued so far that the negative cognitions which high trait-anxious individuals have about themselves and about the opinions which others have of them may cause social problems and failures of communication. However, it is also entirely possible that high trait-anxious or high neuroticism individuals may create potentially stressful social and other situations because of their ineffective or inappropriate behaviour. Evidence for this was obtained by Ormel and Wohlfarth (1991). They distinguished between long-term difficulties which are exogenous (i.e., the consequences of the behaviour of other people or brought about by chance) and those which are endogenous (i.e., possibly brought about by the individual himself or herself). Individuals high in neuroticism had more endogenous long-term difficulties than those low in neuroticism, and this excess of endogenous difficulties was partially responsible for their higher level of psychological distress.

At a more fine-grained level of analysis, there is evidence that the social behaviour of anxious individuals is often less skilled than that of non-anxious ones. Campbell and Rushton (1978) videotaped students while they were discussing their holiday plans. Gaze aversion was much more common in high-neuroticism subjects. This finding was replicated by Daly (1978). He also discovered that highly anxious subjects when listening to someone tended to gaze either fixedly or scarcely at all, whereas non-anxious subjects gazed an intermediate amount. It is possible that the deficit in social skills of anxious individuals may make them more vulnerable to clinical anxiety.

In sum, it is likely that there are bi-directional influences of social cognitions and social behaviour in high trait-anxious normals: Negative cognitions lead to inadequate social behaviour and inadequate social behaviour leads to negative cognitions and stressful events. It is possible that biased social cognitions and ineffective social behaviour both contribute to vulnerability to generalized anxiety disorder, and future research should consider the separate and interactive effects of these two factors. Some evidence suggests that social cognitions may be more important than social behaviour. Stokes (1985) found that the social networks of those high and low in neuroticism were broadly comparable. In spite of this, he discovered that there was a moderately strong relationship between neuroticism and loneliness. As Stokes (1985) concluded, "It is likely that the link between neuroticism and loneliness is at the cognitive level" [p. 988].

Coping Strategies

It is possible that one of the reasons why those high in trait anxiety or neuroticism are vulnerable to clinical anxiety is because they possess less adequate coping strategies than those low in trait anxiety or neuroticism. The first study to examine this issue systematically was by Olah, Torestad, and Magnusson (1984). They asked their subjects to describe in their own words how they would deal with various anxiety-provoking situations, with each response being allocated to one of the three following styles of coping: passive, constructive, or escape.

High trait anxiety was associated with low levels of constructive coping and high levels of escape coping.

Similar findings were reported by Endler and Parker (1990). They developed the Multidimensional Coping Inventory, which provides measures of the usage of task-oriented, emotion-oriented, and avoidance-oriented coping strategies. High trait anxiety and neuroticism were associated with a greater usage of emotion-oriented and avoidance-oriented strategies, and with less reliance on task-oriented strategies.

Parkes (1986) investigated coping strategies in a more direct fashion. Female student nurses reported a work-related stressful episode and indicated how they coped with it on the Ways of Coping Questionnaire. Parkes (1986) found that nurses high in neuroticism made less use of direct coping that those low in neuroticism, and they were more likely to engage in suppression. These findings, together with those of Olah et al. (1984) and Endler and Parker (1990), suggest that high neuroticism or high trait-anxious individuals typically attempt to cope with stressful situations in a passive way rather than by active intervention.

There were further potentially important findings in the Parkes (1986) study. The coping strategies of the nurses low in neuroticism varied in an adaptive fashion as a function of the prevailing work demand: With high work demand, there was reduced use of direct coping and increased use of suppression, presumably because suppression permitted them to meet work demands without distraction. In contrast, the coping strategies used by high-neuroticism nurses remained almost unchanged at all levels of work demand. This failure to adapt to current circumstances may make high neuroticism normals more vulnerable to the adverse effects of stressful events than those low in neuroticism.

In sum, high neuroticism or trait anxiety appears to be associated with deficient and inflexible coping skills. It seems likely that such limited coping skills would increase the likelihood of stressful life events leading to clinical anxiety. However, there are two qualifications that need to be made. First, there is very little evidence relevant to the proposed causal sequence. Second, information about coping strategies has been obtained from questionnaires rather than from direct observation of behaviour, and the validity of such questionnaire assessment is probably rather low.

Cognitive Therapy

There is at present somewhat of a gulf between cognitive therapy for anxiety and laboratory investigations of cognition in anxious patients, although there is obviously some overlap. Cognitive therapy with anxious patients is concerned largely with their misinterpretations, with therapists seeking to correct these misinterpretations. This approach has often proved successful. For example, it was found in a recent study (Salkoviskis, Clark, & Hackmann, 1991) that six out of seven panic patients showed a reduction in frequency of panic attacks following cognitive procedures directed at changing catastrophic misinterpretations related to physical symptoms. There is an obvious link between such forms of therapy and the interpretive bias studied under laboratory conditions.

While most other research discussed in this book does not map so neatly onto cognitive therapy, there are least three ways in which this research is of potential relevance to cognitive therapy. First, it helps to provide solid empirical and theoretical foundations for cognitive therapy. Until comparatively recently, very few of the assumptions incorporated into cognitive therapy had been submitted to detailed experimental test. Second, research suggests that cognitive therapy dealing primarily with patients' misinterpretations may be too narrowly based. As we have seen, the latent cognitive vulnerability factor for generalized anxiety disorder includes a selective attentional bias and an implicit memory bias in additon to an interpretive bias. It is entirely possible that cognitive therapy would benefit from a broader focus which encompassed these other biases.

Third, there are indications in the research literature that certain pre-conscious processes are of importance in anxiety. As well as being of significance in their own right, these pre-conscious processes also undoubtedly influence some of the major conscious processes associated with anxiety. Cognitive therapists concentrate almost exclusively on their patients' conscious awareness, and this may limit the effectiveness of treatment.

SUMMARY AND CONCLUSIONS

The issue of whether or not there is a cognitive vulnerability factor associated with generalized anxiety disorder is important in terms of the potential explanatory value of the cognitive approach. The available evidence suggests that there is probably a latent cognitive vulnerability factor, and that the cognitive differences between anxious patients and normal controls do not simply reflect clinically anxious mood state.

Much of the evidence is consistent with hypervigilance theory, which was presented in Chapter 3. It is clear that the focus within that theory on attentional processes is appropriate. However, hypervigilance theory does not provide a simple explanation of some of the memory findings, and many of its major assumptions need further empirical investigation.

A comparison of the profiles of cognitive biases of generalized anxiety disorder patients, panic disorder patients, and post-traumatic stress disorder patients suggests a reasonably high level of overall similarity. However, generalized anxiety disorder patients differ from the other two groups in not exhibiting an explicit memory bias. This may reflect the lesser severity of generalized anxiety disorder. Alternatively, the fact that generalized anxiety disorder patients experience anxiety much of the time, and in numerous different settings, may lead them to produce memory encodings which are relatively unmemorable because they lack distinctiveness.

The major research discussed in this book does not deal directly with social behaviour or with the possibility that ineffective social behaviour may be a vulnerability factor for clinical anxiety. The research has also not considered the possible role of deficient coping strategies in promoting vulnerability. Finally, the research generally lacks direct implications for cognitive therapy. However, some speculative suggestions were offered as to ways in which these various omissions could be rectified and further progress obtained. But that is another story.

References

Allen, B. P., & Potkay, C. R. (1981). On the arbitrary distinction between states and traits. *Journal of Personality and Social Psychology, 41,* 916-928.

Argyle, M. (1987). *The Psychology of Happiness.* Oxford: Oxford University Press.

Baddeley, A. D. (1986). *Working Memory.* Oxford: Clarendon Press.

Baddeley, A. D., & Hitch, G. (1974). Working memory. In G. H. Bower (Ed.), *The Psychology of Learning and Motivation, Vol. 8.* London: Academic Press.

Bandura, A. (1989). Self-agency in social cognitive theory. *American Psychologist, 44,* 1175-1184.

Barlow, D. H. (1988). *Anxiety and its Disorders.* New York: Guilford Press.

Bartlett, F. C. (1932). *Remembering: A Study in Experimental and Social Psychology.* Cambridge: Cambridge University Press.

Beck, A. T. (1967). *Depression: Causes and Treatment.* Philadelphia: University of Pennsylvania Press.

Beck, A. T. (1976). *Cognitive Theory and the Emotional Disorders.* New York: International Universities Press.

Beck, A. T. (1987). Cognitive models of depression. *Journal of Cognitive Psychotherapy: An International Quarterly, 1,* 5-37.

Beck, A. T., Brown, G., Steer, R. A., Eidelson, J. I., & Riskind, J. H. (1987). Differentiating anxiety and depression utilizing the Cognitions Checklist. *Journal of Abnormal Psychology, 96,* 179-186.

Beck, A. T., & Clark, D. A. (1988). Anxiety and depression: An information processing perspective. *Anxiety Research, 1,* 23-36.

Beck, A. T., & Emery, G. (1985). *Anxiety Disorders and Phobias: A Cognitive Perspective.* New York: Basic Books.

Beck, A. T., Laude, R., & Bohnert, M. (1974). Ideational components of anxiety neurosis. *Archives of General Psychiatry, 31,* 319-325.

Beck, A. T., Shaw, A. J., Bush, B. F., & Emery, G. (1979). *Cognitive Therapy of Depression.* New York: Wiley.

Berlyne, D. E. (1960). *Conflict, Arousal, and Curiosity.* London: McGraw-Hill.

Blackburn, I. M. (1975). Mental and psychomotor speed in depression and mania. *British Journal of Psychiatry, 126,* 329-335.

Blaney, P. H. (1986). Affect and memory: A review. *Psychological Bulletin, 99,* 229-246.

Blankstein, K. R., Flett, G. L., Boase, P., & Toner, B. B. (1990). Thought listing and endorsement measures of self-referential thinking in test anxiety. *Anxiety Research, 2,* 103-111.

Blankstein, K. R., Toner, B. B., & Flett, G. L. (1989). Test anxiety and the contents of consciousness: Thought listing and endorsement measures. *Journal of Research in Personality, 23,* 269-286.

Blaylock, B. A. H. (1963). *Repression-Sensitization, Word Association Responses, and Incidental Recall.* Unpublished master's thesis, University of Texas, Austin, TX.

Borkovec, T. D., & Hu, S. (1990). The effect of worry on cardiovascular response to phobic imagery. *Behaviour Research and Therapy, 28,* 69-73.

Borkovec, T. D., & Inz, J. (1990). The nature of worry in generalized anxiety disorder: A predominance of thought activity. *Behaviour Research and Therapy, 28,* 153-158.

Borkovec, T. D., Metzger, R. L., & Pruzinsky, T. (1986). Anxiety, worry, and the self. In L. M. Hartman and K. R. Blankstein (Eds.), *Perception of Self in Emotional Disorder and Psychotherapy.* New York: Plenum.

Borkovec, T. D., Robinson, E., Pruzinsky, T., & DePree, J. A. (1983 a). Preliminary exploration of worry: Some characteristics and processes. *Behaviour Research and Therapy, 21,* 9-16.

Borkovec, T. D., Shadick, R., & Hopkins, M. (1990). The nature of normal and pathological worry. In R. Rapee and D. H. Barlow (Eds.), *Chronic Anxiety and Generalized Anxiety Disorder.* New York: Guilford Press.

Borkovec, T. D., Wilkinson, L., Folensbee, R., & Lerman, C. (1983 b). Stimulus control applications to the treatment of worry. *Behaviour Research and Therapy, 21,* 247-251.

Bower, G. H. (1981). Mood and memory. *American Psychologist, 36,* 129-148.

Bower, G. H. (1983). Affect and cognition. *Philosophical Transactions of the Royal Society London, B302,* 387-402.

Bower, G. H. (1987). Commentary on 'Mood and Memory'. *Behaviour Research and Therapy, 25,* 443-455.

Bower, G. H., & Cohen, P. R. (1982). Emotional influences in memory and thinking: Data and theory. In S. Fiske and M. Clark (Eds.), *Affect and Social Cognition.* Hillsdale, N.J.: Lawrence Erlbaum Associates Ltd.

Bower, G. H., Gilligan, S. G., & Monteiro, K. P. (1981). Selectivity of learning caused by affective states. *Journal of Experimental Psychology: General, 110,* 451-473.

Breck, B. E., & Smith, S. H. (1983). Selective recall of self-descriptive traits by socially anxious and nonanxious females. *Social Behavior and Personality, 11,* 71-76.

Brewin, C. R. (1988). *Cognitive Foundations of Clinical Psychology.* London: Lawrence Erlbaum Associates Ltd.

Broadbent, D. E., & Broadbent, M. (1988). Anxiety and attentional bias: State and trait. *Cognition and Emotion, 2,* 165-183.

Broadbent, D. E., Broadbent, M., & Jones, J. (1986). Performance correlates of self-reported cognitive failure and of obsessionality. *British Journal of Clinical Psychology, 25,* 285- 299.

Burgess, I. S., Jones, L. M., Robertson, S. A., Radcliffe, W. N., & Emerson, E. (1981). The degree of control exerted by phobic and non-phobic verbal stimuli over the recognition behaviour of phobic and non-phobic subjects. *Behaviour Research and Therapy, 19,* 233- 243.

Butler, G., & Mathews, A. (1987). Anticipatory anxiety and risk perception. *Cognitive Therapy and Research, 11,* 551-565.

Byrne, D. (1964). Repression-sensitization as a dimension of personality. In B. A. Maher (Ed.), *Progress in Experimental Personality Research.* New York: Academic Press.

Calvo, M. G. (1985). Effort, aversive representations and performance in test anxiety. *Personality and Individual Differences, 6,* 563-571.

Calvo, M. G. (1986). Influencia de las condiciones evaluativas sobre la accesibilidad de representaciones aversivas. *Revista de Psicologia General y Applicada, 41,* 565-583.

Calvo, M. G., & Alamo, L. (1987). Test anxiety and motor performance: The role of muscular and attentional demands. *International Journal of Psychology, 22,* 165-177.

Calvo, M. G., Alamo, L., & Ramos, P. M. (1990). Test anxiety, motor performance and learning: Attentional and somatic interference. *Personality and Individual Differences, 11,* 29-38.

Calvo, M. G., & Carreiras, M. (Submitted). Selective influence of test-anxiety on reading processes.

Calvo, M. G., & Ramos, P. M. (1989). Effects of test anxiety on motor learning: The processing efficiency hypothesis. *Anxiety Research, 2,* 45-55.

Calvo, M. G., & Ramos, P. M. (Submitted). Compensatory cognitive resources during reading as a function of test anxiety and task demands on working memory.

Calvo, M. G., Ramos, P., & Estevez, A. (Submitted). Test-anxiety and comprehension efficiency: The role of prior knowledge and working memory deficits.

Campbell, A., & Rushton, J.P. (1978). Bodily communication and personality. *British Journal of Social and Clinical Psychology, 17,* 31-36.

Campbell, D. (1957). *A study of some sensory-motor functions in psychiatric patients.* Unpublished Ph.D. thesis, University of London.

Campbell, J.D., & Fehr, B. (1990). Self-esteem and perceptions of conveyed impressions: Is negative affectivity associated with greater realism? *Journal of Personality and Social Psychology, 88,* 122-133.

Carroll, D. (1972). Repression-sensitization as a dimension of personality. *Perceptual and Motor Skills, 34,* 949-950.

Carter, W. R., Johnson, M. C., & Borkovec, T. D. (1986). Worry: An electrocortical analysis. *Advances in Behaviour Research and Therapy, 8,* 193-204.

Cassiday, K.L., McNally, R.J., & Zeitlin, S.B. (submitted). *Cognitive processing of trauma stimuli in rape victims with post-traumatic stress disorder.*

Cheesman, J., & Merikle, P. M. (1985). Word recognition and consciousness. In D. Besner, T. G. Waller, and G. E. McKinnon (Eds.), *Reading Research: Advances in Theory and in Practice*. New York: Academic Press.

Claeys, W. (1989). Social anxiety, evaluative threat and incidental recall of trait words. *Anxiety Research, 2,* 27-43.

Clark, D. A. (1989). Special review of Brewin's 'Cognitive Foundations of Clinical Psychology'. *Behaviour Research and Therapy, 27,* 691-693.

Clark, D. M. (1988). A cognitive model of panic attacks. In S. Rachman and J. D. Maser (Eds.), *Panic: Psychological Perspectives*. Hillsdale, N.J.: Lawrence Erlbaum Associates.

Clark, D. M., Salkovskis, P. M., Gelder, M., Koehler, C., Martin, M., Anastasiades, P., Hackmann, A., Middleton, H., & Jeavons, A. (1988). Tests of a cognitive theory of panic. In I. Hand and H. U. Wittchen (Eds.), *Panic and Phobias, Vol. 2*. Berlin: Springer.

Clark, D. M., & Teasdale, J. D. (1982). Diurnal variation in clinical depression and accessibility of memories of positive and negative experiences. *Journal of Abnormal Psychology, 91,* 87-95.

Cloitre, M., & Liebowitz, M. (1989). *Memory bias for anxiety information in panic disorder: Elaboration or inhibition of semantic processing?* Paper presented at the World Congress of Cognitive Therapy, Oxford, England.

Collins, A. M., & Loftus, E. F. (1975). A spreading-activation theory of semantic processing. *Psychological Review, 82,* 407-428.

Conley, J. J. (1984). The hierarchy of consistency: A review and model of longitudinal findings on adult individual differences in intelligence, personality and self-opinion. *Personality and Individual Differences, 5,* 11-25.

Cornsweet, D. M. (1969). Use of cues in the visual periperhy under conditions of arousal. *Journal of Experimental Psychology, 80,* 14-18.

Craik, F. I. M., & Lockhart, R. S. (1972). Levels of processing: A framework for memory research. *Journal of Verbal Learning and Verbal Behavior, 11,* 671-684.

Craske, M. G., & Craig, K. D. (1984). Musical performance anxiety: The three-systems model and self-efficacy theory. *Behaviour Research and Therapy, 22,* 267-280.

Craske, M. G., Rapee, R. M., Jackel, L., & Barlow, D. H. (1989). Qualitative dimensions of worry in DSM-III-R generalized anxiety disorder subjects and nonanxious controls. *Behaviour Research and Therapy, 27,* 397-402.

Cronholm, B., & Ottosson, J.-O. (1961). The experience of memory function after electroconvulsive therapy. *British Journal of Psychiatry, 109,* 251-258.

Crowder, R. G. (1982). The demise of short-term memory. *Acta Psychologica, 50,* 291-323.

Crowne, D., & Marlowe, D. (1964). *The Approval Motive*. New York: Wiley.

Culler, R. E., & Holahan, C. J. (1980). Test anxiety and academic performance: The effects of study related behaviors. *Journal of Educational Psychology, 72,* 16-20.

Daly, S. (1978). Behavioural correlates of social anxiety. *British Journal of Social and Clinical Psychology, 17,* 117-120.

Darke, S. (1988 a). Anxiety and working memory capacity. *Cognition and Emotion, 2,* 145-154.

Darke, S. (1988 b). Effects of anxiety on inferential reasoning task performance. *Journal of Personality and Social Psychology, 55,* 499-505.

Deffenbacher, J. L. (1980). Worry and emotionality in test anxiety. In I. G. Sarason (Ed.), *Test Anxiety: Theory, Research, and Applications*. Hillsdale, N.J.: Lawrence Erlbaum Associates Ltd.

(DSM-IIIR) *Diagnostic and Statistical Manual of Mental Disorder* (1987). Washington, D. C.: American Psychiatric Association.

Donat, D. C. (1983). Predicting state anxiety: A comparison of multidimensional and unidimensional trait approaches. *Journal of Research in Personality, 17*, 256-262.

Dornic, S. (1977). Mental load, effort, and individual differences. *Reports from the Department of Psychology*, No. 509. University of Stockholm.

Dornic, S. (1980). Efficiency vs. effectiveness in mental work: The differential effect of stress. *Reports from the Department of Psychology*, University of Stockholm, No. 568.

Dornic, S., & Fernaeus, S.-E. (1981). Individual differences in high-load tasks: The effect of verbal distraction. *Reports from the Department of Psychology*, No. 569. University of Stockholm.

Easterbrook, J. A. (1959). The effect of emotion on cue utilization and the organization of behaviour. *Psychological Review, 66*, 183-201.

Ehlers, A., Margraf, J., Davies, S., & Roth, W. T. (1988). Selective processing of threat cues in subjects with panic attacks. *Cognition and Emotion, 2*, 201-219.

Eitinger, L. (1964). *Concentration Camp Survivors*. London: Macmillan.

Eliatamby, A. (1984). Anxiety and Anagram Solving. Unpublished manuscript.

Ellis, A. (1962). *Reason and Emotion in Psychotherapy*. Secaucus, N.J.: Citadel Press.

Ellis, H. C., & Ashbrook, P. W. (1987). Resource allocation model of the effects of depressed mood states on memory. In K. Fiedler and J. Forges (Eds.), *Affect, Cognition and Social Behaviour*. Toronto: Hogrefe.

Ellis, H., Thomas, R. L., & Rodriguez, I. A. (1984). Emotional mood states and memory: Elaborative encoding, semantic processing and cognitive effort. *Journal of Experimental Psychology: Learning, Memory and Cognition, 69*, 237-243.

Endler, N. S. (1983). Interactionism: A personality model, but not yet a theory. In M. M. Page (Ed.), *Nebraska Symposium on Motivation: Personality—Current Theory and Research*. London: University of Nebraska Press.

Endler, N. S., Magnusson, D., Ekehammar, B., & Okada, M. (1976). The multi-dimensionality of state and trait anxiety. *Scandinavian Journal of Psychology, 17*, 81-96.

Endler, N.S., & Parker, J.D.A. (1990). Multidimensional assessment of coping: A critical evaluation. *Journal of Personality and Social Psychology, 58*, 844-854.

Epstein, S., & Roupenian, A. (1970). Heart rate and skin conductance during experimentally induced anxiety: The effect of uncertainty about receiving a noxious stimulus. *Journal of Personality and Social Psychology, 16*, 20-28.

Erdelyi, M. H. (1974). A new look at the new look: Perceptual defence and vigilance. *Psychological Review, 81*, 1-24.

Eysenck, H. J. (1967). *The Biological Basis of Personality*. Springfield, Ill.: Thomas.

Eysenck, H. J., & Eysenck, M. W. (1985). *Personality and Individual Differences*. New York: Plenum.

Eysenck, M. W. (1977). *Human Memory: Theory, Research and Individual Differences*. Oxford: Pergamon.

Eysenck, M. W. (1979 a). Anxiety, learning and memory: A reconceptualization. *Journal of Research in Personality, 13,* 363-385.

Eysenck, M. W. (1979 b). Depth, elaboration, and distinctiveness. In L. S. Cermak and F. I. M. Craik (Eds.), *Levels of Processing in Human Memory.* Hillsdale, N.J.: Lawrence Erlbaum Associates Ltd.

Eysenck, M. W. (1981). Personality, learning and memory. In H. J. Eysenck (Ed.), *A Model of Personality.* Berlin: Springer.

Eysenck, M. W. (1982). *Attention and Arousal: Cognition and Performance.* Berlin: Springer.

Eysenck, M. W. (1983). Anxiety and individual differences. In G. R. J. Hockey (Ed.), *Stress and Fatigue in Human Performance.* Chichester: Wiley.

Eysenck, M. W. (1984 a). *A Handbook of Cognitive Psychology.* London: Lawrence Erlbaum Associates Ltd.

Eysenck, M. W. (1984 b). Anxiety and the worry process. *Bulletin of the Psychonomic Society, 22,* 545-548.

Eysenck, M. W. (1985). Anxiety and cognitive-task performance. *Personality and Individual Differences, 6,* 579-586.

Eysenck, M. W. (1986). Individual differences in anxiety, cognition and coping. In G. R. J. Hockey, A. W. K. Gaillard, and M. G. H. Coles (Eds.), *Energetics and Human Information Processing.* Dordrecht: Martinus Nijhoff.

Eysenck, M. W. (1987). Trait theories and anxiety. In H. J. Eysenck and J. Strelau (Eds.), *Personality Dimensions and Arousal.* New York: Plenum.

Eysenck, M. W. (1988 a). Trait anxiety and stress. In S. Fisher and J. Reason (Eds.), *Handbook of Life Stress, Cognition and Health.* Chichester: Wiley.

Eysenck, M. W. (1988 b). Anxiety and attention. *Anxiety Research, 1,* 9-15.

Eysenck, M. W. (1989 a). Personality, stress arousal, and cognitive processes in stress transactions. In R. W. J. Neufeld (Ed.), *Advances in the Investigation of Psychological Stress.* New York: Wiley.

Eysenck, M. W. (1989 b). Stress, anxiety, and intelligent performance. In D. Vickers and P. L. Smith (Eds.), *Human Information Processing: Measures, Mechanisms and Models.* Amsterdam: North-Holland.

Eysenck, M. W. (1989 c). Anxiety and cognition: Theory and research. In T. Archer and L.-G. Nilsson (Eds.), *Aversion, Avoidance, and Anxiety: Perspectives on Aversively Motivated Behaviour.* London: Lawrence Erlbaum Associates Ltd.

Eysenck, M. W. (1990 a). Anxiety and cognitive functioning. In G. D. Burrows, M. Roth, and R. Noyes (Eds.), *Handbook of Anxiety, Vol. 3: The Neurobiology of Anxiety.* Amsterdam: Elsevier.

Eysenck, M. W. (1990 b). Cognitive therapy. In M. W. Eysenck (Ed.), *The Blackwell Dictionary of Cognitive Psychology.* Oxford: Blackwell.

Eysenck, M. W. (1991 a). Trait anxiety and cognition. In C. D. Spielberger, I. G. Sarason, Z. Kulczar, and J. Van Heck (Eds.), *Stress and Emotion, Vol. 14.* London: Hemisphere.

Eysenck, M. W. (1991 b). Theoretical cognitive psychology and mood disorders. In P. R. Martin (Ed.), *Handbook of Behaviour Therapy and Psychological Science: An Integrative Approach.* New York: Pergamon.

Eysenck, M. W. (1991 c). Cognitive factors in clinical psychology: Potential relevance to therapy. In M. Briley and S. E. File (Eds.), *New Concepts in Anxiety.* London: Macmillan.

Eysenck, M. W. (1991 d). Anxiety and attention. In R. Schwarzer and R. A. Wicklund (Eds.), *Anxiety and Self-Focused Attention*. London: Harwood.

Eysenck, M. W. (1991 e). Anxiety and cognitive functioning: A multi-faceted approach. In H. Weingartner and R. Lister (Eds.), *Cognitive Neuroscience*. Oxford: Oxford University Press.

Eysenck, M. W. (1992). The nature of anxiety. In A. Gale and M. W. Eysenck (Eds.), *Handbook of Individual Differences: Biological Perspectives*. Chichester: Wiley.

Eysenck, M. W., & Adams, J. (in preparation). An investigation into time orientation with factors producing anxiety and depression.

Eysenck, M. W., & Byrne, A. (in press). Anxiety and susceptibility to distraction. *Personality and Individual Differences*.

Eysenck, M. W., & Calvo, M. (in press). Anxiety and performance: The processing efficiency theory. *Cognition and Emotion*.

Eysenck, M. W., & Graydon, J. (1989). Susceptibility to distraction as a function of personality. *Personality and Individual Differences, 10,* 681-687.

Eysenck, M. W., & Keane, M. T. (1990). *Cognitive Psychology: A Student's Handbook*. London: Lawrence Erlbaum Associates Ltd.

Eysenck, M. W., MacLeod, C., & Mathews, A. (1987). Cognitive functioning and anxiety. *Psychological Research, 49,* 189-195.

Eysenck, M. W., & Mathews, A. (1987). Trait anxiety and cognition. In H. J. Eysenck and I. Martin (Eds.), *Theoretical Foundations of Behaviour Therapy*. New York: Plenum.

Eysenck, M. W., & Mogg, K. (1990). Clinical anxiety and cognition. In R. West, M. Christie, and J. Weinman (Eds.), *Microcomputers, Psychology and Medicine*. Chichester: Wiley.

Eysenck, M. W., & Mogg, K. (1991). Mood disorders and memory. In J. A. Weinman and J. Hunter (Eds.), *Memory: Neurochemical and Abnormal Perspectives*. London: Harwood.

Eysenck, M. W., Mogg, K.,May, J., Richards, A., & Mathews, A. (1991). Bias in interpretation of ambiguous sentences related to threat in anxiety. *Journal of Abnormal Psychology, 100,* 144-150.

Eysenck, M. W., & van Berkum, J. (in press). The structure of worry in high and low trait-anxious groups. *Personality and Individual Differences*.

Fahrenberg, J. (1987). Concepts of activation and arousal in the theory of emotionality (neuroticism): A multivariate concept. In J. Strelau and H. J. Eysenck (Eds.), *Personality and Dimensions of Arousal*. New York: Plenum.

Fahrenberg, J. (1992). Psychophysiology of neuroticism and anxiety. In A. Gale and M. W. Eysenck (Eds.), *Handbook of Individual Differences: Biological Perspectives*. Chichester: Wiley.

Farina, A., Allen, J. G., & Saul, B. B. B. (1968). The role of the stigmatized in affecting social relationships. *Journal of Personality, 36,* 169-182.

Fennell, M. J. V., Teasdale, J. D., Jones, S., & Damle, A. (1987). Distraction in neurotic and endogenous depression: An investigation of negative thinking in major depressive disorders. *Psychological Medicine, 17,* 441-452.

Finlay-Jones, R. A., & Brown, G. W. (1981). Types of stressful life events and the onset of anxiety and depressive disorders. *Psychological Medicine, 11,* 803-815.

Fiske, S. T., & Taylor, S. E. (1984). *Social Cognition*. Reading, MA: Addison-Wesley.

Foa, E. G., & Kozak, M. J. (1986). Emotional processing and fear: Exposure to corrective information. *Psychological Bulletin, 99,* 20-35.

Foulds, G. A. (1952). Temperamental differences in maze performance II: The effect of distraction and of electroconvulsive therapy on psychomotor retardation. *British Journal of Psychiatry, 43,* 33-41.

Fox, E., O'Boyle, C., Barry, H., & McCreary, C. (1989). Repressive coping style and anxiety in stressful dental surgery. *British Journal of Medical Psychology, 62,* 371-380.

Fridhandler, B. M. (1986). Conceptual note on state, trait, and the state-trait distinction. *Journal of Personality and Social Psychology, 50,* 169-174.

Friedman, A. (1979). Framing pictures: The role of knowledge in automatised encoding and memory for gist. *Journal of Experimental Psychology: General, 108,* 316-355.

Gilligan, S. G., & Bower, G. H. (1984). Cognitive consequences of emotional arousal. In C. Izard, J. Kagan, and R. Zajonc (Eds.), *Emotions, Cognitions and Behaviour.* New York: Cambridge University Press.

Gleitman, H. (1987). *Basic Psychology* (2nd edn). New York: Norton.

Goldberg, D. P. , Bridges, K., Duncan-Jones, P., & Grayson, D. (1987). Dimensions of neurosis seen in primary care settings. *Psychological Medicine, 17,* 461-470.

Gotlib, I. H., McLachlan, A. L., & Katz, A. N. (1988). Biases in visual attention in depressed and nondepressed individuals. *Cognition and Emotion, 2,* 185-200.

Graf, P., & Mandler, G. (1984). Activation makes words more accessible, but not necessarily more retrievable. *Journal of Verbal Learning and Verbal Behavior, 23,* 553-568.

Graf, P., Squire, L. R., & Mandler, G. (1984). The information that amnesic patients do not forget. *Journal of Experimental Psychology: Learning, Memory, and Cognition, 10,* 164- 178.

Gray, J.A. (1975). *Elements of a two-process theory of learning.* London: Academic Press.

Gray, J. A. (1982). *The Neuropsychology of Anxiety.* Oxford: Clarendon.

Gray, J. A. (1985). A whole and its parts: Behaviour, the brain, cognition and emotion. *Bulletin of the British Psychological Society, 38,* 99-112.

Graydon, J., & Eysenck, M. W. (1989). Distraction and cognitive performance. *European Journal of Cognitive Psychology, 1,* 161-179.

Greden, J. F., Azbala, A. A., Smokler, J. A., Gardner, R., & Carroll, B. J. (1981). Speech pause time: A marker of psychomotor retardation amongst endogenous depressives. *Biological Psychiatry, 16,* 851-859.

Greden, J. F., & Carroll, B. J. (1980). Decrease in speech pause times with treatment of endogenous depression. *Biological Psychiatry, 15,* 575-587.

Greenberg, M. S., & Beck, A. T. (1989). Depression versus anxiety: A test of the content specificity hypothesis. *Journal of Abnormal Psychology, 98,* 9-13.

Gross, P. R., & Eifert, S. (1990). Components of generalized anxiety: The role of intrusive thoughts vs. worry. *Behaviour Research and Therapy, 28,* 421-428.

Gross, P. R., Oei, T. P. S., & Evans, L. (1989). Generalized anxiety symptoms in phobic disorders and anxiety states: A test of the worry hypothesis. *Journal of Anxiety Disorders, 3,* 159-169.

Haley, G. A. (1974). Eye movement responses of repressors and sensitizers to a stressful film. *Journal of Research in Personality, 8,* 88-94.

Hallam, G. (1985). Anxiety and the brain: A reply to Gray. *Bulletin of the British Psychological Society, 38,* 217-219.

Halperin, J. M. (1986). Defensive style and the direction of gaze. *Journal of Research in Personality, 20,* 327-337.

Hamilton, V. (1978). *The cognitive analysis of personality related to information-processing deficits with stress and anxiety.* Paper presented at the British Psychological Society meeting, London, December.

Haney, J. N. (1973). Approach-avoidance reactions by repressors and sensitizers to ambiguity in a structured free-association. *Psychological Reports, 33,* 97-98.

Harrison, A. J. (1984). *Hypnotic mood induction and subjective judgement of risk.* Unpublished B.Sc. thesis, University of London.

Hemsley, D. R., & Zawada, S. L. (1976). 'Filtering' and the cognitive deficit in schizophrenia. *British Journal of Psychiatry, 128,* 456-461.

Hibbert, G. A. (1984). Ideational components of anxiety: Their origin and content. *British Journal of Psychiatry, 144,* 618-624.

Hill, A. B., & Kemp-Wheeler, S. M. (1989). The influence of anxiety on lexical and affective decision time for emotional words. *Personality and Individual Differences, 10,* 1143-1149.

Hinchliffe, M. K., Lancashire, M., & Roberts, F. J. (1971). Depression: Defence mechanisms in speech. *British Journal of Psychiatry, 128,* 456-461.

Hockey, G. R. J. (1986). A state control theory of adaptation to stress and individual differences in stress management. In G. R. J. Hockey, A. W. K. Gaillard, and M. G. H. Coles (Eds.), *Energetics and Human Information Processing.* Dordrecht: Nijhoff.

Hoehn-Saric, R., McLeod, D. R., & Zimmerli, W. D. (1988). *Subjective and somatic manifestations of anxiety in obsessive-compulsive and generalized anxiety disorders.* Presented at the 141st Annual Meeting of the American Psychiatric Association, Montreal, Canada.

Holender, D. (1986). Semantic activation without conscious identification in dichotic listening, parafoveal vision, and visual masking: A survey and appraisal. *Behavioral and Brain Sciences, 9,* 1-66.

Holroyd, K., Westbrook, T., Wolf, M., & Badhorn, E. (1978). Performance, cognition, and physiological responding in test anxiety. *Journal of Abnormal Psychology, 87,* 442-451.

Hope, D. A., Rapee, R. M., Heimberg, R. G., & Dombeck, M. J. (1990). Representations of the self in social phobia: Vulnerability to social threat. *Cognitive Therapy and Research, 14,* 177-189.

Humphreys, M. S., & Revelle, W. (1984). Personality, motivation, and performance: A theory of the relationship between individual differences and information processing. *Psychological Review, 91,* 153-184.

Ingham, J. G. (1966). Changes in MPI scores in neurotic patients: A three year follow-up. *British Journal of Psychiatry, 112,* 931-939.

Ingram, R. E. (1984). Toward an information processing analysis of depression. *Cognitive Therapy and Research, 8,* 443-478.

Janis, I. L. (1958). *Psychological Stress* (2nd edn). New York: Wiley.

Johnson, E. J., & Tversky, A. (1983). Affect, generalization and the perception of risk. *Journal of Personality and Social Psychology, 45,* 20-31.

Kahneman, D. (1973). *Attention and Effort.* Englewood Cliffs, N.J.: Prentice-Hall.

Karteroliotis, C., & Gill, D. L. (1987). Temporal changes in psychological and physiological components of state anxiety. *Journal of Sport Psychology, 9,* 261-274.

Kemp-Wheeler, S. M., & Hill, A. B. (1987). Anxiety responses to subliminal experience of mild stress. *British Journal of Psychology, 78,* 365-374.

Kendall, P. C. (1978). Anxiety: States, traits, or situations? *Journal of Consulting and Clinical Psychology, 46,* 280-287.

Kennedy, R. E., & Craighead, W. E. (1988). Differential effects of depression and anxiety on recall of feedback in a learning task. *Behaviour Therapy, 19,* 437-454.

Kent, G. (1985). Memory of dental pain. *Pain, 21,* 187-194.

Kent, G., & Jamburathan, P. (1989). A longitudinal study of the intrusiveness of cognitions in test anxiety. *Behaviour Research and Therapy, 27,* 43-50.

Klein, F. B., & Kihlstrom, J. F. (1986). Elaboration organization and self-reference effects in memory. *Journal of Experimental Psychology: General, 115,* 26-38.

Koksal, F., Power, K. G., & Sharp, D. M. (1991). Profiles of DSM III anxiety disorders on the somatic, cognitive, behavioural and feeling components of the Four Systems Anxiety Questionnaire. *Personality and Individual Differences, 12,* 643-651.

LaBerge, D. (1983). Spatial extent of attention to letters and words. *Journal of Experimental Psychology: Human Perception and Performance, 9,* 371-379.

Lang, P. J. (1971). The application of psychophysiological methods to the study of psychotherapy and behaviour modification. In A. Bergin and S. Garfield (Eds.), *Handbook of Psychotherapy and Behaviour Change.* Chichester: Wiley.

Lang, P. J. (1985). The cognitive psychophysiology of emotion: Fear and anxiety. In A. H. Tuma and J. Maser (Eds.), *Anxiety and the Anxiety Disorders.* Hillsdale, N.J.: Lawrence Erlbaum Associates Inc.

Langinvainio, H., Kaprio, J., Koskenvuo, M., & Lonnqvist, J. (1984). Finnish twins reared apart, III: Personality factors. *Acta Geneticae Mediacae et Gemmellologiae, 33,* 259-267.

Lazarus, R. S. (1982). Thoughts on the relations between emotion and cognition. *American Psychologist, 37,* 1019-1024.

Lazarus, R. S., & Averill, J. R. (1972). Emotion and cognition: With special reference to anxiety. In C. D. Spielberger (Ed.), *Anxiety: Current Trends in Theory and Research, Vol. 2.* New York: Academic Press.

Leon, M. R., & Revelle, W. (1985). Effects of anxiety on analogical reasoning: A test of three theoretical models. *Journal of Personality and Social Psychology, 49,* 1302-1315.

Levinson, H. N. (1989). Abnormal optokinetic and perceptual span parameters in cerebellar-vestibular dysfunction and related anxiety disorders. *Perceptual and Motor Skills, 68,* 471-484.

Lewinsohn, P. M., Berquist, W. H., & Brelje, T. (1972). The repression-sensitization dimension and emotional response to stimuli. *Psychological Reports, 31,* 707-716.

Luborksy, L., Blinder, B., & Schimek, J. (1965). Looking, recalling and GSR as a function of defence. *Journal of Abnormal Psychology, 70,* 270-280.

MacLeod, A., Williams, J. M. G., & Bekerian, D. A. (1991). Worry is reasonable: The role of explanations in pessimism about future personal events. *Journal of Abnormal Psychology, 100,* 478-486.

MacLeod, C. (1990). Mood disorders and cognition. In M. W. Eysenck (Ed.), *Cognitive Psychology: An International Review*. Chichester: Wiley.

MacLeod, C., & Mathews, A. (1988). Anxiety and the allocation of attention to threat. *Quarterly Journal of Experimental Psychology, 38A*, 659-670.

MacLeod, C., & Mathews, A. (1991 a). Cognitive-experimental approaches to the emotional disorders. In P. R. Martin (Ed.), *Handbook of Behaviour Therapy and Psychological Science: An Integrative Approach*. Oxford: Pergamon.

MacLeod, C., & Mathews, A. (1991 b). Biased cognitive operations in anxiety: Accessibility of information or assignment of processing priorities? *Behaviour Research and Therapy, 29*, 599-610.

MacLeod, C., Mathews, A., & Tata, P. (1986). Attentional bias in emotional disorders. *Journal of Abnormal Psychology, 95*, 15-20.

Mandler, G., & Sarason, S. B. (1952). A study of anxiety and learning. *Journal of Abnormal Psychology, 47*, 166-173.

Marcel, A. J. (1986). Peer commentary on Holender's "Semantic activation without conscious activation in dichotic listening, parafoveal vision, and visual masking: A survey and appraisal". *Behavioral and Brain Sciences, 9*, 40.

Martin, M., Ward, J. C., & Clark, D. M. (1983). Neuroticism and the recall of positive and negative personality information. *Behaviour Research and Therapy, 21*, 495-503.

Martin, M., Williams, R. M., & Clark D. M. (1991). Does anxiety lead to selective processing of threat-related information? *Behaviour Research and Therapy, 29*, 147-160.

Mathews, A. (1990). Why worry? The cognitive function of anxiety. *Behaviour Research and Therapy, 28*, 455-468.

Mathews, A., & MacLeod, C. (1985). Selective processing of threat cues in anxiety states. *Behaviour Research and Therapy, 23*, 563-569.

Mathews, A., & MacLeod, C. (1986). Discrimination of threat cues without awareness in anxiety states. *Journal of Abnormal Psychology, 95*, 1-8.

Mathews, A., MacLeod, C., & Tata, P. (In press). Supraliminal and subliminal processing of threat in anxiety states.

Mathews, A., May, J. Mogg, K., & Eysenck, M. W. (1990). Attentional bias in anxiety: Selective search or defective filtering? *Journal of Abnormal Psychology, 99*, 166-173.

Mathews, A., Mogg, K., Kentish, J., & Eysenck, M. W. (In preparation). A longitudinal study of cognitive biases in generalized anxiety disorder patients.

Mathews, A., Mogg, K., May, J., & Eysenck, M. W. (1989 a). Implicit and explicit memory biases in anxiety. *Journal of Abnormal Psychology, 98*, 131-138.

Mathews, A., Richards, A., & Eysenck, M. W. (1989 b). The interpretation of homophones related to threat in anxiety states. *Journal of Abnormal Psychology, 98*, 31-34.

Mayer, R. E. (1977). Problem-solving performance with task overload: Effects of self-pacing and trait anxiety. *Bulletin of the Psychonomic Society, 9*, 283-286.

Mayo, P. R. (1983). Personality traits and the retrieval of positive and negative memories. *Personality and Individual Differences, 4*, 465-472.

Mayo, P. R. (1989). A further study of the personality-congruent recall effect. *Personality and Individual Differences, 10*, 247-252.

McKeon, J., Roa, B., & Mann, A. (1984). Life events and personality trait in obsessive-compulsive neurosis. *British Journal of Psychiatry, 144*, 185-189.

McNally, R. J. (1990). Psychological approaches to panic disorder: A review. *Psychological Bulletin, 108,* 403-419.

McNally, R. J., & Foa, E. B. (1987). Cognition and agoraphobia: Bias in the interpretation of threat. *Cognitive Therapy and Research, 11,* 567-581.

McNally, R. J., Foa, E. B., & Donnell, C. D. (1989). Memory bias for anxiety information in patients with panic disorder. *Cognition and Emotion, 3,* 27-44.

McNally, R. J., Kaspi, S. P., Riemann, B. C., & Zeitlin, S. B. (1990). Selective processing of threat cues in posttraumatic stress disorder. *Journal of Abnormal Psychology, 99,* 398-402.

McNally, R. J., Riemann, B. C., & Kim, E. (1990). Selective processing of threat cues in panic disorder. *Behaviour Research and Therapy, 28,* 407-412.

Meichenbaum, D. (1977). *Cognitive-Behaviour Modification.* New York: Plenum.

Metzger, R. L., Miller, M., Sofka, M., Cohen, M., & Perrock, M. (1983). Information processing and worrying. Paper presented at the Association for the Advancement of Behaviour Therapy, Washington, D. C.

Meyer, T. J., Miller, M. L., Metzger, R. L., & Borkovec, T. D. (1990). Development and validation of the Penn State Worry Questionnaire. *Behaviour Research and Therapy, 28,* 487-495.

Miller, E., & Morley, S. (1986). *Investigating Abnormal Behaviour.* London: Weidenfeld and Nicolson.

Miller, W. R. (1975). Psychological deficit in depression. *Psychological Bulletin, 82,* 238-260.

Mineka, S., & Kihlstrom, J. (1978). Unpredictable and uncontrollable aversive events. *Journal of Abnormal Psychology, 87,* 256-271.

Mogg, K. (1988). *Processing of emotional information in clinical anxiety states.* Unpublished Ph. D. thesis, University of London.

Mogg, K., & Marden, B. (1990). Processing of emotional information in anxious subjects. *British Journal of Clinical Psychology, 29,* 227-229.

Mogg, K., & Mathews, A. (1990). Is there a self-referent recall bias in anxiety? *Behaviour Research and Therapy, 28,* 91-92.

Mogg, K., Mathews, A., Bird, C., & MacGregor-Morris, R. (1990). Effects of stress and anxiety on the processing of threat stimuli. *Journal of Personality and Social Psychology, 59,* 1230-1237.

Mogg, K., Mathews, A., & Eysenck, M. W. (in press). Attentional bias to threat in clinical anxiety states. *Cognition and Emotion.*

Mogg, K., Mathews, A., Eysenck, M. W., & May, J. (1991 a). Biased cognitive operations in anxiety: Artefacts, processing priorities, or attentional search? *Behaviour Research and Therapy, 29,* 459-467.

Mogg, K., Mathews, A., May, J., Grove, M., Eysenck, M. W., & Weinman, J. (1991 b). Assessment of cognitive bias in anxiety and depression using a colour perception task. *Cognition and Emotion, 5,* 221-238.

Mogg, K., Mathews, A., & Weinman, J. (1987). Memory bias in clinical anxiety. *Journal of Abnormal Psychology, 96,* 94-98.

Mogg, K., Mathews, A., & Weinman, J. (1989). Selective processing of threat cues in anxiety states: A replication. *Behaviour Research and Therapy, 27,* 317-323.

Monat, A. (1976). Temporal uncertainty, anticipation time, and cognitive coping under threat. *Journal of Human Stress, 2,* 32-43.

Morris, L. W., Davis, M. A., & Hutchings, C. H. (1981). Cognitive and emotional components of anxiety: Literature review and a revised worry-emotionality scale. *Journal of Educational Psychology, 73,* 541-555.

Mowrer, O. H. (1947). On the dual nature of learning — A re-interpretation of "conditioning" and "problem-solving". *Harvard Educational Review, 17,* 102-148.

Mueller, J. H. (1976). Anxiety and cue utilization in human learning and memory. In M. Zuckerman and C. D. Spielberger (Eds.), *Emotions and Anxiety: New Concepts, Methods and Applications.* Potomac: Lawrence Erlbaum Associates Inc.

Murray, F. (1982). Speech patterns in stress and anxiety. In L. Goldberger and S. Breznitz (Eds.), *Handbook of Stress: Theoretical and Clinical Aspects.* New York: Free Press.

Neely, J. H. (1977). Semantic priming and retrieval from lexical memory: Roles of inhibitionless spreading activation and limited-capacity attention. *Journal of Experimental Psychology: General, 106,* 226-254.

Neufeld, R. W. J., & Paterson, R. J. (1989). Issues concerning control and its implementation. In R. W. J. Neufeld (Ed.), *Advances in the Investigation of Psychological Stress.* Chichester: Wiley.

Nicholson, W. M. (1958). The influence of anxiety upon learning: Interference or drive increment? *Journal of Personality, 26,* 303-319.

Nisbett, R. E., & Wilson, T. D. (1977). Telling more than we can know: Verbal reports on mental processes. *Psychological Review, 84,* 231-259.

Norton, G. R., Schaefer, E., Cox, B. J., Dorward, J., & Wozney, K. (1988). Selective memory effects in nonclinical panickers. Journal of Anxiety Disorders, 2, 169-177.

Noyes, R., Clarkson, C., & Crowe, R. R. (1987). A family study of generalized anxiety disorder. *American Journal of Psychiatry, 40,* 1061-1069.

Oatley, K., & Johnson-Laird, P. N. (1987). Towards a cognitive theory of emotions. *Cognition and Emotion, 1,* 29-50.

O'Banion, K., & Arkowitz, H. (1977). Social anxiety and selective memory for affective information about the self. *Social Behavior and Personality, 5,* 321-328.

Olah, A., Torestad, B., & Magnusson, D. (1984). Coping behaviours in relation to frequency and intensity of anxiety provoking situations. *Reports of the Department of Psychology,* No 629. University of Stockholm.

Olson, J. M., & Zanna, M. P. (1979). A new look at selective exposure. *Journal of Experimental Social Psychology, 15,* 1-15.

O'Neill, G. W. (1985). Is worry a valuable concept? *Behaviour Research and Therapy, 23,* 481-482.

Ormel, J., & Wohlfarth, T. (1991). How revolution, long-term difficulties, and life situation change influence psychological distress: A longitudinal model. *Journal of Personality and Social Psychology, 60,* 744-755.

Pallak, M. S., Pittman, T. S., Heller, J. F., & Munson, P. (1975). The effect of arousal on Stroop colour-word task performance. *Bulletin of the Psychonomic Society, 6,* 248-250.

Parkes, K. R. (1986). Coping in stressful episodes: The role of individual stress. In C.L. Cooper and R. Payne (Eds.), *Causes, coping and consequences of stress at work.* Chichester: Wiley.

Paterson, R. J., & Neufeld, R. W. J. (1987). Clear danger: Situational determinants of the appraisal of threat. *Psychological Bulletin, 101,* 404-416.

Patrick, J. R. (1934 a). Studies in rational behaviour and emotional excitement: I. Rational behaviour in human subjects. *Journal of Comparative Psychology, 18,* 1-22.

Patrick, J. R. (1934 b). Studies in rational behaviour and emotional excitement: II. The effect of emotional excitement on rational behaviour in humans subjects. *Journal of Comparative Psychology, 18,* 153-195.

Pedersen, N. L., Friberg, L., Floderus-Myrhed, B., McClearn, G. E., & Plomin, R. (1984). Swedish early separated twins: Identification and characterization. *Acta Geneticae Medicae et Gemellologiae, 33,* 243-254.

Pennebaker, J. W. (1982). *The Psychology of Physical Symptoms.* New York: Springer.

Pennebaker, J. W., & Skelton, J. A. (1981). Selective monitoring of physical sensations. *Journal of Personality and Social Psychology, 41,* 213-223.

Perrig, W. J., & Perrig, P. (1988). Mood and memory: Mood-congruity effects in absence of mood. *Memory & Cognition, 16,* 102-109.

Power, M. J., & Champion, L. A. (1986). Cognitive approaches to depression: A theoretical critique. *British Journal of Clinical Psychology, 25,* 201-212.

Rachman, S., & Lopatka, C. (1986 a). Match and mismatch in the prediction of fear I. *Behaviour Research and Therapy, 24,* 387-393.

Rachman, S., & Lopatka, C. (1986 b). Match and mismatch in the prediction of fear II. *Behaviour Research and Therapy, 24,* 395-401.

Ray, W. J., Katahn, M., & Snyder, C. R. (1971). Effects of test anxiety on acquisition, retention, and generalization of a complex verbal task in a classroom situation. *Journal of Personality and Social Psychology, 20,* 147-154.

Richards, A., & French, C. C. (1990). Central versus peripheral presentation of stimuli in an emotional Stroop task. *Anxiety Research, 3,* 41-49.

Richards, A., & French, C. C. (1991). Effects of encoding and anxiety on implicit and explicit memory performance. *Personality and Individual Differences, 12,* 131-139.

Richards, A., & Millwood, B. (1989). Colour-identification of differentially valenced words in anxiety. *Cognition and Emotion, 3,* 171-176.

Ridgeway, V., & Mathews, A. (1982). Psychological preparation for surgery: A comparison of methods. *British Journal of Clinical Psychology, 21,* 271-280.

Roediger, H. L., & Blaxton, T. A. (1987). Retrieval modes produce dissociations in memory for surface information. In D. S. Gorfein and R. R. Hoffman (Eds.), *Memory and Cognitive Processes: The Ebbinghaus Centennial Conference.* Hillsdale, N. J.: Lawrence Erlbaum Associates Inc.

Rogers, T. B., Kuiper, N., & Kirker, W. (1977). Self reference and the encoding of personal information. *Journal of Personality and Social Psychology, 35,* 677-688.

Rosenhan, D. L., & Seligman, M. E. P. (1989). *Abnormal Psychology* (2nd edn). New York: Norton.

Roy-Byrne, P. J., Weingartner, H., Bierer, L. M., Thompson, K., & Post, R. M. (1986). Effortful and automatic cognitive processes in depression. *Archives of General Psychiatry, 43,* 265-267.

Russell, P. W., & Beekhuis, M. E. (1976). Organization in memory. *Journal of Abnormal Psychology, 85,* 527-534.

Ryle, G. (1949). *The Concept of Mind.* London: Hutchinson.

Sacco, W. P., & Beck, A. T. (1985). Cognitive treatment of depression. In E. E. Beckham and W. R. Leber (Eds.), *Handbook of Depression: Treatment, Assessment, and Research.* Homewood: Dorsey Press.

Salkovskis, P. M., Clark, D. M., & Hackmann, A. (1991). Treatment of panic attacks using cognitive therapy without exposure or breathing retraining. *Behaviour Research and Therapy, 29,* 161-166.

Saltz, E. (1970). Manifest anxiety: Have we misread the data? *Psychological Review, 77,* 568-573.

Sanderson, W. C., & Barlow, D. H. (1990). A description of patients diagnosed with DSM-IIIR generalized anxiety disorder. *Journal of Nervous and Mental Disease, 178,* 588-591.

Sanderson, W. C., DiNardo, P. A., Rapee, R. M., & Barlow, D. H. (1990). Syndrome comorbidity in patients diagnosed with a DSM-IIIR anxiety disorder. *Journal of Abnormal Psychology, 99,* 308-312.

Sarason, I. G. (1956). Effect of anxiety, motivational instructions, and failure on serial learning. *Journal of Experimental Psychology, 51,* 253-260.

Sarason, I. G. (1957). The effect of associative value and differential motivating instructions on serial learning. *American Journal of Psychology, 70,* 620-623.

Sarason, I. G. (1972). Experimental approaches in test anxiety: Attention and the uses of information. In C. D. Spielberger (Ed.), *Anxiety: Current Trends in Theory and Research.* New York: Academic Press.

Sarason, I. G. (1984). Stress, anxiety, and cognitive interference: Reactions to tests. *Journal of Personality and Social Psychology, 46,* 929-938.

Sarason, I. G. (1988). Anxiety, self-preoccupation and attention. *Anxiety Research, 1,* 3-7.

Schachter, D. L. (1987). Implicit memory: History and current status. *Journal of Experimental Psychology, 13,* 501-518.

Schare, M. L., Lisman, S. A., & Spear, N. E. (1984). The effects of mood variation on state dependent retention. *Cognitive Therapy & Research, 8,* 387-408.

Schwartz, G. E. (1983). Disregulation theory and disease: Applications to the repression/cerebral disconnection/cardiovascular disorder hypothesis. *International Review of Applied Psychology, 32,* 95-118.

Schwarzer, R., Jerusalem, M., & Stiksrud, H. A. (1984). The developmental relationship between test anxiety and helplessness. In H. M. van der Ploeg, R. Schwarzer, and C. D. Spielberger (Eds.), *Advances in Test Anxiety Research, Vol. 3.* Hillsdale, N. J.: Lawrence Erlbaum Associates Inc.

Seligman, M. E. P. (1975). *Helplessness.* San Francisco: Freeman.

Shapiro, K. L., Egerman, B., & Klein, B. M. (1984). Effects of arousal on human visual dominance. *Perception & Psychophysics, 35,* 547-552.

Shapiro, K. L., & Johnson, T. L. (1987). Effects of arousal on attention to central and peripheral visual stimuli. *Acta Psychologica, 66,* 157-172.

Shapiro, K. L., & Lim, A. (1989). The impact of anxiety on visual attention to central and peripheral events. *Behaviour and Research Therapy, 27,* 345-351.

Shapiro, M. B., Campbell, D., Harris, A., & Dewsberry, J. P. (1958). Effects of E.C.T. upon psychomotor speed and the 'distraction effect' in depressed psychiatric patients. *Journal of Mental Science, 104,* 681-695.

Shields, J. (1962). *Monozygotic Twins.* Oxford: Oxford University Press.

Simpson, G. B. (1984). Lexical ambiguity and its role in models of word recognition. *Psychological Bulletin, 96,* 316-340.

Spence, J. T., & Spence, K. W. (1966). The motivational components of manifest anxiety: Drive and drive stimuli. In C. D. Spielberger (Ed.), *Anxiety and Behaviour.* London: Academic Press.

Spiegler, M. D., Morris, L. W., & Liebert, R. M. (1968). Cognitive and emotional components of test anxiety: Temporal factors. *Psychological Reports, 22,* 451-456.

Spielberger, C. D., Gorsuch, R., & Lushene, R. (1970). *The State Trait Anxiety Inventory (STAI) Test Manual.* Palo Alto: Consulting Psychologists Press.

Steptoe, A., & Kearsley, N. (1990). Cognitive and somatic anxiety. *Behaviour Research and Therapy, 28,* 75-81.

Sternberg, D. E., & Jarvik, M. E. (1976). Memory functions in depression. *Archives of General Psychiatry, 33,* 219-224.

Stokes, J.P. (1985). The relation of social network and individual difference variables to loneliness. *Journal of Personality and Social Psychology, 48,* 981-990.

Stroop, J. R. (1935). Studies of interference in serial verbal reactions. *Journal of Experimental Psychology, 18,* 643-662.

Swann, W.B. (1987). Identity negotiation: Where two roads meet. *Journal of Personality and Social Psychology, 53,* 1038-1051.

Szabadi, E., Bradshaw, C. M., & Besson, J. A. D. (1976). Elongation of pause time in speech: A simple, objective measure of motor retardation in depression. *British Journal of Psychiatry, 129,* 592-597.

Tallis, F., & Eysenck, M.W. (submitted). *Worry: Mechanisms and modulating influences.*

Tallis, F., Eysenck, M. W., & Mathews, A. (1991 a). Elevated evidence requirements and worry. *Personality and Individual Differences, 12,* 21-27.

Tallis, F., Eysenck, M. W., & Mathews, A. (1991 b). The role of temporal perspective and ego-relevance in the activation of worry structures. *Personality and Individual Differences, 12,* 909-915.

Tallis, F., Eysenck, M.W., & Mathews, A. (1991 c). Worry: A critical analysis of some theoretical approaches. *Anxiety Research, 4,* 97-108.

Tallis, F., Eysenck, M.W., & Mathews, A. (1992). A questionnaire for the measurement of nonpathological worry. *Personality and Individual Differences, 13,* 161-168.

Teasdale, J. D., Proctor, L., & Baddeley, A. D. (1990). *Working memory and stimulus-independent thought: Daydreaming, depression, and distraction.* Unpublished manuscript.

Thorpe, G. L. (1989). Confounding of assessment method with reaction assessed in the three systems model of fear and anxiety: A comment on Douglas, Lindsay and Brooks. *Behavioural Psychotherapy, 17,* 191-192.

Torgersen, S. (1983). Genetic factors in anxiety disorders. *Archives of General Psychiatry, 40,* 1085-1088.

Torgersen, S. (1986). Childhood and family characteristics in panic and generalized anxiety disorder. *American Journal of Psychiatry, 143,* 630-639.

Torgersen, S. (1990). Genetics of anxiety and its clinical implications. In G. D. Burrows, M. Roth, and R. Noyes (Eds.), *Handbook of Anxiety, Vol. 3: The Neurobiology of Anxiety.* Amsterdam: Elsevier.

Trandel, D. V., & McNally, R. J. (1987). Perception of threat cues in posttraumatic stress disorder: Semantic processing without awareness? *Behaviour Research and Therapy, 25,* 469-476.

Tyrer, P., Lewis, P., & Lee, I. (1978). Effects of subliminal and supraliminal stress on symptoms of anxiety. *Journal of Nervous and Mental Disease, 166,* 88-95.

Ullmann, L. P. (1962). An empirically derived MMPI scale which measures facilitation-inhibition of recognition of threatening stimuli. *Journal of Clinical Psychology, 18,* 127-132.

Van Egeren, L. (1968). Repression and sensitization: Sensitivity and recognition criteria. *Journal of Experimental Research in Personality, 3,* 1-8.

Vogel, W., Raymond, S., & Lazarus, R. S. (1959). Intrinsic motivation and psychological stress. Journal of Abnormal and Social Psychology, 58, 225-233.

Von Baeyer, W. (1969). Social and political aspects of anxiety. In M. Lader (Ed.), *Studies of Anxiety.* London: World Psychiatric Association.

Wachtel, P. L. (1967). Conceptions of broad and narrow attention. *Psychological Bulletin, 68,* 417-429.

Wagstaff, G. F. (1974). The effects of repression-sensitization on a brightness scaling measure of perceptual defence. *British Journal of Psychology, 65,* 395-401.

Walker, N. K., & Burkhardt, J. F. (1965). The combat effectiveness of various human operator controlled systems. *Proceedings of the 17th Military Operations Research Symposium.*

Watson, D., & Clark, L. A. (1984). Negative affectivity: The disposition to experience aversive emotional states. *Psychological Bulletin, 96,* 465-490.

Watts, F. N., & Sharrock, R. (1987). Cued recall in depression. *British Journal of Clinical Psychology, 26,* 149-150.

Watts, F. N., Trezise, L., & Sharrock, R. (1986). Processing of phobic stimuli. *British Journal of Clinical Psychology, 25,* 253-261.

Wegner, D. M., & Guiliano, T. (1980). Arousal-induced attention to self. *Journal of Personality and Social Psychology, 38,* 719-726.

Weinberg, R. S. (1978). The effects of success and failure on the patterning of neuromuscular energy. *Journal of Motor Behavior, 10,* 53-61.

Weinberg, R. S., & Hunt, V. (1976). The interrelationships between anxiety, motor performance, and electromyography. *Journal of Motor Behavior, 8,* 219-224.

Weinberger, D. A., Schwartz, G. E., & Davidson, J. R. (1979). Low-anxious, high-anxious, and repressive coping styles: Psychometric patterns and behavioural and physiological responses to stress. *Journal of Abnormal Psychology, 88,* 369-380.

Weiskrantz, L. (1990). Blindsight. In M. W. Eysenck (Ed.), *The Blackwell Dictionary of Cognitive Psychology.* Oxford: Blackwell.

Weissman, M. M. (1990). Panic and generalized anxiety: Are they separate disorders? *Journal of Psychiatric Research, 24,* 157-162.

Weltman, G., & Egstrom, G. H. (1966). Perceptual narrowing in novice divers. *Human Factors, 8,* 499-506.

Weltman, G., Smith, J. E., & Egstrom, G. H. (1971). Perceptual narrowing during simulated pressure-chamber exposure. *Human Factors, 13,* 99-107.

Williams, J. M. G., Watts, F. N., MacLeod, C., & Mathews, A. (1988). *Cognitive Psychology and Emotional Disorders.* Chichester: Wiley.

Wine, J. (1971). Test anxiety and direction of attention. *Psychological Bulletin, 76,* 92-104.

York, D., Borkovec, T. D., Vasey, M., & Stern, R. (1987). Effects of worry and somatic anxiety induction on thoughts, emotion and physiological activity. *Behaviour Research and Therapy, 25,* 523-526.

Young, G. C. D., & Martin, M. (1981). Processing of information about self by neurotics. *British Journal of Clinical Psychology, 20,* 205-212.

Zaffy, D. J., & Bruning, J. L. (1966). Drive and the range of cue utilization. *Journal of Experimental Psychology, 71,* 382-384.

Zajonc, R. B. (1980). Feeling and thinking: Preferences need no inferences. *American Psychologist, 35,* 151-175.

Zajonc, R. B. (1984). On the primacy of affect. *American Psychologist, 39,* 117-123.

Zeitlin, S. B., & McNally, R. J. (Submitted). Implicit and explicit memory biases for threat in post-traumatic stress disorder.

Author Index

Subject Index

motivation and 145, 146
performance and 144-150
schema theory of 20
Dichotic listening 8-10, 60, 70, 158, 159
Distractibility 58-68

Effort 127, 129, 138-143
Evolutionary perspective 5, 10, 11

Failure feedback 121, 150

Generalized anxiety disorder:
    aetiology of 31, 36, 37, 44, 45, 153-157
    distractibility and 60-68, 154
    definition of 29, 35
    hypervigilance and 45, 46, 52, 155, 156
    implicit memory bias and 93-97, 154
    interpretive bias and 82-85, 154
    modified Stroop and 66-68, 154
    negative memory bias and 92-94, 154
    panic disorder and 157-161
    post-traumatic stress disorder and 159-161
    selective attentional bias and 73-76, 154
    worry and 5, 6, 29, 100, 101, 108, 109, 162
Gray's theory 14-18

Hypervigilance theory 21, 43, 44, 46, 50, 52, 54, 57, 155, 156, 165

Incentives 140
Interpretive bias 40, 80-85, 154, 158, 160

Letter-transformation task 59, 134-136
Lexical decision 73, 74

Memory:
    implicit bias 80, 90-97
    negative bias 21, 22, 25, 85-90
    short-term 127, 128, 133, 134
Modified Stroop 64-68, 76, 77, 94, 154, 155, 159, 160
Mood-congruent effects 23-27, 32, 79, 80

Naming task 81
Neuropsychology 14-18

Panic disorder 31, 45, 87, 101, 157-159, 165
Perceptual defence 9, 69
Performance:
    cognitive interference and 126, 127
    effort and 132, 145, 146
    motivation and 127, 128, 130, 150
    processing efficiency theory of 130-144
    stress and 125, 126
    working memory and 133-138
    worry and 131, 133, 137, 144, 150
Post-traumatic stress disorder, 159-161
Pre-conscious processes 9, 10
Primary appraisal 17, 18
Priming 27-30

Recovered anxious patients:
    distractibility and 61, 62
    implicit memory bias and 94-97
    negative memory bias and 92
    selective attentional bias and 73, 74
    vulnerability and 36, 48, 49
Repressors 2, 3, 57, 68-70, 81, 105-107
Response bias 69, 84, 85, 90
Response systems 1, 2